The Musical World of Halim El-Dabh

The Musical World of

Halim El-Dabh

Denise A. Seachrist

The Kent State University Press ▣ Kent and London

Frontis photo by Jerry Simon.

© 2003 by The Kent State University Press, Kent, Ohio 44242-0001
All rights reserved

Accompanying photos and illustrations courtesy of Halim El-Dabh and the
author from their personal collections.

Library of Congress Catalog Card Number 2002003878
ISBN 0-87338-752-X
Manufactured in the United States of America

07 06 05 04 03   5 4 3 2 1

Library of Congress Cataloging-in-Publication Data
Seachrist, Denise A.
The Musical World of Halim El-Dabh / by Denise A. Seachrist.
p.   cm.
Includes bibliographical references (p.   ) and index.
ISBN 0-87338-752-X (pbk. : alk. paper) ∞
1. El-Dabh, Halim, 1921–
2. Composers—United States—Biography.
I. Title.
ML410.E395 S43 2003
780'.92—dc21
2002003878

British Library Cataloging-in-Publication data are available.

For my father
Glen W. Seachrist
(1924–1964)

Contents

Foreword

BY AKIN EUBA

I do not recall precisely when I started taking a scholarly interest in modern African composition, but by the late 1960s or early 1970s I was already collecting the scores of Ghanaian colleagues such as J. H. Kwabena Nketia, Ephraim Amu, and Ato Turkson. This activity was at first intuitive, and it was only later that I theorized that modern African composition could one day become important. The theory is based on two premises. First, the historical and social context of modern African composition is similar to that of modern African literature, and it is likely that the two would share similar paths of development. If modern African literature rose from obscurity to international prominence, it were likely (I surmise) that modern African art music would one day do the same.

The second premise is grounded on my comparison of the circumstances leading to the international recognition of Asian (especially the Chinese and Japanese) and Latin American composers. Assuming that Asian, Latin American, and African composers share similar social and historical contexts, I reason that African composers could one day become as important on the international scene as their Asian and Latin American colleagues.

My interest in collecting the works of African composers was boosted during the period 1986 to 1991 when I worked as a research scholar at Iwalewa-Haus, the Africa Center of the University of Bayreuth in Germany. My job there was mainly to do with developing an archive of modern African music. My predecessor in the archival work, Wolfgang Bender, had concentrated on popular and Christian religious music, and my principal contribution to the archive was in the area of neo-African art music.

By the time I arrived in Bayreuth I was already aware of the status of Halim El-Dabh in African composition and regarded him as the most important modern African composer. I therefore sought to collect as many of his works as possible and was able to obtain currently available compositions from C. F. Peters Corporation. It was already apparent at the time that there was a paucity of recordings of El-Dabh's music, and this is something that Denise Seachrist also comments on. Indeed up until recently the only recording of El-Dabh's music that I owned was one that was made at a concert organized by me. This is a cassette recording of *Mekta' in the Art of Kita'* (Book III), one of the items in a recital titled "Towards an African Pianism" given by Timothy Peake at the first biennial international symposium and festival on the theme "New Intercultural Music," which I directed for the Centre for Intercultural Music Arts (CIMA) London in 1990.

I first met Halim El-Dabh during a summer program in African music that took place at Howard University, Washington, D.C., in 1969. El-Dabh was at the time teaching at Howard and this, according to Seachrist, would have been shortly after he had turned his back on fame and embraced academia. Although it was not until much later (and especially since reading Seachrist's biography) that I understood El-Dabh's stature not only in African composition but also in twentieth-century music in general, I was already highly impressed with his achievements. Here was a senior colleague pursuing the same goals (a neo-African idiom of composition) toward which I aspired, and he instantly became one of my role models. Looking at that period retrospectively, El-Dabh emerges as a deeply modest person, for he did not in any way reveal to me information about his famous period.

Materials (El-Dabh's and others) that I collected for the Iwalewa-Haus archive formed the basis of my first major essay on modern African art music in which El-Dabh features prominently. In this essay I postulated the notion that intercultural music, of which El-Dabh's is a good example, would become increasingly important and that composers from non-Western cultures would become more and more influential internationally. The position that I took in that essay has since been frequently validated by the activities of African composers and the opening up of various avenues for the promotion of their works.

Before going to Bayreuth in 1986 I organized a series of four concerts of modern African art music in the United Kingdom, the first of which took place in the auditorium of the Faculty of Music, University of Cambridge, in July 1985, although I do not recall that any of El-Dabh's works were featured in these concerts. In 1989 to mark the launching of an LP of my piano music, I performed a joint recital with German concert pianist Irene

Hegen on the theme "Towards an African Pianism," and her section of the recital included El-Dabh's *Mekta' in the Art of Kita'* (Book 3). The concert took place in the auditorium of the Jugendskulturzentrum, Bayreuth. The concept of African pianism became the focus of several subsequent recitals and a flag carrier for the general idea of neo-African art music. El-Dabh's *Mekta'* (Book III) was often featured in these recitals (performed by pianists other than myself) and itself became an epitome of African pianism.

In October 7–9, 1999, I organized a symposium and festival on the theme "Towards an African Pianism: Keyboard Music of Africa and the Diaspora," which took place in Pittsburgh and attracted composers, performers, and scholars from Ghana, Nigeria, Uganda, South Africa, the United Kingdom, and the United States. Reflected in the theme of this event is the idea that the composers of Africa and the diaspora tread similar paths and hence derived my new commitment toward presenting them on the same platform. Denise Seachrist read a paper on El-Dabh at the symposium, and El-Dabh, unable to attend, submitted a paper that was read on his behalf by Seachrist.

My aim in recounting various activities in the field of modern African art music is to place Halim El-Dabh in context and also support my views on the ascendance of African composition.

The biennial international symposium and festival on the theme of new intercultural music has continued (and is now organized by Dr. Robert Kwami, who took over from me as the director of the Centre for Intercultural Music Arts in 2001). Whether consciously or unconsciously, the 1999 Pittsburgh event on African pianism marked the beginning of a new series devoted to neo-African art music. In August 2–4, 2001, I organized a symposium and festival on the theme "Composition in Africa and the Diaspora" at Churchill College, University of Cambridge. The event was dedicated to Halim El-Dabh and J. H. Kwabena Nketia in celebration of their eightieth birthdays and in recognition of their exemplary contributions to African composition. In addition to a keynote address titled, "This Building Is Going to Fly: Halim El-Dabh and the Columbia-Princeton Electronic Music Center," delivered by Seachrist, and other scholarly presentations, the event featured thirteen concerts, including performances of several compositions by El-Dabh. Significantly both El-Dabh and Nketia were present to receive the accolade of their peers.

According to Seachrist, El-Dabh enjoyed fame for a period of years before going into academia, and the move into academia resulted in the loss of fame that he has not quite been able to recapture. I would like to offer a complementary perspective by placing El-Dabh in the context of the history of composition in Africa and its diaspora. In my view El-Dabh is part of an African and diasporic history that also includes the Sierra Leonean British composer Samuel Coleridge-Taylor, the African American composer William Grant Still, and the Nigerian composer Fela Sowande. Like El-Dabh, Coleridge-Taylor and Still experienced a degree of lost fame for various reasons. At the start of his career Coleridge-Taylor was considered by no less a personality than Edward Elgar to be superior to his British contemporaries, but toward and after his death his fame declined considerably in British society. The reason, I believe, was that he had dared to attempt to give his work an African-black identity. In other words, moving away from British perceptions towards African perceptions resulted in his being disowned by the British. Still, too, was enthusiastically supported by the white American avant-garde establishment until he began composing in an idiom that was more accessible to black audiences. In the case of Sowande (1905–87), he too was as good as if not better than his British contemporaries as long as he remained within the orbit of British society. When he moved to Nigeria to become a broadcasting executive and later an academic he became less productive as a composer and his British and international fame declined.

Although the circumstances were different, I believe that there is a link among the experiences of Coleridge-Taylor, Still, Sowande, and El-Dabh. When placed within a Western frame of reference (and it must be admitted that in modern art music, this is synonymous with the international frame of reference) and as long as Western criteria of evaluation are applied, the fame of these composers may be perceived to have declined. When placed within an African frame of reference, however, their fame may be perceived to increase in value, whether or not the composers are dead or remain active. In other words, the true value of Coleridge-Taylor, Still, Sowande, and El-Dabh can best be evaluated by African historians of music (such as Kofi Agawu, Daniel Avorgbedor, and Bode Omojola) and sympathetic Westerners (such as Denise Seachrist and Dominique-René de Lerma) and not by the average Western scholar whose horizons are basically Eurocentric and whose ideological and professional commitments are to sustain the Western canon.

El-Dabh's position in twentieth- and twenty-first-century composition is further enhanced when viewed in the context of theories of contemporary music, at least those that I pioneered, namely the theories of African pianism, intercultural composition, and creative ethnomusicology. El-Dabh is one of the world's leading exponents of all three theories. The theory of African pianism has been widely adopted and was the topic of the 1999 Pittsburgh symposium and festival mentioned above. El-Dabh's contribution to African pianism is well documented, and Linda Burman-Hall's penetrating study provides the North African background against which it may be better understood. El-Dabh's status in intercultural composition is highlighted by the preeminence of Asians, Africans, and Latin Americans as intercultural composers. Although interculturalism was not invented in Asia, Africa, or Latin America, these regions were subjected to intensive colonization and cultural influence, resulting in the creation of new musical idioms that reflect the blending of European and local elements. Moreover, there were sub-regional interactions that produced music in which elements from different sub-regions were fused. There is no living composer that better articulates the concept of intercultural composition than El-Dabh, and in view of the historical, social, and political background of Egypt's modern composers, El-Dabh's compositions are almost inevitably intercultural. Some of his works stand out, however, as validators of intercultural practice, and these include sets of piano music, namely "Ifriqiyaat" (based on the African forms) and "Arabiyaat" (based on the Arabic forms). El-Dabh also wrote music in which Indian and Egyptian instruments are featured, for example "Hindi-Yaat No. 1" for percussion ensemble and "Tabla Dance" for piano and percussion ensemble. From whichever cultures the elements of his music derive, they invariably include the Western, if only insofar as elements from non-Western cultures are presented in the context of Western techniques of composition.

El-Dabh's achievements in the area of creative ethnomusicology are in the best traditions of Ukrainian Mikhail Lysenko (1842–1912) and Hungarian Béla Bartók (1881–1945). Creative ethnomusicology may be described as the transformational zone between research and composition. Lysenko's practice of this concept derived from a need to create a Ukrainian identity in composition in an energetic reaction to an all-too-thorough Russification of Ukrainian culture that existed in his days. He conducted field research and used the results in composition. Bartók's approach to creative ethnomusicology was fueled by a need to forge a Hungarian identity and thus counteract the overwhelming domination of Hungarian composition by German methods. Bartók was very critical of those of his compatriots who sought to impart a Hungarian identity to their music by absorbing the elements of Hungarian folk music via its interpretation by gypsy musicians who performed in the coffee houses of

Budapest. Instead he recommended that the best way to absorb the true elements of Hungarian folk music was to observe this music at its source, that is, in its village setting among the peasants. In other words, Bartók regarded fieldwork as an essential part of composition (in the same way that fieldwork is regarded as an essential aspect of ethnomusicology).

El-Dabh did extensive fieldwork in Africa and Latin America and, whether or not he was consciously following the Bartókian approach, he is a creative ethnomusicologist in the best sense of the word. Ironically the delving into ethnomusicology that resulted in loss of fame on the New York scene would have been applauded by Bartók as a move toward an elevated sphere of composition. Earlier in this essay I traced an African line of descent that links Coleridge-Taylor, Still, Sowande, and El-Dabh, and it is now possible to trace another line based on creative ethnomusicology that connects Lysenko, Bartók, and El-Dabh.

The successful combination of ethnomusicology and composition that marks the careers of Lysenko, Bartók, and El-Dabh leads one to question the wisdom of Alain Daniélou's statement that "a composer should not be involved in ethnomusicology" and that "ethnomusicology and composition were two different and separate activities which should remain isolated one from the other." I would venture further to say that one of the more tedious aspects of the careers of non-Western composers and scholars is having to suffer the kind of irrational and Eurocentric attitude implied by Daniélou's statement.

Seachrist's biography of El-Dabh is a most welcome contribution to the growing literature on the new art music of Africa and its diaspora. Now that this music is on the threshold of international recognition, it is necessary to develop parallel traditions of scholarship and pedagogy, and it is gratifying to see a young and gifted scholar such as Seachrist deeply engaged in the musicology of neo-African art music.

Also gratifying is the growing number of activities and institutions that support the composers of Africa and the diaspora. The International Centre for African Music and Dance (whose founder and first director is the preeminent African musicologist Professor J. H. Kwabena Nketia) has as one of its priorities the promotion of neo-African art music. The Centre for Intercultural Music Arts, a U.K.-based charity, has a strong African input within its overall aim of supporting intercultural composers worldwide. Also based in the United Kingdom is the International Society–African to American Music (IS-AAM), whose founder and chairman is Mike Wright. The society has been very active in compiling a database and archival resources on modern art music in Africa and the diaspora. Even more recently (since October 1999) a new organization, the International Consortium for the Music of Africa and Its Diaspora (ICMAD), has emerged with objectives that include the art music of Africa and the diaspora.

Beginning in 2001 ICMAD has been organizing an annual Festival of African and African American Music; the first took place in St. Louis (organized by the St. Louis African Chorus), the second in New Orleans (under the joint patronage of the Jefferson Performing Arts Society and Dillard University), while the third will be hosted in Windhoek by the Namibian Ministry of Culture.

Mention should also be made of the Ensemble Noir based in Canada, whose founder and artistic director is the twenty-five-year-old South African composer Bongani Ndodana. In a short space of time the ensemble has made an impact on the concert scene in Toronto. Another important ensemble is the St. Louis African Chorus under its energetic director Fred Onovwerosuoke from Nigeria, which over the last few years has piled up a strong record of achievement. A New York branch of the chorus is shortly to be started.

Activities and institutions similar to those cited in the course of this essay are crucial to the development of new art music in Africa and the diaspora, and it is significant that these activities and institutions already constitute a community of composers, performers, and scholars who meet regularly, whether at CIMA events, at ICMAD events, or in the course of those that I organize at Churchill College, University of Cambridge.

Preface and Acknowledgments

A prophet is not without honor except in his own country and in his own house. —Matthew 13:57

Halim El-Dabh may not be a prophet, but he has been blessed with a divine gift of exceptional musical creativity and expression, yet throughout his career he has often been discounted and misunderstood by those closest to him. Because El-Dabh has never been a self-promoter, many of his closest associates and colleagues are not fully aware of the accomplishments of this internationally renowned composer and performer.

A recipient of numerous honors, awards, and grants, including two Rockefeller fellowships (1962, 2001), two Fulbright fellowships (1950, 1967), and two Guggenheim fellowships (1959, 1961), El-Dabh has heard his compositions performed at the Metropolitan Opera House, the Cairo Opera House, and the Edinburgh Festival, as well as in Amsterdam, Athens, Paris, London, and Rome. His music is well known in his birthplace, Egypt, where pieces he wrote for the *Sound and Light of the Pyramids of Giza* (1960), a spectacle that captures the mystery of the ancient structures in narration, lights, and music, are performed daily at the pyramids.

During his time in New York City, he was critically acclaimed and honored by many recognized giants of twentieth-century music and dance—Leopold Stokowski, Leonard Bernstein, Aaron Copland, Martha Graham, and Jerome Robbins, to name just a few. In the 1950s, El-Dabh worked with electronic music pioneers Otto Luening and Vladimir Ussachevsky at the Columbia-Princeton Electronic Music Center, and Graham, a choreographer and modern dance innovator, commissioned him to write the music for *Clytemnestra* (1958) and *A Look at Lightning* (1961).

On the brink of imminent acclaim and recognition, El-Dabh chose to leave New York to conduct research in Egypt and Ethiopia, and he never quite recaptured his opportunity for celebrity. Although recognized for his achievements with biographical entries in such major musical references as *The New Grove Dictionary of Music and Musicians, The New Grove Dictionary of American Music, The New Grove Dictionary of Opera, Baker's Biographical Dictionary of Musicians, The International Cyclopedia of Music and Musicians, Who's Who in American Music,* and *The International Who's Who in Music and Musicians' Directory,* little of El-Dabh's creative output has been well known until recently.

For more than thirty years, Kent, Ohio, has been the place El-Dabh has called home. Accepting an academic appointment in 1969 to teach in the ethnomusicology division of the School of Music and the Center of Pan African Culture at Kent State University, the composer and his family came to the campus one year before the tragic event of May 4, 1970, in which four students were killed and nine others were wounded when the Ohio National Guard fired into a crowd of Vietnam War protestors. A period of great personal turmoil and struggle was precipitated by that horrific event, but he decided to remain nonetheless at Kent State. El-Dabh was awarded the status of University Professor in 1989, a first for the School of Music in the College of Fine and Professional Arts. Since its inception on May 23, 1968, only eleven professors have achieved that special academic status at Kent State University. In that capacity he continued to maintain an office on the campus even after his retirement in 1991.

The opportunity to work personally with the composer arose when I received an invitation to write his entry in *The International Dictionary of Black Composers* (Chicago: Fitzroy Dearborn, 1999), a project of the Center for Black Music Research, Columbia College, Chicago. This research was later supported by a Summer Regional Campuses Faculty Professional Development Award from Kent State University, which led to a second invitation to author his entry in the recently published second edition of *The New Grove Dictionary of Music and Musicians* (New York: Macmillan, 2001). At the urging of two colleagues, Terry E. Miller and Kazadi wa Mukuna, I agreed to undertake the daunting task of writing this biography.

Throughout 1995–1996, El-Dabh and I met regularly, and I interviewed him and attempted to organize his personal papers and music manuscripts. Working with this energetic, ebullient man has been most rewarding. I have been overwhelmed by his creative genius and astounded by the clutter and chaos that surrounds a life unfettered by convention. The journey of the tenacious, organized researcher and the scattered, carefree composer has produced mutual respect and appreciation. Through it all, music has been the focal point. It is obvious that El-Dabh's music has a tremendous impact on listeners. Talented pianists such as Tuyen Tonnu and Felipe Hall deliberately have programmed El-Dabh's compositions in their recitals, doing so not only to challenge themselves by learning these innovative works but also to introduce his music to new audiences. Also, choreographers such as Cleo Parker Robinson, well versed in the history of the Graham–El-Dabh collaborations, request new commissions for the opportunity and privilege of working with a composer who fully understands and appreciates their art.

At a symposium and festival (October 7–9, 1999) at the University of Pittsburgh, I was amazed by the audience's response to audio samples of El-Dabh's compositions—*Mekta' in the Art of Kita'* (1955), "Misriyaat" (1954), "Ifriqiyaat" (1954), and "Arabiyaat" (1954). Symposium participants clamored to learn where they could purchase recordings of these pieces. Their disappointment at learning that none were available was evident. One woman stated, "I would buy anything by Halim El-Dabh." Leo Sarkisian, a writer and radio broadcaster for the Voice of America, pressed his business card into my palm with instructions to contact him. It was his desire to devote a program entirely to El-Dabh and his music.

Other well-known and respected African-born composers credit El-Dabh with providing them inspiration in their own works. Akin Euba and J. H. Kwabena Nketia, the revered elders of the symposium, spoke at length of El-Dabh's individuality and his creative impact on them. Younger audience members were dismayed that they were only now learning of this composer and his musical contributions; they were incredulous that his work had not been known to them before.

This is the paradox of Halim El-Dabh. The man and his music have been internationally celebrated, but most of his work has remained unknown. He has traveled the world and socialized with royals and celebrities, but he has been settled in a small university town for more than thirty years. He has been honored and acclaimed but at the same time largely ignored and forgotten. It is hoped that this biography will present the musical world of Halim El-Dabh in the proper context of twentieth-century music history and allow him to be recognized for his many innovations and contributions to our collective creative world.

The overwhelming support and assistance of those aiding and encouraging this work is greatly appreciated and must be acknowledged. I am especially indebted to the cooperation of Halim El-Dabh and his wife, Deborah, for willingly allowing me access to their lives while conducting the research for this biography. It also gives me great pleasure to acknowledge others who graciously offered assistance throughout this process. Special thanks is given to Dr. Terry E. Miller, Kent State University professor of ethnomusicology, who first proposed my undertaking this task and whose friendship and mentorship have guided me for many years.

As an academic, I have benefited from the supportive and collegial atmosphere fostered at Kent State University and its Trumbull Campus. Dr. Nawal Ammar, associate dean of arts and sciences and associate professor of justice studies; Dr. Salah Blaih, assistant professor of chemistry; Dr. Irene Ginakos, assistant professor of psychology; Dr. Harold Zellner, professor emeritus of philosophy; Father Dennis Mikelas of St. Demetrios Hellenic Orthodox Church in Warren (Ohio); and Ms. Koula Glaros, student, were extremely helpful in clarifying issues related to Egyptian and Greek cultures.

I would like to thank the following for their assistance with my myriad research queries: Ms. Evelina Smith and the Kent Trumbull Library staff; Ms. Jeanne Somers, associate dean of libraries and media services, and the Kent State University special collections and archives staff; Ms. Jean Morrow, director of libraries at the New England Conservatory of Music; Mr. David Herzel of the University of New Mexico Fine Arts Library; Warner Lawson Jr., Howard University professor of law; Ms. Tamra Hess of the East Palestine (Ohio) Memorial Public Library; Mr. Jerome Stephens of the Warren (Ohio) Public Library; Ms. Louise Kiefer, college historian at Baldwin-Wallace College; the Boston Public Library music reference staff; and Nicholas Riddle, managing director, and Gene Caprioglio, rights clearance division director, of the C. F. Peters Corporation. The entire staff of The Kent State University Press, particularly Joanna Hildebrand Craig, assistant director; Will Underwood, director; Kathy Method, managing editor; Susan Cash, marketing manager; Christine Brooks, design and production manager; and John Hubbell, director emeritus, have been tremendously encouraging and helpful throughout the creation of this work.

I appreciate the efforts of Aaron Sherber; Christina Dakin; Maxine Glorsky; Josephine Irvine; and Verdery Roosevelt, executive director of the Ballet Hispanico, who assisted me in locating Ms. Hope Ryan, who oversees the estate of her late cousin, Eugene Lester; and Tan Crone, who put me in contact with Mrs. Sluijters, who oversees the estate of Guus Hoekman in Holland. Thanks to Glorsky and Richard Daniels, for providing biographical information about Yuriko, and to David Peter Coppen, special collections librarian at the Sibley Music Library of the Eastman School of Music. Philip Blackburn, senior program director at Innova Recordings; Sahama El-Kholy, former president of the Egyptian Academy of Arts at the Egyptian Ministry of Culture and widow of Gamal Abdel-Rahim; Sherif Mohie El Din, director of the Arts Center at the Bibliotheca Alexandrina; Shady Abdel Salam, assistant to maestro Sherif Mohie El Din; and Dr. Diedre Badejo, chair of the department of pan-African studies at Kent State University have been very generous with their support of this project. I also want to thank Mike Hovancsek for sharing information regarding the performances of *Opera Flies* during the twenty-fifth anniversary commemorations of May 4, 1970, Nicholas D. and Sara Ohly for providing information about the sculpture that ultimately inspired the work "Pirouette Continuum" (Track No. 12 on the companion CD), and Margrit and Yehoshua Lakner for graciously allowing the publication of the photograph of Aaron Copland with Lakner and El-Dabh, which was from their own personal collection.

I am especially indebted to George Faddoul, who, along with James Meyers, Joel Jacobson, and Julie Grant, freely shared his expertise with sound recording, which proved invaluable in creating the compact disc to accompany the text. David Badagnani, who compiled the annotated discography, ably assisted with countless other tasks related to the production of this book. I also want to thank Badagnani and Hardin Butcher, Al Couch, Kent Larmee, Dennis Nygren, Tuyen Tonnu, Blake Tyson, and Liana Tyson for their roles in creating such a memorable trip to Egypt in celebration of the reopening and rededication of the Bibliotheca Alexandrina. It was an honor for me to be in the company of such superior musicians.

Finally, I want to recognize my mother, Eloise Seachrist; my brother, Daniel Seachrist; and my husband, Charlie Wentz, who have supported, challenged, and loved me throughout the journey.

I

From Childhood to Young Manhood

As a deafening crack of thunder reverberated throughout the heart of Cairo's oldest section, Balsam El-Dabh gave birth to the last of her nine children. A healthy baby boy, Halim Messieh, was born on March 4, 1921, in a spacious eight-bedroom apartment occupying the entire third floor of an enormous old house on Sharia Al-Gameel, the "Street of the Beautiful." Weeping with exhaustion and joy, Balsam declared to the midwife that surely the fierceness of the storm had heralded the arrival of a most blessed and special child. After instructing the midwife to prepare the baby for presentation to his anxiously awaiting father, Abdul Messieh (who had been standing like a sentry on one of the house's several balconies), Balsam summoned her eldest daughter, Victoria, already a mother herself, to come sit with her. When the midwife returned with the baby and his proud father and placed the infant on the mother's breast, Balsam became convinced that this child was the reason she had so fervently insisted that her husband move the family from central Egypt to Cairo, where the nation's main universities were, in order for their children to obtain better educations. The move had proved financially beneficial to Abdul Messieh, whose agricultural-produce business flourished in Cairo, enabling him to support properly his large family of three girls and six boys. Victoria, Labeeb, Bushra, Alice, Adeeb, Regina, Michael, and Selim had all been born in Upper Egypt. That only Halim had been born in Cairo was another reason that his mother was certain that her youngest child was indeed special.

Balsam Benyiamin Fam was only fourteen years of age when she married the handsome, nineteen-year-old Abdul Messieh El-Dabh in an arranged ceremony within the small walled city of Zarabi, in the province of Asyut. Abdul Messieh pursued his family's profession, grain farming, of which Asyut was considered the center. The name El-Dabh can be traced back three hundred years to a great-grandfather who had lived in Zarabi and had, it was said, single-handedly captured a hyena. The hyena had become the family's symbol, and a gate of the walled-in area had been named in honor of the bravery of the great-grandfather. Sometimes depicted ideographically as a jackal or a pharaoh, the name El-Dabh is found also in northern Egypt, where some Muslim members of the family live. A variant, Al-Dabaa, is the name of a small town in the northwestern part of the country.

Balsam Fam's Coptic (Orthodox Christian) family, known for its interest in theology, came from Abu Tieg, also in the province of Asyut. Balsam's parents had promised her in marriage to Abdul Messieh once she completed her education at a missionary school near Abu Tieg, where she was a bright student. The pretty, intelligent, but rather shy, schoolgirl studied English and demonstrated an excellent knowledge of history and Egyptian politics. Balsam's parents were proud that their daughter had completed the eighth grade, a considerable achievement for a young woman at that time, and the marriage contract with the eligible Abdul Messieh El-Dabh was considered beneficial to both families.

Balsam and Abdul Messieh were married in a double ceremony, the other groom being Abdul Messieh's cousin Garris, who later became a well-known doctor and the physician to King Fu'ad. On the wedding day, the two nervous young brides were veiled in traditional garb and were brought to the elaborately decorated tent upon a single-hump camel. A file of musicians with flutes, double-reed *mizmar*[1] pipes, and trumpets, as well as *naqqarah*[2] kettledrums hanging from the sides of another camel, played fanfares and festive marches to announce the arrival of the veiled brides and their attendants. Balsam had never seen her future husband, except between heavy window shutters as he rode by on horseback; she now confused Garris for Adbul Messieh and positioned herself beside him. During the ceremony, Balsam's mother noticed that the two young women were standing beside each other's intended spouses and interrupted the ceremony to reposition the couples. Following the wedding, the Fam and El-Dabh families began a lavish forty-day public celebration, in which the entire town of Zarabi was invited to partake of lamb and other delicacies.

The marriage proved a most fruitful union, and Balsam thrived in her role as wife and mother. Her firstborn son, Labeeb, displayed a bright and curious mind at a very early age. Until the birth of her youngest child, Balsam favored Labeeb, encouraging his intellectual curiosity and exulting in his decision to attend medical school and become a physician. A fastidious and meticulous housekeeper, Balsam overlooked Labeeb's obsession with human and animal skulls. He had a collection of the latter in his bedroom; she voiced displeasure only when he was caught teasing his youngest brother with them. Bushra, however, was openly acknowledged as his father's favorite son; although Abdul Messieh supported his intention to study philosophy and literature in college, he was thrilled when Bushra agreed to become his assistant and enter the family business.

The third son, Adeeb, also pursued business and commerce in college; however, realizing that he could never measure up to Bushra in their father's eyes, Adeeb pursued a career with Egypt Air. He was ultimately to be the most accomplished and commercially successful of the El-Dabh siblings. He would be responsible for opening a direct line between Cairo and Moscow, and he was to visit TWA's headquarters in St. Louis, Missouri, becoming the first of the El-Dabh children to visit the United States. Eventually, Adeeb would leave the airline and enter the maritime travel business, out of the port of Alexandria. Michael, the strongest of the sons, was the only one to earn his living relying on physical prowess rather than mental aptitude. He was to become famous throughout Egypt as a championship figure skater. Although an injury ended his dream of competing in the Olympic Games, his reputation enabled him to earn a living as a coach to aspiring figure skaters and ballet dancers as well. As for Selim, like his oldest brother Labeeb he demonstrated a keen intellect at a very young age. He would study engineering in college and become an employee of the British Shell Company, a subsidiary of Dutch Royal Shell. Selim would travel throughout the Arab world supervising the drilling of oil wells.

Victoria, Alice, and Regina, the three daughters of Balsam and Abdul Messieh, were afforded elementary educations equal to those of their brothers. All three were instructed in foreign languages, history, and the piano; however, none was encouraged to pursue a college education. Although Victoria, a strikingly beautiful and vivacious young woman, was acknowledged to be the intellectual equal of her brothers Labeeb and Selim, she and her two sisters as well appeared content to fulfill their predetermined roles of marriage and motherhood, of which Balsam had provided the perfect example.

Notwithstanding her apparent submission to her role as a woman, Balsam exerted tremendous power and influence on her children and also on her husband, who grew to adore her. One area in which she did so was religion. As was true in many prominent families in Egypt at the beginning of the twentieth century, some members of the El-Dabh family retained the ancient Coptic religion, while others chose to practice Islam. When the family moved (at Balsam's insistence) to the large house on the Street of the Beautiful, Abdul Messieh's brother, after working in southern Sudan, announced that he had joined the Reformed church, and he urged his brother and sister-in-law to leave the Coptic Orthodox tradition and convert with him. Abdul Messieh was a deeply religious man who gathered the family to pray and sing every day prior to leaving for work across the Nile; however, tradition compelled him to follow his older brother to the Reformed church. Balsam, not wanting to cause a rift within the family, acquiesced and attended services with her husband and the children; however, she remained steadfast to her own beliefs and soon began attending the Orthodox church as well. The children attended church primarily with their father, but on occasion they accompanied their mother, whose dedication to her convictions greatly influenced them, especially her youngest child Halim.

Abdul Messieh and Balsam El-Dabh created an environment that exposed their children to a variety of people and to different ways of thinking and of experiencing the world around them. This was particularly true by the time the youngest child was born. For instance, Abdul Messieh's mother lived with the family until she was ninety-seven years old, and often Balsam had the toddler kiss his grandmother's hands and receive her blessings; having the revered matriarch of the family living with them was considered an honor. It was also considered an honor to be visited by relatives, and the young boy relished the frequent presence of members of his extended family, who brought many village products with them. Laden with pomegranates, oranges, lettuce, live chickens, and turkeys, they came from Asyut, Tell El Amarna, Luxor, and Aswan. These visits implanted the notion that life was connected to the earth. Also, the child spent untold hours talking with his mother, as he ground wheat into flour for her between granite stones, about history, America, and happenings in the world. Often the conversations were quite political, as she told him stories of the king, of Arabia, and of Islamic development in general.

Because the family was large and because Adbul Messieh was affluent enough to afford their salaries, there were many servants who lived with the family. The doorman, the two cooks, and several maids were considered a part of the household. The staff would bring their own musical instruments to join in the festive family gatherings. At the end of the day, the doorman played his lyre in front of the door, singing traditional songs from Nubia, Upper Egypt, and Central Egypt—one of the first musical exposures for the youngest El-Dabh child.

Every Wednesday his mother laundered the family's clothes in the basement, with two or three maids assisting her. Balsam would boil the water over a small burner to prepare to wash the garments. Then she would distill the essence of orange blossoms, jasmine, and roses, whose sweet fragrances she kept in small decorative bottles, to flavor the strong Turkish coffee she enjoyed each morning sitting at her balcony. Her youngest child later in life would regard these moments with his mother as an invaluable part of his education; he would consider her to have been the first, and one of the more essential, of his informal educators.

Another of El-Dabh's informal teachers was the man known only to the young boy as the "Orange Man." Once every two weeks he would walk six miles from downtown Cairo to the El-Dabh house, a huge basket containing three bushels of oranges adeptly balanced atop his elderly head with its mane of long white hair. The Orange Man would stay with the family for the entire day, for breakfast, lunch, and dinner, before returning home with an empty basket. Occasionally, he stayed so late that Balsam would insist he spend the night in a spare room. The days the Orange Man came were major events for the household. The youngest El-Dabh would eagerly anticipate the moment the ancient figure, with his gnarled hands and weathered face, would appear with the fruit and the wonderful stories of happenings at the palace and around the country.

Others of El-Dabh's everyday instructors were street puppeteers. Traditionally in Egypt there were two types. A puppeteer of the first kind toted on his back a bench and a box, resembling an Islamic citadel;[3] he was often accompanied by a man playing a long trumpet and another beating a drum. A troupe would go into the crowded streets as the children were dismissed from school and set up on a street corner. The blaring trumpet and pounding drum drew the children, who would scurry to find places on the bench to watch the show. The puppeteer's "citadel," the stage, had scrolls on two sides and a cloth over the front. When the cloth cover was opened, three screens of transparent glass were revealed, with the ends of the scrolls beautifully illuminated with pictures between them. As the audience watched the pictures passing between the glass panes, the puppeteer would begin an elaborate tale—often biblical, koranic, or historical—and the squirming children quickly quieted into calm fascination. Often a little monkey came around collecting money. If the children did not have any money, which was often the case, they paid for the performance with glass bottles they had brought with them—the clearer the glass, the more valuable.

The other kind of puppeteer carried a triptych, or three-sided framework, which would be opened to form a makeshift stage. Covering himself with a cloth, the puppeteer would manipulate hand and stick puppets to enact the plays. Old-time puppeteers placed metal *swazzles*[4] in the roofs of their mouths to create a puppet's voice. There was a great deal of political allusion in the puppeteers' tales, so though the performances were mainly for children, adults also enjoyed them.

El-Dabh's first formal education occurred at the school across the street from his house. He was enrolled when he was just four years old. The close proximity of the school was very appealing to his parents, who were overly protective of their youngest child. However, when the boy came home one day speaking Hebrew, Abdul Messieh and Balsam decided to remove him from that school and find another. Everyone had opinions regarding which school the ninth child should attend, but eventually it was determined that he should enter the Jesuit school, Khouranfish—where he stayed until he was eleven years old and where he first learned to speak French. Young El-Dabh often was transported to the Khouranfish school by his own driver in a horse-drawn carriage; however, the boy preferred to ride the school bus along with the other children. He enjoyed the social interaction with his classmates, but mostly he enjoyed traveling by school bus, because the thirty-minute trip went over the Red Mountain, Mukatam, and he loved the scenery.

It was a very different world for him at the French school, where the students, dressed uniformly in black tunics, were very regimented. The priests, also attired in black tunics, were strict disciplinarians who required the students to silently walk two by two, in pairs of files. This was an aspect of the education for which El-Dabh did not care. Once while walking in the file outside in the school's courtyard, he noticed through the school's entrance several large posters on the theater across the street. The posters advertised the theater's attractions; one depicted women with their legs exposed.[5] Transfixed by the sight, El-Dabh forgot he was in the file, forgot about the priests, and ran straight to the movies for the remainder of the day. The next day a priest stood waiting for the impetuous youth as he

Halim El-Dabh, age nine, with his dog, Antar (1930).

arrived at the school. The priest gruffly escorted the boy to a corner of the classroom and, pointing an ebony stick at him, sternly demanded, *"Cinéma! Qu'est-ce que vous vue?"* "What did you see?" In particular, had he seen women?

"Oui, mon père, oui," the frightened boy replied. "Yes, Father, yes."

The priest continued to hold that threatening stick over the boy's head until, apparently, he received some satisfaction through the fear in the youth's eyes. After hearing what he wanted, the priest commanded, "Don't do that again. Don't leave the line."[6]

Nonetheless, El-Dabh flourished at Khouranfish, where he excelled in many sporting activities including fencing and barrel running. He dominated in stilt walking; eventually he was a member of a team that played a type of kickball on stilts. Academically he was at the top of his class as well. Because he showed such great aptitude in the second grade, he was promoted early to the third grade, where he also continued to thrive, so he was placed in the fourth grade. (However, that move pushed him too far; he could no longer keep up and found himself at the bottom of the class. The bright boy became frustrated; in tears, he demanded to return to the third grade.) For his scholastic achievements, El-Dabh was given special privileges and duties. One such duty was the *moulin,* or "wind-mill." Students who had been caught misbehaving were forced to walk around a fountain in the middle of the school's courtyard for the entire recreation period; as his reward, the young El-Dabh was selected to su-pervise the activity. However, he was not fond of the job, nor was he well suited to it. Instead of ensuring that his peers were toeing the line, the outgoing boy would stand at his post and engage in conversation with them. Eventually, he was removed from his position of authority.

In 1932, the El-Dabh family moved from the Street of the Beautiful to the Street of Ismailia,[7] in Heliopolis, the "City of the Sun," and the eleven-year-old El-Dabh was placed in a public orientation program to prepare him for entrance into the regular government school for the remainder of his Egyptian education. When he first entered into the program, El-Dabh felt that his time among the Jesuits at Khouranfish had been a detriment to his progress; however, he soon realized that his varied educational ex-perience had been very beneficial, because in addition to learning French, he had been exposed to Catholics, Protestants, Copts, and Jews.

El-Dabh was very close to his wide assortment of friends, a trait he would possess throughout his life. Although reared Coptic, he was to be comfortable in the company of his Muslim friends, and he was welcomed by Islamic society in Cairo. As long as he was with his friends, he would be equally at ease in a mosque or a church. His exposure to many reli-gions and his eclectic education enabled him to adapt to a variety of situ-ations of the multifaceted society into which he had been born. He would often join in the prayers of any denomination or religious group; it did not make any difference to El-Dabh. Later, as he worked in the villages, he found that the mosque was the best place to find clean water when he wanted to bathe.

Following his orientation program, in 1932 El-Dabh entered an Ara-bic middle school where he was exposed to intensive study of geography and mathematics. It was also in 1932 that the eleven year old discovered his passion for music.

Halim El-Dabh, age eleven (1932).

The El-Dabh house contained an old, upright monstrosity of a piano, on which all the siblings learned to play. However, Halim, as the ninth child, was often pushed aside by the others when it came his turn, and this treatment made him more determined to play. He credits his brothers Bushra and Adeeb for encouraging his musical talent. Bushra, who was twenty years older than his youngest brother, played the *ud*[8] and was one of the young boy's greatest inspirations. Adeeb, eleven years older than Halim, was a self-taught pianist, who by the time he was fifteen years old often was asked to perform on the radio. He possessed a natural talent for playing by ear; he would delight his family and friends by attending concerts and then returning to play all he had heard. It was acknowledged that Adeeb could have been a professional musician; however, the family did not encourage or support such an endeavor. It was Bushra who recognized his youngest brother's musical talent and decided that he should have standard lessons. The boy was taken to downtown Cairo and enrolled in the Sculz Conservatory, where he worked out exercises in musical theory and harmony and learned to play Beethoven's "Für Elise."[9]

For several years El-Dabh would periodically study at the Sculz Conservatory, developing his playing technique and performing concerts. His first concert occurred only one month after he was enrolled at the conservatory. Exploiting his natural ability, the staff utilized him as a promotional vehicle to attract more students. In 1932 King Fu'ad convened a major musical symposium, to which he invited several international composers, including Béla Bartók[10] and Paul Hindemith.[11] Bushra arranged to take his young brother to the event, which would be the first time Halim El-Dabh was exposed to sounds that had been captured on a wire recorder, a device that recorded sound on a steel wire by magnetizing the wire as it passed an electromagnet. The young El-Dabh was awestruck.

Following his middle school years, the budding musician attended Kubeh High School, where he was introduced to English and reintroduced to French. The Kubeh High School administration took pride that the teachers of English were actually British and that the French teacher was a native of France. El-Dabh, with his natural gift for imitating sounds, soon spoke the two languages with little trace of an accent. In addition to languages, he studied geography, a course that included in-depth examination of the cultures of North and South America. He also enjoyed learning algebra, trigonometry, and physics. But El-Dabh most enjoyed fraternizing with a group, known as The Bones, of about ten young men who met after school to discuss such philosophical issues as the meaning of life, the origin of the universe, and, of course, girls. In the final year of high school, El-Dabh and his classmates were required to select a major concentration of study from among pure science, literature, languages, and medicine. He opted to enter the science orientation, a prerequisite for continued study at the medical school, the scientific school, or the agricultural school. He planned to follow his father and brother Bushra into the family business by matriculating in the agricultural school when he entered college in 1941.

The agriculture curriculum covered a wide variety of topics, including the planting and rotation of crops and veterinary medicine, because the students were expected to be knowledgeable about all aspects of operating a successful farm. The course work was so intense that with only a few more courses one could qualify as a veterinarian. Some of the classes—for example, bacteriology—were taken at the medical school. Because it was necessary for the students to be able to analyze soil and know how to establish and operate profitable farms, chemistry and economics were required courses. The agriculture students were expected to study different methods of growing various crops throughout the world, so El-Dabh and his classmates learned about systems of agriculture other than that of Egypt.

The curriculum included many trips into the countryside, and El-Dabh always enjoyed the trips. One of his favorite teachers often took the students on trips to learn the best methods to reclaim desert—how to develop it, how to bring water to it, and to make it arable. El-Dabh and his classmates relished entering the villages dressed in white, as though they were medical doctors. The students visited towns and cities all over Egypt, from the northern Delta to deep in the South, to experience first-hand how the land was developed in each region. El-Dabh greatly enjoyed meeting and working with individuals from all over Egypt. He felt that agriculture was a noble and humane profession because of the great effort that was put into renewing the land. He experienced the cyclic rhythm of nature when he learned to plant *berseem*[12] to hold the nitrogen in the soil, then to plant beans and peas to make the land fertile enough for wheat or corn. Later, when the land was stronger still, cotton could be planted. Learning this renewal process and then digging into the irrigation system to comprehend how water is distributed to the land taught the agriculture students how families and animals utilized an area. This new knowledge was very stimulating to El-Dabh.

As he advanced in his course work, El-Dabh and the other more experienced students were selected to travel to villages, where usually ten families would be living on approximately a hundred acres. The students were sent into these areas to offer advice about how best to utilize the land, and invariably they would be invited to stay for a gathering in their honor or to help celebrate a special feast day or harvesting day with singing and dancing, accompanied by clarinets, especially the long *arghūl*,[13] oboes, trumpets, flutes, and drums.

El-Dabh quickly learned that the people in the villages were deeply connected to the land and that the land was rich not only in agricultural products but in music. The realization that the lives of people working the land were so connected to music provided tremendous comfort to the young man, who was wrestling with the difficult task of expressing to those closest to him a strong new desire, to study music formally. This desire was sparked in 1942 by his first real exposure to the public as a musician when he was awarded the first prize in a piano competition at the Egyptian Opera House (where Giuseppe Verdi's *Aida*[14] had received its premiere in 1871). Because he had grown up in a culture in which musical expression was a way of life but not a living, El-Dabh struggled to balance working toward his degree in agriculture, traveling to the villages, and composing and performing music as a diversion. He felt restless and unfulfilled. He had no idea at the time that the exposure to the Egyptian folklore, music, and people would prove an important and vital aspect of his musical education, that the decade of his life involved in agriculture was preparing him well for his life to come as an ethnomusicologist and composer.

Following his graduation in 1944, El-Dabh was hired to work at a firm that rapidly promoted him to manage the entire agricultural zone of Central Egypt. As a reward for his hard work, he was provided with an office next to the agricultural school in Cairo. He prospered in his job, but he was disappointed that its demands took up the time he wanted to devote to his music. Once again, his brother Bushra recognized his youngest brother's frustration, and he provided him an opportunity to find his creative voice. Bushra, who had married and moved into a house with a large balcony facing the side street at the back of his parents' house, often would invite his youngest brother to stay with him when his wife was away visiting her family. The younger El-Dabh relished these visits with his beloved older brother, who encouraged him to compose at all hours of the night. The young composer frequently arose at 2:00 A.M. to experiment with the various capabilities of Bushra's grand piano; it was now that the young composer became enamored of tone clusters.[15] The hot and stifling early morning air induced El-Dabh to throw open the windows, bringing the cool breezes in and letting the musical sonorities out. He soon had quite a nocturnal audience—people who, having opened their windows because of the heat, were compelled to listen to the music. (Track No. 2 on the companion CD.)

Word of Halim El-Dabh's musical talent spread throughout the community. He was invited to join a social group composed of French, Lebanese, and Syrian men who met after work to play music and dance. Occasionally the group took weekend camping trips, and during one of these outings El-Dabh learned that his acquaintances Munir Yunan, Henri Shalala, and Kamal Iskander were very knowledgeable about and interested in avant-garde music and musicians. The four men spent the remainder of the camping trip engaged in lively discussions of their favorite contemporary composers, and they formed a close bond that continued throughout their lives.

Iskander, the most influential of the group, was in contact with the several classical music societies in Cairo, and when one of the more prestigious, with a branch in France, announced a commitment to promote the music of Egyptian composers, Iskander informed it that his friend Halim El-Dabh was a young composer to watch. The other members of the society had never heard of El-Dabh but wondered if he would be interested in performing for them; Iskander assured them that he would make the necessary arrangements. However, when Iskander approached his friend for the society, El-Dabh declined, stating that he was working in agriculture and only dabbled in music. Iskander implored him to reconsider, but El-Dabh was adamant. Although Iskander continued to promote El-Dabh's music, their friendship was strained for some time afterward.

At the same time, El-Dabh's brother Michael was successfully cajoling him to enter the business of manufacturing cheese. Returning from America, a friend of Michael's had begun to acquire surplus milk from the palace; however, the friend had no idea what to do with it. Michael presumed that with his brother's knowledge and connections in agriculture they could make a great profit converting the milk into cheese for sale. The younger brother reluctantly agreed to join Michael and his friend in this pursuit. The three rented a villa outside Cairo and filled it with large tanks to process the cheese. Unfortunately, Michael had overestimated his brother's ability in this area; the cheese spoiled, and their business venture failed. However, the villa was to serve as a backdrop for Halim El-Dabh's only venture in the lucrative Egyptian film industry.

As Virginia Danielson points out in her work *The Voice of Egypt*, "Although production costs were generally high, if financing could be arranged, the profits and fees were much greater [in Egyptian song films] than those from any other source."[16] As early as 1929 there were "fifty cinema halls in Cairo and the provincial capitals,"[17] and by 1946 Cairo had at least forty major film-making firms,[18] which distributed films especially for India, the largest market for the Cairo movie industry. While El-Dabh was making a name for himself in agriculture and becoming known in certain musical circles, a movie director by the name of Husayn Helmy, famous for habitually smoking a *shisham*[19] (which resulted in a perpetual apparently stoned state), approached him to compose music for a movie on which he was working. El-Dabh declined Helmy's request as he had dismissed Iskander's: he wanted to concentrate on agriculture.

Helmy, however, was not convinced and was not used to being denied. Consequently, the next day he dispatched two muscular and threatening-looking men to El-Dabh's cheese-making villa. They informed him that Helmy wanted to see him immediately; El-Dabh brusquely responded that he was too busy. However, the men were undeterred and hoisted the startled El-Dabh into the waiting truck and transported him the fifty miles back to Misr Studios, where Helmy was waiting. There Helmy smugly instructed El-Dabh to sit at a grand piano in the center of the studio and informed the composer that, as his latest film was projected on several screens throughout the room, El-Dabh was to improvise while photographers took shots of him from various angles. El-Dabh's hands were to be made to seem those of the actor cast in the lead role of a conductor and pianist. El-Dabh was so relieved that only the photographers were going to be "shooting" him that he eagerly began playing, working at the studio throughout the entire night before being returned to the villa.

For several months Helmy dispatched his two accomplices to "kidnap" El-Dabh to work on the film, regardless of the inconvenience. One time the henchmen tracked El-Dabh to a barbershop and removed him against his will from the chair. Fortunately, in the film's credits El-Dabh was acknowledged for both his "role" and as having written the musical score. The film, *Azhar wa Ashwaq* (*Roses and Thorns*), released in 1946, was shown in Cairo and throughout India. Moreover, he was paid a hundred Egyptian pounds (five hundred U. S. dollars) for his services.

The involvement with *Azhar wa Ashwaq* prompted El-Dabh to embark on an active period of composition, although his commitment to agriculture kept him from producing a large body of work. The pieces he created during the years before he left the agricultural life in Egypt for a musical life in the United States were inspired by specific events and circumstances. "Prelude Sheroude" (1946), for solo piano, was his response to the feelings of isolation and confusion he experienced as his desire to compose began to overwhelm him. Frequently he caught himself daydreaming about what it must be like to live as a composer. When he acknowledged to himself his conflict and uncertainty, he recalled the many times during his adolescence when he had felt the same way and had run away from the house, as if to escape his troubles.

The word *sheroude* has many meanings; two of the more common are "daydreamer" and "one who is lost"—exactly how El-Dabh viewed himself during this period. He spent hours wandering aimlessly around Cairo, losing himself in the myriad sights and experiences of the city. He was particularly fond of roaming the streets at night and listening to the music emanating from clubs. As a teenager he had fantasized about the world; as an adult he fantasized about a career in music. The circumstances were different, but his response was the same. The desire to dream about and then to pursue new and unfamiliar experiences would constantly manifest throughout Halim El-Dabh's life. The strong urge to be a composer was simultaneously frightening and stimulating. He now remembered having once become lost in the city when he was a teenager, with his sister Victoria's daughter, Rawheiya. As the hour grew late, the teenagers had grown scared, hungry, and tired. Yet after their tears subsided and they pooled their money to purchase a few tomatoes, they realized with excitement that they were responsible for themselves, with no adult supervision. These images of confusion and fear coupled with hope and dreams were now reflected in the "Prelude Sheroude."

In 1947 El-Dabh attended a performance at the Opera House of a ballet troupe from Belgium, and he became enamored of their dancing and music. Shortly after, he was invited to perform some of his music on the radio, and the broadcast was heard by Hassan Tussan, one of the princes in King Farouk's palace. One day soon after his radio performance, El-Dabh and his family were shocked when a bright red Rolls-Royce sports car pulled up in front of the family home—the king had decreed that only the royal family could drive red automobiles. To the family's amazement, the young prince entered the house and requested that the composer come with him to the palace in Abdeen to perform his music for the royal family. Without hesitation El-Dabh left with the prince, who broke all speed limits returning from Heliopolis to the palace.

El-Dabh was awestruck by the splendor of the palace, which was like an art gallery, full of the most magnificent artifacts that he had ever seen. King Farouk's sisters greeted him warmly, and the young man believed them to be most beautiful women; he wondered what their diet must be that allowed them to be so beautiful. A party soon began, and El-Dabh was instructed to play a large grand piano for the guests; when he finished, the prince performed pieces by Chopin and Beethoven. The party lasted until dawn, when the composer was returned to his anxiously awaiting family. The experiences of seeing the Belgian ballet troupe, being paid for his radio performance, and entertaining the royal family were to be the inspiration for his "Egyptian Suite Ballet" (1947), for piano.

When Gamal Abdel Nasser[20] became president of Egypt, El-Dabh composed *Ya Gamul Ya Nasser* (1947), for orchestra, in his honor. (This was not, however, the first instance of El-Dabh's paying a musical tribute to an Egyptian leader. The "Homage to Muhammad Ali al-kabir" (1946), for violin, cello, and piano, had been composed for the celebration of Muhammad Ali's[21] birthday. It had premiered on a Cairo radio station,

marking the first time El-Dabh earned money for one of his compositions.) El-Dabh was thoroughly enamored of Nasser and his ideology,
which envisioned unity throughout the Arab world. Nasser was a very
powerful and charismatic political figure who "used many references to
the people of Egypt and later to the unity of Arab peoples. He coupled the
language of oratory with that of ordinary speech. He played on Egyptian
heartstrings by championing sovereignty and Egyptian control of resources
to create a renovated version of 'Egypt for Egyptians.'"[22] El-Dabh composed *Ya Gamul Ya Nasser* to capture Nasser's attempt to return to a
period of an enlightened Arabic civilization that had combined religion
with the study of philosophy, language, mathematics, music, and medicine. Years later, when El-Dabh was in Ethiopia, the Ethiopian people
were still enthralled by Nasser, and elementary schoolchildren carried
his picture everywhere.

As El-Dabh was finding his musical voice and beginning to receive positive responses to his compositions, he continued to make a name for himself in agriculture and came to be considered quite an astute businessman.
Although he had an impressive and comfortable office in downtown Cairo,
he most enjoyed the days he had to travel with an affiliate into the villages
to work among the farmers for a few days. Eventually, El-Dabh realized
that he experienced great exhilaration outside the office but that he dreaded
paperwork and meetings, which he found tedious and insipid.

He now acknowledged to himself that his passion was music and that
he desired to devote his life to composition. The realization filled him
with elation that bordered on pure mirth; however, he also encountered
great torment as he struggled to reconcile the two passions of his life—
music and agriculture. As a response to this conflict, El-Dabh composed
Atshan Ya Sabaye (1947), for string orchestra, a piece inspired by a village song of the same name. The lyrics are:

> There is plenty of water, my countrymen, but I am thirsty.
> I am thirsty, my countrymen, even though the rivers are full of water.
> Everything is full of water, but I am still thirsty.[23]

The lyrics reflect need and the desire to be fulfilled. He had plenty of
money and had a good life working in agriculture, but he was still hungering and thirsting for music. For months he said nothing about it to his
family and close friends, yet he felt as though he died a little each morning when he arose to spend the day inside his office.

It was on one such morning that El-Dabh received a message from his old friend Kamal Iskander to contact him. Iskander implored his friend to reconsider the request to perform for the prestigious classical music society that was promoting the music of Egyptian composers. This time El-Dabh acquiesced, and in February 1949, at the Assembly Hall of All Saints' Cathedral in Cairo, he premiered his piano work "It Is Dark and Damp on the Front" (1949), a work about the mass Jewish emigration from Germany into Palestine and the resulting war. The composer said of the work, "The war is dark and damp in the heart of human beings. There is something there that is going to haunt people for years and years and years and years. War truly begins in the heart of every human being."[24] During the concert, El-Dabh also performed his "Prelude Sheroude," "Egyptian Suite Ballet" (1947), and "Fantasia-Amira" (1946), a work for solo piano he had composed for an eleven-year-old prodigy. However, the audience responded most enthusiastically to "It Is Dark and Damp on the Front" in which he utilized superimposed multiple chords, plucked the strings from inside the piano, and modified the sound of the instrument by inserting various items around the strings. (Track No. 5 on the companion CD.)

The day following the performance, Halim El-Dabh's name was in all the Egyptian newspapers. A Swiss critic, A. J. Patry, who had previously objected to the unknown pianist's appearance in such a prestigious hall, wrote a front-page story in Cairo's French newspaper, *La Bourse Egyptienne*, hailing the composer for his innovative use of sound and pedal technique. He wrote, "El-Dabh touches the instrument in a fashion of his own; he molds and fuses the sonorities of the piano producing sounds and feelings pertaining to a basic cult (race). He has exposed the European ear to a different way of playing. One must notice the way in which he uses the pedals, producing from simple elements complex superpositions of harmonies."[25]

An overnight sensation, El-Dabh was approached by a Mr. Black, cultural attaché of the American embassy, and asked to repeat his concert at the Oriental Hall (so named for its beautiful Islamic decorations) of the American University in Cairo. An announcement that El-Dabh would be performing was placed in the newspaper, and the result was staggering. The auditorium was filled to capacity, and latecomers were forced to stand outside listening to the performance through the open doors. The response to this second performance, which Iskander recorded, was equally remarkable, and arrangements were made to have "It Is Dark and Damp on the Front" performed during an exhibition of contemporary art at the local

MUSIC AND THE ARTS

ASSEMBLY HALL, ALL SAINTS' CATHEDRAL,
SHARIA MASPERO.

ENTRANCE FEE (to cover taxes and expenses)
P.T.9.5 *(front rows P.T.19.5)*

PIANOFORTE RECITAL

Friday, 11th February 1949, at 9.15 p.m.

Compositions by HALIM EL DABH

1) Prelude - Sheroude (Day-dreaming)
   First Theme : Calmness and relaxation
   Second Theme : Echo or illusions and dreams
   First Theme repeated.

2) Suite - Egyptian Ballet in the Romantic Style.
   1. The Palace
   2. The Arrival of the People
   3. The Dance of the Queen
   4. Departure.
   A Queen living in a palace in the desert governs
   the surrounding villages by her magic charms
   and dances, for which a yearly Festival is held.

3) Fantasy - Amira
   Written for an artist girl of eleven years' old
   to express the inate growing power of such young
   artists in finding their ways through the boundaries
   and worries of our social defects.

4) Espoir.

5) "It is dark and damp on the Front."
   Expressionist music of the darkness and damp-
   ness that are germinated in the psyche of man
   whilst fighting at the front in wartime.

HALIM EL DABH

INTERVAL

Recital by LINETTE TAMIM

1) Mozart . . . . Sonata in A major
   Andante con variazione
   Minuetto
   Trio
   Alla Turca

2) Mendelssohn . . 1. Songs without Words in
   F sharp minor
   2. Rondo Capriccioso

3) Chopin . . . . 1. Nocturne in D flat major
   2. Polonaise in A flat major.

Refreshments obtainable at the Interval by ticket
TEA - COFFEE P.T.2   LEMON P.T.1¹/₂   SANDWICH P.T.1

Amalgamated Press, Cairo

YMCA, marking El-Dabh's first collaboration with visual artists. An isolation booth was erected that contained a copy of the music on tape; a listener could enter the booth, sit on a stool, and listen to a recording of the piece while reading about it.

So keen was Patry's interest in the music of the young Egyptian composer that, following the performance at the Assembly Hall of All Saints' Cathedral, he sought out El-Dabh and arranged for a meeting to discuss El-Dabh's compositional style. This was the first time anyone had ever posed such a question to him, and El-Dabh was hesitant to discuss with words what he could effortlessly express through the piano. Nonetheless, the critic was persistent, and eventually El-Dabh was able to verbalize the concept behind his compositional process.

The exercise of articulating his art to a sympathetic audience proved quite liberating and inspired "Evolution and Decadence" (1949), for piano, a piece that examines the idea of music evolution. In the interview El-Dabh began by reflecting on very simple sounds—for instance, a single tone—and then explored its evolution through time and through the different elements of the universe until that single sound converged with other sounds. He asserted that there was really only one tone in the world and that all sounds came from that single pitch, which traveled throughout the universe. All sound was just one tone; that was all that was needed.

Patry withdrew from their meeting quite perplexed and convinced that El-Dabh was mocking him. However, El-Dabh left the exchange energized and immediately commenced developing his concept that sounds were traceable to a single tone, which then divided like a fertilized egg. He explored the idea that sounds were first developed in ancient Egypt before evolving diversely as they reached Europe. El-Dabh began studying the choral descants of the Baroque composers Dietrich Buxtehude[26] and Johann Sebastian Bach.[27] Feverishly analyzing the music of the Romantic period and the twentieth century, he became fascinated with the exploration of noise and sound. El-Dabh's new philosophy dealt with how the elements that cause a tone to emerge are also the elements that cause it to decay. In "Evolution and Decadence" he expresses that concept: as the tone evolves, it simultaneously begins to decay.

During this period of musical validation, El-Dabh's uncle returned from America for a brief visit with his family. As Balsam El-Dabh's eldest brother,

Opposite: 1949 program from the famed concert at All Saints' Cathedral in Cairo.

Aziz Benyiamin Fam exercised great influence on his sister's family, and all his nieces and nephews had great respect for him. Naively believing that his Uncle Aziz was acquainted with influential people in America, the newly motivated composer requested that he take some of his compositions back to the United States to show to anyone who might be interested. His uncle agreed; however, as Benyiamin Fam departed for the airport, he haphazardly stuffed the music sheets into his pockets. Witnessing his uncle's indifferent behavior, El-Dabh became distressed and angry; he vowed that he would follow his uncle to America within the year to make his music known himself.

El-Dabh would soon learn that the American cultural attaché had already begun to make that pledge a reality. Within weeks of the celebrated performance of "It Is Dark and Damp on the Front," Black contacted El-Dabh with the express purpose of encouraging him to apply for a Fulbright scholarship. Black was convinced that El-Dabh needed to be in the United States. El-Dabh was intrigued by this opportunity to study in America; however, his written English skills were so deficient that he struggled just to complete the application form. Black strongly supported his application, and despite his not passing the written portion of the test, a requisite for acceptance, Halim El-Dabh was selected to be one of seven chosen from over five hundred applicants to travel to the United States. Clearly Black's having been at the performance, the power of the music, and the audience's response had been critical factors.

Excited about traveling to America, El-Dabh feverishly attempted to learn everything he could about American music. Imploring a young Egyptian woman working at the embassy to bring him all the recordings of American music it had, he was dumbfounded to hear for the first time on some of the 78 rpm recordings she dutifully handed him American Indian music. He was intrigued by these people known as Hopi and Pueblo, and when he received word that he would be studying at Juilliard, he assumed that "Juilliard" was the name of another Native American tribe. Even when his misconception was discovered and clarified, El-Dabh contended that he wanted to learn more of the Native American music and inquired if there was not a school in the United States where he could hear and learn of the music of the Hopi and Pueblo. Black and others informed him of Juilliard's fine reputation, but the Egyptian composer held his ground, arguing that he did not think he would like New York's climate.

Amazingly, the Fulbright committee reconsidered, and El-Dabh was thrilled to receive a cable that he was to attend the University of New

Mexico to study music composition. However, first he was required to participate in a six-week intensive program at the University of Denver to remedy his English-language deficiency. Later, he learned that extra money would be supplied from the Surplus of Arms Fulbright Program. In essence, he would be receiving a double grant—one to study English and one to study composition in the United States. El-Dabh was struck by his good fortune that was precipitating his career change from agriculture to music, but only after several years had passed would he fully realize and appreciate the extraordinary treatment he had received.

In June 1950, two weeks before he was to leave for America, El-Dabh approached his boss, Abdul Monein Ashur, who had been in agricultural development in the United States, with the news that he would be leaving soon for America to study music. Ashur was flabbergasted and did not take the announcement well. Shaking his head, he inquired what he had done wrong as a boss. Then he became infuriated and pointed out that as manager of the entire area of agricultural land in Central Egypt, El-Dabh had been provided with an office in the city. He reminded El-Dabh that he was wealthy and that he had everything a young man needed. Ashur began screaming and cursed El-Dabh, prophesying that he would starve as a musician. The sensitive composer retreated from Ashur's office visibly upset; however, he was eager to travel to the United States to study musical composition, and he vowed never to second-guess his decision to leave Egypt and agriculture.

2

Denver, New Mexico, and Boston

Visiting *Amreeka*[1] was something the twenty-nine-year-old El-Dabh often had fantasized about as a young boy listening to his mother's tales while she tended the family's laundry. Yet when the time came for him to leave his beloved Egypt and embark on his adventure to the United States during the summer of 1950, he grew apprehensive that he was not fully prepared. His trepidation waned, however, when he arrived in New York City, where he was immediately enthralled by the sights and sounds of the metropolis. He deeply regretted that he had only one week to absorb everything before traveling to the University of Denver.

During his brief stay in New York, El-Dabh was drawn to the George Washington Bridge; the massive structure of concrete, steel, and asphalt captivated him. He spent hours standing on the bridge[2] gazing at the traffic and the lights, transfixed by the stratification of the overlapping ramps winding in and out before terminating at the various levels of the structure. To El-Dabh this architectural engineering was the visual equivalent of the cacophony of the subway system. He delighted in the experience and reflected on Arnold Schoenberg's *Pierrot Lunaire*,[3] a work he had heard shortly before his departure from Egypt and discussed with his close friends and fellow devotees of contemporary music, Munir Yunan, Henri Shalala, and Kamal Iskander. The time spent on the George Washington Bridge prompted El-Dabh to reexamine his relationship to the world, specifically to recall and to contemplate the pyramids, which had always filled him with the same feelings of awe and wonderment that he was experiencing in New York. As is often the case when one travels to a foreign country for the first time, El-Dabh discovered that the act of leaving his homeland had expanded his image of it, that he now appreciated Egypt and the entire African continent with a fuller sense of perspective. Feeling for the first time that his vision was not limited, El-Dabh felt confident that he was prepared to learn more about musical composition and to comprehend more about himself.

The stay at the University of Denver afforded El-Dabh the opportunity to become friendly with several members of the Denver Symphony Orchestra, who were housed with him in one of the university's dormitories. He valued the time he spent with the young and vivacious musicians. Because there were not many foreign students in Denver in 1950, the musicians in turn were fascinated by the young Egyptian. However, the musicians were astounded when El-Dabh, who was housed in a private apartment fully equipped with a modern kitchen, complained to the administration that as the youngest of nine siblings he had never learned to cook for himself; one of the cultural attaché's personal assistants flew in from Cairo for the express purpose of instructing him in the operation of his kitchen.

Assuming him to be a member of the Egyptian elite, the American musicians who had befriended him immediately invited him to attend Colorado's Aspen Music Festival. Arranging with the backstage manager for El-Dabh not to have to purchase tickets, the musicians enabled their exotic new friend to attend the festival any time he pleased, just by showing up at the backstage door with them. One evening during the festival the musicians eagerly awaited the arrival of the celebrated composer Igor Stravinsky,[4] who was to arrive the next morning to begin rehearsing for a performance of his *Firebird*, which he was to conduct personally. The enthusiastic musicians insistently reminded the often-preoccupied El-Dabh to be certain to awake early the next morning to accompany them to the festival grounds for the much-anticipated first rehearsal. Unfortunately, El-Dabh stayed up late studying for his English exam and overslept. Distraught that he might miss the prodigious opportunity and disappoint his friends, El-Dabh dressed in haste and thought he could walk to the site. Soon it was clear that only by hitchhiking could he arrive in time; El-Dabh forlornly stood at the side of the road and stuck out his thumb. Within minutes, and much to his delight, a large black sedan pulled over and stopped. He approached the vehicle and bent to peer through the tinted glass of the passenger window—and was startled to see Stravinsky squinting back at him. Gathering his courage, El-Dabh crawled into the back of the automobile and began speaking in French to the great composer, who was so captivated by the young Egyptian that by the time they arrived at the grounds, he had invited him to be his assistant during his tenure at the festival.

El-Dabh readily assumed the responsibilities of shadowing Stravinsky, toting his scores, locating his conducting or reading glasses, and helping the maestro maintain an organized schedule—which El-Dabh's friends viewed as most amusing. El-Dabh enjoyed an immediate and remarkable rapport with Stravinsky, who introduced him to several visiting New York opera directors and conductors and generously acquainted them with some of El-Dabh's scores. "It Is Dark and Damp on the Front" was particularly well received—an irony, since an old friend, Henri Shalala, had once cautioned El-Dabh never to show the piece to Stravinsky, because the composer, he was certain, would attempt to pass it off as his own. Never imagining he would have an opportunity to meet Stravinsky, El-Dabh had dismissed Shalala's well-intentioned warning at the time, but now here he was, enjoying a favorable relationship with the man. The serendipitous meeting and subsequent experience with Stravinsky seemed ever more surreal, and El-Dabh was eager to write his old friend to inform him of his good fortune.

El-Dabh thrived upon all this attention and enjoyed attending Stravinsky's rehearsals of *The Firebird* and Mozart's *Symphony No. 1* (K. 16), until one day he tried too hard to impress the maestro by initiating a discussion of the twelve-tone compositions of Arnold Schoenberg. The minute El-Dabh mentioned Schoenberg, Stravinsky became very upset and agitated; he walked away from the young man, who soon learned through another aide that his position as the maestro's assistant had been terminated. On several occasions following their split, El-Dabh and Stravinsky encountered each other at festival parties and other functions, and quite frequently someone unaware of their past relationship would attempt to introduce the two. Each time Stravinsky would bristle and announce curtly that they had already met. El-Dabh was confused and hurt by the brusque treatment from Stravinsky. When El-Dabh later heard a performance at Harvard University of Stravinsky's *Septets* (for clarinet, bassoon, horn, piano, violin, viola, and cello), which employed Schoenberg's twelve-tone system, he was baffled that Stravinsky had become angry when he had broached the subject of Schoenberg's compositional technique.

It was not until several years later that El-Dabh learned that during the first decade of the twentieth century, when the Schoenbergs struggled with financial difficulties, Mathilde Schoenberg had contacted Stravinsky, beseeching him to assist her husband. Stravinsky had refused, and his relationship with the Schoenbergs had remained strained for several years. El-Dabh was ignorant of the Schoenberg-Stravinsky rift, but Stravinsky took great offense at the mention of Schoenberg's name, and he never fully forgave El-Dabh his perceived transgression. In fact years later, when the two were reintroduced following the Boston premiere of Stravinsky's *The Rake's Progress*, Stravinsky graciously shook El-Dabh's hand, but he was still quite cold. The meeting had occurred following an incident of déjà vu, when transportation difficulties forced El-Dabh to hitchhike to the Tanglewood Festival site in Massachusetts. He had the good fortune to be picked up by soprano Arlene Stone, who later became so enamored of El-Dabh and his music that she invited him to be her guest for the premiere. Delighted, El-Dabh readily accepted Stone's invitation and was greatly amused when, following the performance, Stone escorted him to Stravinsky for an introduction.

Following his intensive English-language study at the University of Denver, El-Dabh traveled on the *Santa Fe Chief* to attend classes in composition at the University of New Mexico. He was met at the train station by a wiry and energetic woman who appeared to be ninety years old. Her large felt hat was adorned with a long pheasant feather, which tickled El-Dabh as she enthusiastically pumped his hand while introducing herself as Mrs. Creswell. Impatiently motioning El-Dabh to place his suitcases in the trunk of her large black sedan, Creswell explained that she held an important literary position with the International Institute of Education, which was based in Cairo with representatives in Albuquerque; curiosity had compelled her to volunteer to meet the new student from Egypt. Charmed by her candor, El-Dabh relaxed as he settled into the seat beside her; however, his mood changed to panic as they sped off toward town, nearly colliding with two parked cars.

When queried where he wished to live while attending the University of New Mexico, El-Dabh had naively replied that the dormitory would be fine. However, he was disappointed to discover that the student housing at the University of New Mexico was different from the facilities he had been accustomed to at the University of Denver; they appeared crowded and noisy. Fearing that he would not be able to concentrate enough to compose, he petitioned Mrs. Creswell to find him alternative housing. She immediately arranged for him to stay in a room at the spacious residence of a pharmacist named Miller, who generously invited students who boarded in his home to accompany his family on weekend outings to explore the state of New Mexico. These outings greatly appealed to the former agriculturalist, and El-Dabh particularly enjoyed some of the American Indian areas, where he investigated the brooks and rivers among the mountains of Jemez Springs.

Additionally, it was at the Millers' home that he was introduced to a pretty and vivacious dark-haired young woman named Marybelle Hyde, from Missouri. Mary, as she was known, also lived with the Millers and was pursuing an undergraduate degree in social work among the American Indians in the area. The Egyptian seized on the opportunity for extensive conversations with the attractive student about the music of these American Indian tribes. Although he was sincerely interested in learning more about Hopi and Pueblo music, it was obvious to the Miller family that the young man was also deeply interested in learning more about Mary.

El-Dabh's reputation as a composer had preceded him to New Mexico, where he was enrolled in the graduate program. However, because he was primarily self-taught as a musician, he was required to attend the freshman music-theory class as part of his training. El-Dabh appreciated this rudimentary instruction, and he enjoyed his experience in the freshman class. He also relished the awe of the younger students in the presence of the Egyptian composer about whom everyone was talking. El-Dabh flourished in his advanced counterpoint, composition, and conducting classes, but he especially enjoyed the class on the twelve-tone system taught during the summer of 1951 by visiting composer Ernst Krenek,[5] who commenced his discussions of Arnold Schoenberg and Alban Berg[6] with explorations of Johann Sebastian Bach's counterpoint.

In Krenek's class one extremely hot Friday afternoon, El-Dabh realized that he had not yet composed a symphony, and he felt compelled to write one. Following class he purchased a ream of orchestral manuscript paper and headed for the Millers' large enclosed porch, where he commenced work on *Symphony No. 1* (1951), for full orchestra. With huge sheets of paper spread out in front of him, he sat on the floor for hours that first evening; Mary was forced to step over him when she returned from a late date. El-Dabh was not accustomed to American dating practices, and Mary was not knowledgeable about the compositional process; accordingly, they were intrigued with each other and stayed up well past dawn engrossed in conversation, which marked the beginning of their romance.

After working intensely on his own for several weeks, El-Dabh took his symphony to his music history teacher, Hugh Milton Miller,[7] for consultation. Miller asked why the work had not been shown first to El-Dabh's composition instructor, John Donald Robb,[8] dean of the College of Fine Arts; the young man sheepishly confessed that Robb was frequently annoyed with his assigned homework. Miller remarked sympathetically that he had observed the growing friction between El-Dabh and Robb; however, he convinced his student that it was appropriate to take the work to him. Neither Miller nor El-Dabh was aware that Robb had received a letter from the American Cultural Center in Cairo stating that it was preparing to send a delegation to observe how El-Dabh was developing; Dean Robb was apprehensive and suspicious about this visit.

When El-Dabh finally brought the composition to Robb, the dean immediately insisted that El-Dabh make a piano reduction to facilitate reading through it. Believing that to comprehend fully how to compose a symphonic work one needed to tackle the undertaking completely, from the flutes to the double basses, El-Dabh adamantly refused. He insisted day after day on bringing the full score for Robb's critique. Robb tried to convince El-Dabh, but he became so frustrated that he shook his head and remarked insultingly, "Well, what can I expect? You're just an African!" He regretted the comment instantly, but without hesitation El-Dabh replied, "Dean Robb, that's the best compliment I've ever heard, and I love you for it. Thank you. I've always wanted somebody to tell me that."[9]

However, the teacher-student relationship was strained. Although he attempted to brush off the insult, El-Dabh related the story to one of the delegates during the visit. Robb soon received a letter from both the Cairo and New York offices of the International Institute of Education informing him that El-Dabh was not happy and should receive better treatment. Robb was also informed that both offices required verification that El-Dabh was receiving the full benefit of his Fulbright opportunity. Astonished that the situation had escalated to such a degree, Robb summoned El-Dabh into his office and suggested that if he was having problems with the composition class, perhaps he should consider majoring in musicology. El-Dabh insisted on continuing with composition as his major concentration, but he continued to refuse to produce a piano reduction of his symphony for Robb. He later recognized that he had scored the double basses too low. Instead of E as their lowest tone, El-Dabh had scored them down to E-flat. This "error," later repeated in El-Dabh's *Symphony No. 2* (1951), in which the basses are required to play as low as B and even G (two full octaves below the cello's G string), was ridiculed by Howard Hanson when it was considered for inclusion at the Eastman School of Music's Festival of American Music in 1954.[10]

Luigi Dallapiccola and their friend Rosa with Halim El-Dabh (1951).

Symphony No. 1 was an enormous undertaking for El-Dabh; however, he regarded it as one of his most valuable learning experiences, and
while struggling with it he decided to submit examples of his music to
the leading composers in the country, including Cole Porter[11] and Paul
Hindemith. Typically, El-Dabh mailed one or two pages from a composition; however, because the pages of "It Is Dark and Damp on the Front"
were already stapled together, he sent Irving Fine[12] the entire piece. Fine,
impressed with the work, immediately offered El-Dabh a scholarship to
study at the Berkshire Music Center at Tanglewood in Lenox, Massachusetts. El-Dabh immediately relayed the good news to the members of the
Fulbright committee.

Recognizing the significance of this opportunity, the committee unanimously agreed to extend El-Dabh's Fulbright support for another year,
which enabled him to travel to the Berkshires for study with Irving Fine,
Aaron Copland,[13] and Luigi Dallapiccola.[14] Again, it was several years later
before El-Dabh fully realized how special was the treatment he had received not only from the cultural attaché but from the American Cultural
Center in Cairo, the International Institute of Education, and the Fulbright committee, to name only a few benefactors. At the time he took

Composers at work in a class at the Berkshire Music Center, 1952. Left to right:
Yehoshua Lakner of Tel Aviv, Israel; Aaron Copland, head of Tanglewood's
composition department; Ben-Zion Orgad of Tel Aviv; and Halim El-Dabh.
(Photo courtesy of Margrit and Yehoshua Lakner.)

everything in stride and only focused on the moment—a personality trait
he maintained throughout his life.

Arriving at the Berkshire Music Center in early summer of 1951, El-
Dabh attempted to absorb as much music as possible. In the midst of this
intensely musical experience, the radio broadcasting network of the U.S.
government, Voice of America (VOA),[15] became interested in chronicling
and telecasting the Egyptian composer's experiences in America. From
its studio in New York, Voice of America broadcast many of El-Dabh's
piano works, his *String Quartet No. 1: Metamorphosis and Fugue on
Egyptian Folklore* (1951), and his "Drum-Takseem" (1951, for solo percussion). Interviews with El-Dabh explaining his drumming technique,
of the composer demonstrating on various African drums, and even entire drum performances were recorded and aired for VOA's *Handshakes
across the Ocean*[16] program. (Unfortunately, El-Dabh never was able to
obtain copies of any of the programs.)

String Quartet No. 1 was based on the theme of "Atshan Ya Sabaye,"
the village song that had served as the basis for his 1947 string orchestra

composition of the same name. Shortly after his arrival in the Berkshires, El-Dabh composed an expanded version of *String Quartet No. 1* and presented it to Fine for a critique; Fine was so impressed that he offered to instruct El-Dabh in scoring the appropriate slur and phrasing indications. Fine became quite engaged with the piece and personally rehearsed the string quartet for its premiere at Tanglewood. (This engendered a strong bond between the two men, which later resulted in an invitation by Fine to El-Dabh to study at Brandeis University.) When the work was later performed in Jordan Hall in Boston, Klaus George Roy, in a review for the *Christian Science Monitor*, wrote, "By far the most absorbing offering was the String Quartet No. 1 by the young Egyptian composer Halim El-Dabh. The Quartet was fascinating in color and at times compelling in motion. A lento mysterioso [*sic*] movement of consistently dissonant chords was highly evocative of Egyptian sights and sounds. Surely more authentic than Aïda! The final fugue proved not at all academic but strikingly original in themes and formal growth."[17]

When El-Dabh departed the University of New Mexico to begin his study with Irving Fine and Aaron Copland at the Berkshire Music Center, Mary Hyde followed him. He had not entreated her to accompany him; however, she believed she was in love and took advantage of the fact that her sister and brother-in-law lived at the foot of the Berkshires in Northampton. Mary knew she would be welcome to stay with them. Aware of Mary's feelings for the composer, her sister often encouraged her to invite El-Dabh to dinner with them. El-Dabh, however, although he was very fond of Mary, dated others as well. He particularly enjoyed the company of a beautiful young woman named Rosa, who also dated the composer Luigi Dallapiccola. El-Dabh's relationship with Rosa caused some friction with Dallapiccola, who often asked if El-Dabh's fatigued appearance in class was a result of late evenings with Rosa.

Eventually, nonetheless, his relationship with Mary blossomed, and they decided to marry—without his family's approval. When he announced his plan to his family, his uncle Aziz Benyiamin Fam became highly distressed. Benyiamin Fam quickly announced that he had found a rich woman for his nephew to marry instead; he insisted that Halim return to his successful career in agriculture, with music as a sideline. Uncharacteristically, El-Dabh refused his uncle's mandate, which so incensed Benyiamin Fam that he contacted Mary's father to see if he could prevent the wedding.

Despite grave misgivings by both families, the couple married on August 6, 1952; however, the ceremony did not go smoothly. Because El-Dabh did not possess a valid driver's license, Mary was forced to drive them to obtain the marriage license on the way to the ceremony, which was to be performed by the justice of the peace at New Lebanon, New York. The nervous bride promptly drove the car into a ditch. Fearing that the disgruntled families had cursed their union, the couple decided to delay the ceremony, but a congenial tow-truck driver, learning they were on their way to be married, offered to drive them to the office of the clerk of courts for the license and then on to the justice of the peace. Arriving at the clerk's office, El-Dabh produced his visa from Egypt, and Mary presented her papers certifying that New Mexico was her state of residence. The New York clerk found everything in order with El-Dabh's visa; however, he did not recognize New Mexico as part of the United States and refused to issue the license. Mary burst into tears, and a heated and emotional exchange between El-Dabh and the clerk ensued. Finally the clerk agreed that he would accept the word of the town's doctor. The tow-truck driver carried the three of them to the doctor, who verified that New Mexico was indeed a state in the Union; the satisfied clerk issued the license; and the distraught couple proceeded to the justice of the peace to be married.

Shortly after the wedding, Irving Fine suggested that El-Dabh pursue a master's degree in music at the New England Conservatory, studying theory and composition with Francis Judd Cooke.[18] Following his mentor's advice, El-Dabh applied for admission and was elated to be notified that he had been awarded a two-year scholarship. The most beneficial experience for El-Dabh during his tenure at the New England Conservatory was to be his weekly composition class with Cooke. Each Friday the composition students were required either to have their pieces performed or to perform them themselves in free public concerts in Jordan Hall. For these performances, El-Dabh frequently played the drums or improvised new compositions on the piano. Many of these improvisations, unfortunately, are lost, but one that was later notated was his fifteen-minute "Meditation on the Nile" (1951), for piano. Following its premiere on December 15, 1952, Harold Rogers wrote the following for the *Christian Science Monitor*:

> El-Dabh, an Egyptian, performed his "Meditations [*sic*] on the Nile" for piano and revealed a concept of superb originality. He works economically, he seeks and finds surprising timbres; his writing is filled with melodic and rhythmic intrigue. But there is far more to El-Dabh's "Meditations" than meets the ear. These pieces are infused with the

mystery of the East. The Time motif, as serene as the Pyramids, reappears cyclically as an interlude. There is captivating fugal treatment in the "Life and Motion" section, and for the flood El-Dabh actually achieves watery timbres.[19]

El-Dabh thought very highly of Francis Judd Cooke and his classes, in which the students were immersed fully in contemporary musical thought through analysis of the compositions of Béla Bartók, Arnold Schoenberg, Alban Berg, and Igor Stravinsky. To give his students a better appreciation and understanding of the history and pedagogy of music theory, Cooke required them to sing Palestrina[20] and Buxtehude. While some of the students bristled at connecting contemporary music to the works of Renaissance and Baroque masters, El-Dabh found the experience extremely beneficial in developing and enhancing his own compositional style. He believed the connection to the past enabled him to expand his innovations while simultaneously evoking his Egyptian heritage. This duality is evident particularly in his piano works, in which the historical connections—represented by mbiras, sanzas, marimbas, and xylophones, and by harps, lyres, dulcimers, psalteries, and lutes—are integrated into the sonorities and essence of the piano.

At the New England Conservatory, El-Dabh struggled to express the real meaning of what he was attempting to convey musically. The other students spoke in advanced theoretical terms, and El-Dabh, wanting to impress his mentor, attempted to explain his *Symphony No. 2* to Cooke similarly. Cooke, who admired El-Dabh's employment of sustained violas throughout the piece, laughed at the less than articulate El-Dabh and responded, "Don't worry. God is sitting at your elbow. Let the others worry. You know, there are thousands of theorists who will figure it out, but it's perfect."[21] Cooke's comment had a tremendous effect on El-Dabh's compositional life, because it allowed him the freedom he required to compose.

Symphony No. 2 was dedicated to Francis Judd Cooke, who certainly did not maintain the typical professor-student relationship with El-Dabh. Cooke made a great many allowances for his prize pupil that he never would have considered granting to the average composition student. If, for example, Cooke believed El-Dabh had stayed up all night composing, he instructed the other students not to awaken him. Whenever El-Dabh elected not to join the class in the morning, his professor would arrange to convene with him at noon. Often El-Dabh was invited to dinner with Cooke and his British wife and their many children at their home in

Halim El-Dabh in silhouette (1952). (Photo by Gordon N. Converse.)

Lexington. Once again, it would be several years later before El-Dabh would recognize how very atypical was his relationship with Cooke.

"Osmo-Symbiotic" (1952), for two pianos, was composed for the husband-and-wife duo-piano partners Ivan and Suzan Waldbauer, members of the New England Conservatory faculty. Although the family name was a German one, Ivan was Hungarian and related distantly to Bartók, whose use of asymmetrical meters and compound rhythmic structures was very influential at that time. When the couple suggested that El-Dabh compose a work for two pianos, he opted to pay homage in it to Bartók be-cause of their personal connection. "Osmo-Symbiotic" combined El-Dabh's agri-cultural life with his musical world. When he was working in agricul-ture, El-Dabh had experimented with the process of osmosis in the rich, black Egyptian soil—two organisms would rise to the top of a liquid solu-tion and there exist through each other symbiotically. The piece may be viewed as an expression of El-Dabh's prior agricultural life in Egypt against the background of the social environment he discovered as a composer in the United States. The work was premiered by the faculty duo in Jordan Hall before they assumed faculty positions at the University of Rhode Island, where Ivan became involved in archiving Bartók's manuscripts.

"Osmo-Symbiotic" is also known as "Duo-Tahmeel No. 1." *Tahmeel,* or *tahmeela,* is a poetic Arabic word with different meanings in various Arab countries. In Lebanon, for example, *tahmeela* means "suspenders." *Tahmeel* is also a musical form that developed only in Egypt; however, as it developed during the eleventh century in Egypt, Morocco, and Algeria, a *tahmeela* was based primarily on poetry. In this composition, *tahmeela* reflects word placement in a specific poetic form. El-Dabh, fascinated by the actual poetic form of the word *tahmeela,* incorporated the idea into this piece but took the concept a little further. Like the *nawba,* a suite that developed in Egypt and Morocco and influenced compositional forms employed by the Meistersingers[22] and the troubadours,[23] the *tahmeela* was a type of concerto grosso,[24] in which a smaller ensemble is a foil for a larger group. "Osmo-Symbiotic" (or "Duo-Tahmeel No. 1") was performed again in 1954 when Darius Milhaud[25] was invited to Brandeis University for a reception in his honor. The concert was performed outdoors, under a huge tent; however, in the middle of the concert a torrential rain col-lapsed the tent. Milhaud, along with everyone else, was drenched, and El-Dabh, who had met Milhaud briefly prior to the concert, was unable to locate him following the downpour.

In the winter of 1952, El-Dabh and Mary decided to travel to New Hampshire to visit his friend, pianist Nadia Kelada, one of seven Egyp-tians who had received Fulbrights with him. Nadia and several of her friends invited the couple to join them on their way to Dartmouth Col-lege to attend Winterfest, an elaborate festival of winter sports and games. Prior to his departure, El-Dabh received word that his *String Quartet No. 1* had been selected to represent the New England Conservatory of Music at the International Federation of Music Students Sixth Annual Sympo-sium of Contemporary Music, sponsored by a consortium of the conservatory, Juilliard, the Yale University School of Music, the Eastman School of Music at the University of Rochester, the Curtis Institute of Music, and the Royal Conservatory of Music of Toronto. It was Juilliard's turn to host the event in 1952. El-Dabh's delight that his work had been selected by the symposium committee continued throughout the Winterfest. El-Dabh found the snow exhilarating and snowmen hilarious, and he and Mary savored life at Dartmouth.

When he returned to the New England Conservatory on Monday, however, Francis Judd Cooke announced that, due to a previous engagement, the symposium's first violinist had been forced to withdraw from the performance;[26] the committee had to reach a decision by the following Friday concerning which alternate composition could be substituted. Furious to learn that he had less than a week to submit a suitable piece for consideration, El-Dabh began to work frantically on "Monotone, Bitone, and Polytone" (1952), for wind sextet and percussion. He did not bother with a preliminary sketch of his ideas but commenced writing down the new work in ink. Working feverishly all night long, El-Dabh triumphantly entered Cooke's composition class on Tuesday morning and announced that he had completed a movement of a piece for wind ensemble and percussion called "Monotone." Thrusting the composition into the hands of his startled teacher, El-Dabh spun on his heel and strode from the classroom. To the delight of his fellow classmates, El-Dabh returned the next morning with another movement, entitled "Bitone." The next morning his classmates and teacher anxiously and eagerly awaited the final movement of the work; however, exhaustion after two days without sleep forced the composer to remain at home. Following some much-needed sleep, he again worked relentlessly throughout the night and on Friday morning emerged with "Polytone." Cooke delivered the work ahead of the deadline to the symposium committee, which unanimously selected "Monotone, Bitone, and Polytone" to represent the New England Conservatory at the Juilliard Symposium in March 1952. El-Dabh was asked to conduct the piece; however, as he stood before the musicians at the first rehearsal, he realized that the exhaustion brought on by the work's hasty creation had resulted in anxiety and tension, and he requested that someone else conduct the piece. (Track No. 6 on the companion CD.)

"Monotone, Bitone, and Polytone" is also known as "Sextet" because when first questioned at the symposium about the meaning of the title, El-Dabh responded that it was a sextet. In 1959, El-Dabh added a second percussion part to the original wind sextet; however, he soon realized that the part was too difficult for one percussionist to play alone. With a second percussionist the work required eight performers, and the title changed to "Thumaniya" to reflect the fact that it had emerged as an octet for winds and percussion; however, El-Dabh eventually returned to the preferred original title.

The performance of "Monotone, Bitone, and Polytone" at the Juilliard Symposium was critiqued during a panel discussion led by John Cage,[27] Gian Carlo Menotti,[28] and Vincent Persichetti,[29] who maintained their philosophical differences throughout the debate. Cage praised the work for its innovative use of blocks of sounds and timbres throughout various ranges of instrumentation. He appreciated its organic development and relationship among sounds rather than thematic expansion in the melody. Conversely, Menotti and Persichetti harshly criticized the work; El-Dabh perceived that, for these two, if Cage liked a work it must be terrible. He never fully comprehended the uproar caused by "Monotone, Bitone, and Polytone," but he was pleased that his former teacher Aaron Copland attended the symposium and offered him support, stating that he was impressed by El-Dabh's ease and facility in composition. However, the critique that meant the most to the composer was to come when Balsam El-Dabh first heard her son's very avant-garde work. She declared that it sounded like the village and brought to her mind the image of a cow wearing blinders walking in a circle, pulling a huge rotating wheel attached in the middle to a geared horizontal shaft. The mechanism scooped water in ceramic buckets from a trough and then emptied them onto the land, and as the buckets submerged into the water, the gears squeaked. For her, this is the essence of "Monotone, Bitone, and Polytone."

In 1952 El-Dabh composed a work scored for full orchestra; however, it cannot be termed a symphony. Francis Judd Cooke was very intrigued by the piece and encouraged El-Dabh to submit it for a competition to be held in Belgium. *The Legend* (1952) treated the fermata[30] as a point of activity in itself rather than as a lengthening of a pitch or a rest, often at a cadential point at the end of a phrase. In addition to the fermata, El-Dabh employed a symbol he referred to as an "antifermata," which he drew as a coil to represent the shortening of a pitch or a rest from its usual value.

In the score El-Dabh wrote that the work was:

> a visual rendition of frozen sound within vertical bars. The bar lines are indicators only for chronological time. Individual instrumental-

ists are free to choose their own active time according to what they're playing. The opening first movement is a guide. The indications of fermata and antifermatas is an indication of this free over lapp [*sic*] of active time over the chronological bar organization. The chord as a unit is a frozen painting in movement 1. It is up to the *conductor* to bring the overlapping times into the frozen vertical position whenever he desires to do so. This is true with all the movements except the last where point to point relation were [*sic*] meant to be so.[31]

Unusual characteristics of the piece include the composer's requiring the first violin to play an E-flat to an E-1/4-sharp on the D string, and combining the harp and the strings of the piano, plucked on the inside of the instrument, as continuations of each other. Although the harp and piano are indicated in the fourth movement of the work, these instruments are omitted from the list of instruments on the front page of the score. The harp and piano later are combined with the strings of the orchestra to produce an ethereal effect as they play harmonics. Later the horns are required to play into the piano, which produces greater resonance of the sound. Included in the battery of percussion instruments is a set of Afro-Caribbean drums (bongos, timbales, and conga), as well as xylophone, vibraphone, marimba, cymbals, gong, and a set of four chromatic timpani (played by two performers) ranging from high B to low F. The bongo player is instructed to use shoe polish or rosin on the right hand thumb and to press and release near the edge of the bongo while striking the instrument. Analysis of the score indicates that the "voice of the legend" referred to in the composition's title is realized in the English horn part.

In 1954, as El-Dabh was finishing his graduate degree at the New England Conservatory, he received an invitation to study with the influential conductor and teacher Nadia Boulanger[32] at Fontainebleau, outside Paris, France—an opportunity that he considered a dream come true. The timing was fortuitous, because he already had made arrangements to travel to Paris and home to Egypt following graduation, while Mary returned to Missouri to visit with her family. He planned to contact Boulanger at Fontainebleau as soon as he arrived in Paris; however, El-Dabh was soon distracted by Parisian life. He experienced a revitalization, an energy that he had not felt since living in Cairo, and he became engrossed in a festival celebrating Egyptian music and fashion. During this festival, El-Dabh was introduced to the president and chief executive officer of France Batîment

Industrie, a major producer of steel. The man was also a tenor; he wined and dined the Egyptian in his chateau with the hope that El-Dabh would compose music for him. Before a commission took place, however, El-Dabh learned that his high-school friend Pierre Nouri, a former member of The Bones, was to be ordained a priest at the monastery located at Soubise, on the Seine. Nouri invited his friend to come and stay at the monastery with him, and without hesitation El-Dabh left to spend eighteen days with the priests. He reveled in their activities and most enjoyed singing Gregorian chants at four o'clock in the morning; the priests were equally taken by the Egyptian and his music. One Scandinavian priest sight-read "It Is Dark and Damp on the Front," and the composer was quite impressed. The atmosphere at the monastery was very inviting, and as his third week there came to an end, El-Dabh informed Nouri that if he did not leave soon and return to his wife, he might never want to leave at all.

Soon after, El-Dabh received a cable from his mother chiding him for not visiting his family back in Egypt. He dutifully complied, and in his hurry to appease his mother he promptly forgot about the scholarship to Fontainebleau; for the remainder of his life he would receive criticism for not taking advantage of this opportunity. In Egypt, El-Dabh received a cable from his former teacher Irving Fine, who was now teaching at Harvard. Fine announced that he had been offered the chairmanship of the newly created School of Music at Brandeis University and asked El-Dabh to pursue an advanced degree there. Although intrigued by this prospect, El-Dabh had promised to stay with his mother in Egypt until December. Fine cabled back that he would hold a place for El-Dabh until his return. However, because he was less than careful with paperwork, the Egyptian encountered difficulties when he finally decided to return to America. He was not permitted to reenter the United States because, technically, he was no longer eligible for a student visa. And since he had married an American woman he could not receive a visitor visa either. El-Dabh contacted Fine, who arranged for El-Dabh to reenter the country on a special visa reserved for scholars possessing exceptional knowledge or unique talent.

El-Dabh accepted a graduate assistantship at Brandeis, which involved teaching Arabic, and he became very well known and popular across the campus. He also entered into the beginning of a very creative period in terms of his composition, thriving in the rich musical environment, which was replete with composers such as Arthur Berger[33] and Harold Shapero,[34] as well as Fine. Milton Babbitt[35] and Leonard Bernstein[36] often visited the campus as well. El-Dabh was pleased that both Fine and Aaron Copland

Egyptian felucca boats.

attended his many performances at Brandeis, including the premiere of "Felucca, the Celestial Journey" before an audience of twenty thousand.

"Felucca, the Celestial Journey" (1953), for solo piano, relates the legend of the Egyptian god Ra[37] in his journey across the celestial sky. Transported on a *felucca*, depicted in renderings of ancient Egyptian boats as a small vessel with its sails tilted in a particular way, Ra entered into the body of the goddess Nut[38] and the following day emerged from her mouth, shining with great splendor. Frequently when El-Dabh had traveled to Aswan via a modern-day felucca, he had been greeted by small children running alongside the riverbank chanting, singing, or playing in the river with their own small boats made of tin. In this piece, El-Dabh combined the images of the children chanting as they played with their boats and of the pharaonic temples surrounding Luxor and Aswan, which reminded one of the stories of Ra and ancient Egypt. The work's three movements have appeared under different titles. Once they were identified as "Dimensions," "Transformation," and "Celebration"; however, they more frequently are labeled as "Ra," "The Journey," and "The Festival of Nut."

When the piece premiered at the first Boston Festival in 1953, the *Boston Herald* headline declared, "Twenty Thousand People Listen to Halim El-Dabh Play 'Felucca.'"[39] Four years later, while collaborating with choreographer Martha Graham[40] on the ballet *Clytemnestra* (1958), a work that proved to be a major vehicle for both, El-Dabh learned that Graham and her musical director, Eugene Lester, had been two of the twenty thousand

Halim El-Dabh in profile (1954).

in attendance for the premiere. He believed this to be an act of divine intervention, because it was at Brandeis that El-Dabh began combining music with dance and the visual arts, working with fellow student Saga Vuori, a talented dancer from Finland, who approached El-Dabh with a request to be allowed to choreograph his music. El-Dabh was flattered by the young woman's attention and started spending a great deal of time watching her rehearse with a small group of dancers. To his wife's increasing concern, El-Dabh and Vuori became very close friends. He composed "Frieze in Body Movement" (1954, for violin, piano, timpani, and harp) for Vuori to choreograph. Originally titled "Impressions from Gauguin, Léger and Dali," paintings by the three artists were displayed at the work's premiere. El-Dabh selected Paul Gauguin[41] for his earthiness, his women, and his lushness; Fernand Léger[42] for his imagery of the mechanical body; and Salvador Dali[43] for the surrealism in the painting *Watch* and the superconsciousness it depicted.

As her husband became increasingly well known, Mary immersed herself in her own career in social work. El-Dabh focused on completing his degree. El-Dabh received a master's in fine arts in 1954,[44] which was considered a terminal degree, because no doctoral program had been developed at Brandeis. His was one of the first master of fine arts degrees conferred by Brandeis, and he was appointed a marshal for the School of Music's first graduation ceremony.

Mary was now eager to start a family and wanted her husband to secure a teaching position at a university, which would provide them with benefits and financial security. El-Dabh was not averse to a teaching career; however, he did not want to be associated with any one particular institution of higher learning in the traditional sense. Rather, he wanted to work with various institutions, on his own terms. Hoping to balance teaching with composition, he inquired of the deans of the Boston Conservatory and the Peabody Institute if they were interested in hiring him. However, he soon realized that his ideas were considered too advanced and he himself was considered a dangerous species for a higher-education setting. Feeling restless and confined in Boston, he frequently traveled to Egypt, France, and throughout the United States freelancing as a composer, leaving Mary behind. Dissatisfied with her marriage to a man she found increasingly capricious and impetuous, Mary seriously contemplated divorce. She planned to confront him as soon as he returned to their home in Union Park, Massachusetts. An unexpected telephone call from her physician, however, altered her plans. When her wandering husband returned, Mary greeted him with news of her pregnancy.

3

Massachusetts and New York

Named by her maternal grandmother after a famous Egyptian singer, Shadia El-Dabh[1] (whose name means "song" or "inner light") was born July 25, 1955, and the impact of her birth was so great that her jubilant father vowed to renounce his wanderlust and to purchase a more spacious house in the respectable suburb of Brookline, Massachusetts. Mary El-Dabh was delighted by this demonstration of commitment by her husband, and the couple entered into a very satisfying phase in their relationship. The move to Brookline proved very profitable as well for El-Dabh in terms of his creative output. He was recognized for his innovative compositional style at a competition sponsored by the Brookline Library Music Association. El-Dabh's "Thulathiya," for violin, oboe and piano[2] (1955), was awarded the first prize in 1955. Writing for the *Christian Science Monitor*, Harold Rogers observed,

> His music is highly original in its Eastern inflection, yet easily accessible to the Western ear. El-Dabh feels that it is his duty to find the music expression that will speak to the world. He has already attained marked success in this direction. He is able to produce the most ingenious timbres that bespeak an extremely sensitive ear and heart. His melodies for the violin and oboe, with melismatic embellishments, run parallel without any apparent relation to each other, yet they evolved simultaneously in the composer's thought. There is a rightness in his use of dissonance, as if it happens through logic, not through will.[3] [Track No. 7 on the companion CD.]

El-Dabh's *Sonics* (1955), for solo *derabucca*,[4] were also performed by the composer at the Brookline Library and reviewed by Rogers for the *Monitor*. The entire sound spectrum available to the instruments is reflected in these works, which explore the timbre of the drum, the expansion of its sound possibilities, and the delicacy of the instrument. El-Dabh was interested in the myriad sounds the drum is capable of producing as both a quiet and powerful instrument and includes an in-depth, detailed description of drumming technique, in which he indicates how to obtain those delicate, subtle sounds. Although the rhythm is rendered in customary Western musical notation, El-Dabh created a "drum-sign-symbol-notation" that denotes "placement," "curvature and touch," "position," and "resonance." The qualities of the sounds to be produced are indicated by the terms *dum, dhôuumm, tik, mma,* and *tak*. The score of *Sonics* indicates that if a *derabucca* is not available, Indian *tabla*, timbales, or tom-tom may be substituted. (Track No. 3 on the companion CD.)

Rogers wrote that the *Sonics* are "not mere displays of rhythmic possibilities. By the dexterous use of his fingers and knuckles, by controlling the tension of the drum head, by inserting his arm into the open end, he can produce an almost infinite variety of tones and timbres; and his rhythms have a subtle complexity almost unfathomable by the Western mind and ear."[5] For a subsequent performance, Eric Salzman of the *New York Times* wrote that the *Sonics* "contained the composer's art in its essential form. Rhythmic cells and patterns grew out of a predetermined fixed order that gave character to each particular piece. Added to this was a fantastic variety of colors that the composer-performer drew out of the eighteen-inch drum."[6]

In 1955 El-Dabh composed two works that typified his compositional style and his belief that sound is meaningful irrespective of what generates it. In other words, he was interested in the exploration of pure sounds and the manner in which the instruments of the symphony orchestra combine to capitalize on different sound spectra, different sound textures, and different sound expansions of each instrument. "Spectrum No. 1: Symphonies in Sonic Vibration" (1955, for strings of the piano and drums of wood and pottery) and *Mekta' in the Art of Kita'* (1955), for solo piano, formed the basis of El-Dabh's harmonic style. "Spectrum No. 1: Symphonies in Sonic Vibration" was recorded and released in 1958 as Folkways FX-6160 under the supervision of Moses Asch,[7] owner of Folkways Records, a company involved in folk, ethnomusicological, and contemporary music. In the recording's liner notes, written by Eugene Bruck, one learns that the composer described his work as follows: "In my 'Symphonies in Sonic Vibration,' I make use of traditional musical instruments (old and modern, such as bongos strapped to a piano) for the main purpose of producing vibrations, tonal shades, timbres and sound spectrums rather than melodies or harmonic progressions. The resulting vibration, an entity in itself, is used as direct expression for communication."[8] In 1959, El-Dabh arranged this work for four harps and violins.

The title of *Mekta' in the Art of Kita'* comes from a specific type of poetry found in the oasis area of Egypt that explores the juxtaposition of ideas and evolution of ideas. It derives from a basic philosophy that the whole is part of the unit, and the unit is part of the whole. Therefore, in El-Dabh's conception, each tone that he explores actually consists of all the elements of everything he composes, and all the elements are in each tone. The words *kita'* and *mekta'* are used to describe musical feelings in Arabic. *Kita'* is the whole, and *mekta'* is the segment; the segment contains the whole, and the whole is in the segment. If one experiences the segment, one also experiences the whole; if one experiences the whole, one also experiences the segment. *Sama,* the Arabic word for "music," is defined as the art of listening. As El-Dabh explains, "So when I listen, the music is created. I listen . . . I take it in. I can't just play something without being *sama* myself. I'm listening as well as I'm playing."[9] Under this concept, the primary focus is on the listener rather than the composer/performer. Music involves the individual/performer (the *mekta'*) and the group/audience (the *kita'*) in a shared experience.

The conceptualization behind El-Dabh's harmonic style is that in order to break the regimentation of tempered tuning,[10] he determined that a new harmony could be created from "frictions" (dissonances, usually of the interval of a major or minor second) around points of unison in superimposed melodic lines. For El-Dabh, these points of unison and frictions create the harmonic reality and also allow the tones to "curve" without actually changing the tuning of the piano. He accepted the piano as a tempered instrument and realized that he had to work within its confines. These frictions create a specific tension, which is a result of complex acoustical beating. From this perspective the sound itself becomes more alive to El-Dabh, who found European chordal progressions rather limiting because, when utilizing this system, his concept of melody was devoured by the harmony. In his view, Johann Sebastian Bach successfully managed to transcend that limitation by his contrapuntal relationships. Bach's thinking was basically not chordal progressions but rather linear contrapuntal processes. El-Dabh felt that conventional chordal progressions created a chasm or a separation from the melody, which hindered him; therefore, he was not comfortable with such chordal progressions.

Analysis reveals how El-Dabh's premise of the "curving of sound" is manifested in the pieces, which utilize repeated short fragments and unusual key signatures, often different in each hand. While one may argue that, in the work, El-Dabh is really thinking in terms of bitonality, his theory of the expansion of sound is really that of a single tonality extending into different realms. El-Dabh stated, "I'm not doing bitonality. It's really one melody expanded."[11] Queried if it was simplistic to suggest that he was thinking in terms of a heterophonic texture, El-Dabh replied:

My heterophony is a friction of the notes to create harmony. So it is really "heteroharmony," not heterophony exactly. It's a "heterofriction" that creates harmony, but the harmony is created from the friction around elements of points of unison. The points of unison and the friction create the harmonic reality and also allow the tones to curve without actually changing the tuning of the piano. I accepted the piano as a temperate instrument, and then I had to work with it. I accepted the fact that everybody tunes to the piano. When you're sitting in an orchestra, everybody tunes in on the piano. So if you want something different, you have to create signs in between, and it becomes like effects rather than an organic element of the music. Many contemporary composers wanted the relationship, especially since the 1950s, but it became like a deviation, rather than an organic relationship. For me, this is an organic relationship that keeps evolving and exploring the possibilities of the color of the orchestra, the texture of the orchestra, the rhythms, the melodies. Everything is freer to me with this involvement. So, it's not a matter of just heterophony for the sake of heterophony. You could use heterophony as an effect, but this is an organic basis of the music. It's that friction that creates a unison and also creates a harmony around it. Most traditional Egyptian music contains the idea of one tune played against another. It is essentially linear. In my music, many linearities [sic] clash with each other to create harmonic depth.[12]

Mekta' in the Art of Kita' is published in two volumes. The first volume comprises Books I and II, and each book contains three pieces bearing

Sketch of "Soufiane," dedicated to Edward MacDowell, part five of *Mekta' in the Art of Kita'*, Book III (1955).

the titles "Basseet," "Samaï," and "Soufiane." Throughout Book I, an intense use of unison appears in two lines. Tone clusters are featured in Book II. Book III, in the second volume, is expanded to five pieces entitled "Basseet," "Samaï," "Nawakht," "Sayera," and "Soufiane." The books are arranged in an obvious progression in degree of difficulty; El-Dabh has noted that the first two books are not often performed, because they appear too easy; however, "even though they look so simple, they're really not that simple."[13] On one occasion, the composer was asked to play the individual works and then discuss them. When he attempted to play from the printed score, El-Dabh often hesitated; when it was suggested he play from his own handwritten manuscript, the result was remarkable. Playing from his manuscript, El-Dabh had the music in his fingers and was able to play with the command of someone who had practiced for a performance. El-Dabh had been distracted by the appearance of the printed score. The change in the visual representation of the notes altered the way he thought about the tones he was producing. All five pieces in Book III were given individual dedications that do not appear in the printed score: "Basseet" for El-Dabh's daughter Shadia; "Samaï" for his wife, Mary; "Nawakht" for a family friend, Vera; "Sayera" for the pianist Allen Barker; and "Soufiane" a homage to Edward MacDowell.[14] (Track No. 13 on the companion CD.)

In 1956, to his wife's great dismay, El-Dabh accepted an invitation to stay for six months at the MacDowell Colony, an artists' retreat in Peterborough, New Hampshire. The colony had been founded in 1907 by the pianist Marian Nevins MacDowell as a memorial to her composer husband. There El-Dabh finished *Mekta' in the Art of Kita'* and began to explore the possibility of utilizing magnetic tape in his compositions. He created an atmosphere in which to work by stretching piano strings throughout the library and strategically placing drums. He then altered the strings and drums and recorded his experimentations with "sound expansion." Otto Luening[15] and Vladimir Ussachevsky,[16] two of the other guests invited to create undisturbed at the retreat, witnessed what El-Dabh was doing. These two pioneers in electronic music encouraged him to expand his experimentation in the retreat's electronic music studio, and later they were to be instrumental in persuading El-Dabh to study at the Columbia-Princeton Electronic Music Center[17] in New York City. El-Dabh enjoyed the MacDowell Colony, where he found a "good life energy."[18]

Two years later in the *Christian Science Monitor* Robert A. Wilkin quoted El-Dabh with crediting the picturesque retreat as having been where he "really learned to think."[19] It was there that El-Dabh "discovered hidden relations of tone and distance, of vibration and mood. He learned to capture on paper a surging tide of strange, modern-ancient sounds that welled up in his consciousness during his days at the mountain idyll."[20] El-Dabh also made many important contacts during his stay in Peterborough, contacts that caused his world to shift from Boston to the broader influence of New York City. Suddenly acquaintances in New

York were encouraging him to relocate in order to advance his career. In mid-1957, fearful that Mary would object to his uprooting the family and knowing how unhappy and disappointed she had been with his decision to leave her and the baby for six months to go to MacDowell, he secretly contacted Leon Polk Smith,[21] the great visual artist, for advice. The two had spent many hours at MacDowell discussing the relationship between music and the visual arts, and the gregarious Smith had remarked that an apartment he shared with a roommate on 12th Street near the New York School of Social Research had an extra room, which he offered to El-Dabh unconditionally should he ever decide to visit New York. Smith fueled El-Dabh's belief that everyone of importance was in New York and that if he did not relocate El-Dabh would be "only a big toe in Boston. That was all."[22] Two nights later, El-Dabh informed an unsuspecting Mary that he was languishing in Boston and had made arrangements to take the train to New York the following morning. She was too stunned to respond and was still speechless the next day when her husband left for the train station with the promise that he would send for her and Shadia when he had established himself in New York.

Leon Polk Smith delighted in escorting his new friend to New York's finest art galleries and exposing him to exhibits while discussing paintings and querying El-Dabh on his perception of how the Dada[23] period related to music. At the end of El-Dabh's first week in New York, Smith threw an elaborate party in his honor at his capacious apartment, which was filled with Mondrian[24] paintings. El-Dabh captivated the guests by performing on his *derabucca*. Eugene Lester,[25] Martha Graham's musical director, attended the soirée and told El-Dabh of having heard him play the piano at the first Boston Festival in 1953. Graham had performed there at the same time and she would be very interested, he said, to learn El-Dabh was now in New York.

Two of the other guests were Edward Marks and his wife, owners of the popular Edward B. Marks Music Publishing Company. Marks announced that he and his wife were leaving the next morning for three months in Los Angeles and inquired if El-Dabh would be willing to stay in their penthouse on the corner of 12th Street and Fifth Avenue in their absence. Thrusting his spare set of keys into El-Dabh's hand, Marks and his wife left the party, leaving a flabbergasted El-Dabh to realize slowly that in one week's time he had been handed the keys to a penthouse and had received a promise that Martha Graham would be made aware of his presence in New York. He could not believe his good fortune. When a few days later Eugene Lester contacted him to inquire if he could bring some recordings of his music to Miss Graham's studio, the composer enthusiastically agreed. El-Dabh felt New York City was calling out to him, opening its arms, and embracing him. He later recalled reading the work by Nigerian writer Wole Soyinka,[26] *The Lion and the Jewel*, in which the main character arrives in the big city and proclaims, "To town me come." El-Dabh felt that was exactly how it was for him—"to New York me come." He had not gone to New York; rather, New York had called him. When El-Dabh recounted this story later to others, he was often teased and asked, "What kind of English is that?" El-Dabh always responded that it was real—the town had been alive and had been calling him. For El-Dabh it really was "to town me come" rather than "I am going to town." He felt New York City calling out to him, and he believed that the timing was excellent, everything was perfect, and he was ready.

On a hot evening in July 1957, El-Dabh entered the subway armed with several hours' worth of recordings of his music. Leaving the subway at 59th Street, he walked up to East 63rd, perspiring because of his heavy burden and his mounting anticipation of meeting the famous dancer. Martha Graham lived in an apartment in a huge building on the corner of 63rd and York; she had to walk only two blocks to her studio, between First and Second Avenues. Entering the dark, cavernous studio, surrounded by mirrors, El-Dabh immediately spied a large grand piano along one side and was greatly impressed by the fifty-foot-square floor with low tables for seating. Warmly greeting him, Lester instructed El-Dabh to sit on one of the low tables while he brought in the tape machine. Just as everything was ready, Graham dramatically entered the dimly lit room, dressed in black gauze and lace. She approached El-Dabh, extended her hand, and inquired after his health. He took her hand and kissed it in the Parisian manner. The three then sat in silence for over two hours, while El-Dabh handed the tapes one after the other to Lester, who carefully placed them on the machine. Throughout the entire session, Graham listened in intense silence, never making a comment or otherwise revealing her reactions to the music she was hearing. Finally she abruptly stood, extended her hand to El-Dabh, said "Thank you," and disappeared. El-Dabh was stupefied and turned for guidance to Lester, who simply thanked El-Dabh for his time and promised he would be in touch.

A week passed before El-Dabh received the anxiously awaited telephone call from Lester; Graham wished a second hearing of El-Dabh's tapes. The delighted composer agreed to meet them the next evening.

The second meeting went exactly like their first. El-Dabh experienced déjà vu as he took the same subway, walked the same streets, and toted the same materials to the same studio. Again he perspired in reaction to the oppressive heat, the weight of his heavy burden, and his ever-increasing tension. Graham, attired in the same outfit, made her grand entrance precisely as before. Again she extended her hand to the composer, who kissed it once more in a courtly manner, and again she sat listening intently to his tapes without uttering a word. When the music ended, Graham gracefully rose and thanked El-Dabh for his time. It was an eerily exact repetition of their first meeting, and El-Dabh was quite perplexed as he returned to the penthouse.

His confusion changed into mirth when Lester telephoned El-Dabh the next day, explaining that Miss Graham had requested the second hearing because she was not certain if what she had heard the first time was real. El-Dabh's music had left her feeling awestruck. For many years she had been working on an untitled work with Aegisthus (the lover of Clytemnestra) as the subject, and now she was convinced that El-Dabh was the one to compose the music for it. El-Dabh agreed to a meeting to stipulate the terms of his contract. This was never a part of the collaborative process that El-Dabh enjoyed, but he found Lester to be such an agreeable man that the two became close friends. They spent many hours together playing chess, composing and playing music, and grilling steaks on the penthouse's balcony.

The next time El-Dabh and Graham met, at the studio in her second-floor office, she mentioned the subject of Clytemnestra rather than Aegisthus and disclosed that she had booked the Adelphi Theater on 54th Street for a performance scheduled on October 3, 1957; Graham questioned the feasibility of El-Dabh's having even a short piece ready by October 1. With great bravado, not wanting to disappoint Graham or to jeopardize his opportunity, El-Dabh immediately agreed to her timetable; Graham was impressed and gave him several books of Greek tragedy to help him prepare for his collaboration. During the next two weeks El-Dabh totally immersed himself in the lives of Aeschylus and the characters Agamemnon, Clytemnestra, and Orestes and commenced writing music with abandon. When he had composed a substantial amount, El-Dabh contacted Lester to arrange a meeting with Graham. When she first heard the music, Graham sat erect, listening in stony silence; El-Dabh perceived a negative reaction. Turning to her, the composer asserted that he felt she did not like his work;

making a dramatic gesture of his own, he gathered the score, tore the sheets in half, and declared that he would start over.

El-Dabh worked frenetically, imagining the dancers and sketching pictures of them in a notebook. Observing Graham conducting classes in the studio, he mused, "There she is. Clytemnestra is right in front of me."[27] While reading of Clytemnestra's struggle with her husband, Agamemnon, El-Dabh had learned that Graham and her husband, Erick Hawkins, were experiencing their own marital strife; he was also compelled to reflect on his relationship with Mary. These strained relationships stimulated El-Dabh's creativity. Working on the piano and orchestral scores simultaneously, El-Dabh began composing "The Furies." To help Lester explain to Graham what El-Dabh had in mind, the composer indicated the orchestral instrumentation on the piano score.

Graham became enthralled with the collaboration and permitted El-Dabh access to her studio from nine o'clock in the evening to dawn. She even revealed the small closet in the corner where she kept her surreptitious supply of Old Grand Dad bourbon. El-Dabh was very glad to have access to the studio. He would usually call Graham around midnight to inform her that he had finished a section; feeling the pressure of the October deadline and wanting to be certain that what he was doing was acceptable, El-Dabh wanted Graham to be apprised of everything. Graham would walk to the studio with her sister, Geordie, and Geordie's small dog. Lester, who lived on Second Avenue, would be summoned to play El-Dabh's piano scores for them. If she approved of El-Dabh's efforts, Graham would announce that the next morning they would choreograph, and by eleven o'clock in the morning the company would be hard at work, learning and practicing the new routine. Graham was pleased enough with the emerging results to postpone the October opening until April 1, 1958, so that the proposed fifteen-minute work could be transformed into a two-hour masterpiece.

The first time Graham had invited El-Dabh to her apartment to discuss the work, he had been awed by a large canopied Chinese bed in the center of her living room; desiring to inspect this piece of the décor, he immediately approached the bed. Graham shrieked that he must stay away. Horrified, she explained that the bed was there for the spirit of an elderly Chinese woman, who was living in it.[28] Realizing that Graham was sensitive to Eastern philosophy, El-Dabh apologized to the spirit and suggested to Graham that instead of discussing the practicalities of the music and the choreography, the two of them share their thoughts and ideas about Clytemnestra and ancient Egypt. Graham was charmed, and this marked the first of many evenings in which the two spent hours discussing Greek and Egyptian mythology.

Originally, Graham had envisioned Clytemnestra as condemned by the spirits; El-Dabh preferred to see Clytemnestra forgiven and desiring the option of rebirth and renewal. He explained that, according to ancient Egyptian tradition, if one experienced the energies of the underworld, one had the choice of being reborn. After much deliberation, it was decided that El-Dabh should go with his instincts and end the work according not to Greek mythology—total condemnation after death—but rather according to Egyptian mythology—that is, with rebirth. He further justified his new ending on the grounds that Mysia[29] was connected culturally to Egypt. During Clytemnestra's lifetime many Greeks had traveled to Egypt to present offerings to Osiris and Isis; El-Dabh felt a spiritual connection to the gods and goddesses of that period. Graham was strongly drawn to the new ending.

One evening the studio administrator became furious with El-Dabh for opening the heavy metal door to the studio without first checking to see who was outside. El-Dabh had heard banging on the door and forgot that he was not supposed to open it to anyone in the middle of the night. When he did, El-Dabh was shoved aside by several people who pushed their way in, announced that they were chasing someone, and ran up to the roof and disappeared. The administrator admonished El-Dabh that they could have ruined the entire place.

Sometimes Graham's sister, Geordie, would visit El-Dabh at the dance studio in the middle of the night. Often she would catch him frenetically dancing around the piano and inquire if he had seen the studio's ghost. Laughing, he would joke that it was the ghost that had given him such energy. Geordie was convinced there was a spirit inhabiting the studio and often thought she saw it in flashes of light. Holding tightly to her small dog, Geordie would ask El-Dabh why he was not afraid to be in the studio alone with it; he would respond that he loved the ghost and its company.

Although he heard people speaking of its dangers, El-Dabh felt New York City contained a kind of life and vitality that he had not experienced in Paris. Leaving Graham's apartment or studio at four or five o'clock in the morning and walking down Fifth Avenue to 12th Street, it never occurred to him to be afraid. Although El-Dabh could speak French as well as a native, he could not connect with anyone in Paris as he could in New York and Cairo, cities with a creative immediacy that El-Dabh enjoyed. Although the streets of Cairo were much safer, it did not bother El-Dabh to walk through the streets or ride the subways of New York late at night. He reveled in the great excitement and vibrant energy he encountered in the off hours. Stopping sometimes at Tiffany's for breakfast was a very enjoyable routine for him; he was inspired by the light of dawn as the sun was about to rise between the huge buildings. As he walked the streets, El-Dabh found the city full of dazzling sounds and colors.

Although El-Dabh was living rent-free in a penthouse and had a signed contract to open on a Broadway stage what would become one of his greatest works, he realized that he needed more money and sought employment at the New York Public Library on 42nd Street. There he was hired immediately in the Preparation Division. It was his responsibility to identify titles of foreign-language books and determine if the library already owned them or if they should be ordered. El-Dabh's routine consisted of composing until five o'clock in the morning, working at the library from seven until eleven o'clock in the morning, and then sleeping until it was time for him to return to the studio at nine o'clock in the evening. Enjoying his library position, El-Dabh spent many hours lost among the library's stacks, and because his job was not intellectually stimulating, El-Dabh found it a perfect foil to the intensity of the compositional process.

At this time, El-Dabh's good friend Raffaele Stocchino, an artist from Boston, contacted him announcing that he too wanted to live and work in New York City. Excited at the prospect of his friend coming to New York, El-Dabh asked Mrs. Moromovich, his supervisor, to find a library position for Stocchino. Well aware that Mrs. Moromovich was quite fond of him and enjoyed the manner in which he laughed and joked with her all day long, El-Dabh promised that Stocchino would smile and laugh as well. He also asserted that since Stocchino was fluent in Italian, English, and French, he would be an asset; finally, he halfheartedly threatened to quit if his friend was not hired. Mrs. Moromovich agreed to employ Stocchino sight unseen. Because the Markses soon were due to return from their summer vacation, El-Dabh prepared to move from the penthouse and arranged for Stocino to share an apartment with him in the Latin quarter of the Bronx. The arrangement worked very well for the two friends, who had quite a flair about them, which especially was apparent during their coffee breaks at the library. The typically reserved library staff did not always know how to handle the Egyptian and the Italian, and the usually sedate, quiet library quickly acquired a livelier atmosphere. El-Dabh planned to work indefinitely at the library; however, when the *New York Times* printed a column

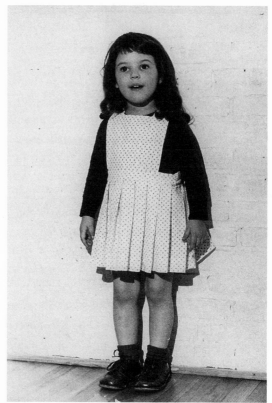

Shadia El-Dabh, age three (1958).

by Howard Taubman[30] stating that Halim El-Dabh was collaborating on a work with Martha Graham, he decided it was time to leave.

Eventually Mary realized that her husband was not going to be content being a "big toe" in Boston, and she consented to move to New York with Shadia; however, the Bronx did not appeal to her. Elated that his wife had agreed to finally join him in New York, El-Dabh sought more suitable accommodations for his family and located a house for rent in Demarest, New Jersey. The owners of the house were a married couple who were doctors, one a cancer specialist, the other an obstetrician (who would later deliver El-Dabh's second daughter, Amira). The couples became very good friends, and often the doctors drove El-Dabh into New York City with them.

In the weeks prior to the first performance of *Clytemnestra*, it became necessary for El-Dabh to move back to New York City. Knowing that sometimes hotels maintained rooms for artists and performers, he inquired whether the Winslow Hotel, located at 55th Street and Madison Avenue, had a special place or small room where he could stay by the week. For nineteen dollars per week he was provided an ideal accommodation—a room with a telephone and room service. Tirelessly he worked on the music for *Clytemnestra*; a courier appeared at his room each night to take the new pages to the twelve copyists hired to work on what would become an eight-hundred-page score. The copyists often teased El-Dabh that his music would not work. Unfazed, El-Dabh instructed them just to copy the music.

The energy of New York gave El-Dabh the feverish strength to complete the work. April 1, 1958, the opening night of the ballet *Clytemnestra*, proved to be a very powerful experience for both Martha Graham and Halim El-Dabh. The work was scheduled for a two-week run at the Adelphi Theater, however, there was a full house every night, and Graham had to extend it by adding a Sunday performance for the benefit of Broadway actors who were working and unable to attend a scheduled performance. Never before had Graham worked so closely with a composer, and she was delighted by the experience. In the past she had given either an idea or a theme to a composer, who would then write the music. Sometimes the composer would simply mail the music back for her to give to her conductor and begin the choreography. Marcelle Hitschmann, of the *Foreign Press News*, reported of Graham: "Of Hamid [*sic*] El-Dabh she said: 'He was brought to me by Eugene Lester, when I was working on 'Clytemnestra.' He sang and played the drums . . . and I said this is it. The richness, the appetite for sound, the tradition of rhythmic complexity for emotional reasons, which I was looking for. It was the most marvelous collaboration I ever had. . . . I thought of El-Dabh as an Egyptian writing on a world theme—Clytemnestra has many sisters in the world."[31] *Clytemnestra* was critically acclaimed in the newspapers following its premiere and subsequent early performances. John Martin, for the *New York Times* wrote:

> For once a composer has no end in view for his music beyond making it an inseparable element in a theatrical collaboration. Part of the time a chorus of two, a man and a woman dressed in impeccable modern evening clothes, sits just inside the proscenium, scores in hand, half-singing, half-speaking explanatory passages and introductions of the central figures. Sometimes they resort to wordless chanting with almost Kabuki[32] vocal coloration. The air of remoteness and

objectivity they contribute is remarkably valuable. Elsewhere the orchestra groans and shrieks and mutters and throbs, in timbres as odd as that of the movement on stage and in melodic snatches as inhibited. It is a fine job, indeed, all the way round.[33]

Four days later Martin, again for the *Times*, remarked, "To this general theatrical texture the music score of Halim El-Dabh makes a notable contribution. Here is music actually written for the work in hand, an unusually close instance of collaboration. The composer has not only emphasized the dramatic atmosphere and shaped the rhythmic phrases from time to time, but he has also captured in the quality and timbre of his writing the distinctive color and the very bone and muscle of the movement style."[34]

A review in the *New York Herald Tribune* by Walter Terry declared, "Ageless in its ritualized form and in its theme and wholly contemporary and brilliantly theatrical in its method of presentation, this *Clytemnestra* would, I think, be as at home in an ancient Greek amphitheatre as it is in a Broadway house. Part of this dual potency is due to the remarkable score by Halim El-Dabh."[35] Miles Kastendieck observed for the *Christian Science Monitor*:

> An important aspect of the work as a whole is the score by the Egyptian composer Halim El-Dabh. Far from being independent so that it might be heard in concert, the music is so complementary to the action that it appears to be the result of close collaboration. Mr. El-Dabh's score is frankly rhythmic, frequently percussive, and only occasionally melodic. That it should be primarily functional may account for the archaic atmosphere it creates and the texture of sound it generates. Indeed, the kind of sound assumes a most significant position in its general value. Most interestingly it all appears quite appropriate. A suggestion of the Greek chorus is attained through the use of two singers standing at each side of the stage. They help elucidate the story through an English text.[36]

The following appeared in *Variety*: "Miss Graham has been able to create with Egyptian composer Halim El-Dabh a dance occasion that is a true creative fusion of music and dance design."[37] The review in the *New York Journal-American* stated, "Completely integrated with the stage movement is a musical score of truly functional nature. The collaboration between Halim El-Dabh and Miss Graham strengthens the work impressively."[38] (Track No. 9 on the companion CD.)

In 1958, El-Dabh was at the peak of his success. *Clytemnestra* created great excitement and brought attention to El-Dabh, who received several congratulatory cables from Egypt about the piece. His parents were thrilled by their son's success. The work achieved worldwide attention when the ballet company took it on tour to Jerusalem, Tel Aviv, Bangkok, Italy, Paris, Greece, Portugal, and Edinburgh. Following a performance in Jerusalem, Y. Boehm wrote in the *Jerusalem Post*, "The impression that it successfully transmits to the listeners is that this is archaic Oriental music, functional, effective, a good blend of modern technique in composition with an ancient heritage, creating something timeless with an authentic ring."[39] As a result of the performance in Greece, El-Dabh was commissioned by the noted Greek choreographer Rallou Manou[40] to compose *Theodora in Byzantium* (1965).

Still living in the Winslow Hotel, El-Dabh appeared to be on top of everything, including Madison Avenue. Leonard Bernstein was interested in working with him, and he was approached to compose the music for a Broadway show (these ventures never materialized). During this triumphant period, El-Dabh attended several parties with Martha Graham. At one such event he became acquainted with the great harpist Carlos Salzedo,[41] and the two discussed Egyptian harps and how sometimes as many as three hundred harps had been played simultaneously in ancient Egypt. Salzedo opined that it would have been impossible to tune all those harps perfectly together and pressed El-Dabh for his assessment; El-Dabh, committed to the concept that the very essence of music was sonority and vibration, philosophized that the incredible sound emerging from three hundred harps, plus the shivering *sistrum*,[42] would have shaken the entire world. Salzedo replied that if El-Dabh were to compose a work for twenty-five harps, Salzedo knew he could get the twenty-five harpists together for a performance in New York; that would be the inspiration for arranging "Spectrum No. 1: Symphonies in Sonic Vibration" for four harps and violins.

El-Dabh thrived on the artistic setting of New York, both visual and literary, as well as musical. He was introduced to many artists and authors, including Isamu Noguchi,[43] who had created the sculptures at the United Nations gardens and had produced the sets for *Clytemnestra*. During his tenure at the MacDowell Colony, El-Dabh had met Oscar Williams,[44] the anthologist of Pulitzer Prize–winning American playwright Arthur Miller.[45] Williams and El-Dabh had enjoyed each other's company at MacDowell and when El-Dabh received acclaim for his collaboration with Graham, he was invited to Williams's apartment in the Wall Street district for a party honoring Miller and his second wife, Marilyn Monroe.[46] El-Dabh engaged in a long conversation with the famous actress, whom he found to be a very philosophical, insightful woman whose internal beauty was greater than the external beauty for which she was known and marketed.

The United Nations Orchestra was being formed, and El-Dabh was commissioned by the Contemporary Music Society to compose a work for it to be conducted by Leopold Stokowski.[47] "Fantasia-Tahmeel: Concerto for Derabucca and Strings" (1958) was the result. Although the solo part was composed for *derabucca*, the score indicates that timpani can be used instead. However, it was determined that the timpani does not work very well. El-Dabh traveled to Stokowski's Fifth Avenue apartment for a consultation and was struck to see the maestro's three-year-old son riding a tricycle through the apartment. The child, a product of Stokowski's marriage to Gloria Vanderbilt, pedaled while the men pored over the score, and eventually El-Dabh became annoyed by the distraction. He was also disturbed that Stokowski, complaining that the rhythms were too difficult and complicated, kept making cuts in the score.

Nonetheless, the concert ultimately took place at the Grace Rainey Rogers Auditorium of the Metropolitan Museum of Art on December 3, 1958. El-Dabh was delighted to hear Henry Cowell's[48] *Persian Set* that night. In a review for the *New York Herald Tribune,* Francis D. Perkins wrote, "Mr. El-Dabh rapped out a skillfully wrought array of rhythms in the hard and incisive sounds of his derabucca; these overlay a melody presented in a rather turbid timbre by the strings."[49] Because Cowell was a good friend of John Cage, El-Dabh was invited on several occasions to visit with the two at Cowell's New York home. There El-Dabh was first exposed to the Japanese flute, the *shakuhachi;*[50] he thought he had never heard such a beautiful sound. El-Dabh enjoyed these evenings; as for Cowell, who owned and played Indian tabla drums, one time when he traveled to Tehran, the capital of Iran, to speak about contemporary Western music and its relationship to the world, he took along recordings of El-Dabh's music to illustrate his points.

Because many of the composers at Columbia University, including Otto Luening, attended the performance and were impressed with "Fantasia-Tahmeel," El-Dabh was invited to work at the Columbia-Princeton

Electronic Music Center and received both a Guggenheim grant and a small grant from the university. Columbia University had its own substantial studio in the basement, next to the McMillin Theatre, which housed fifteen-inch recording machines, oscillators, and an enormous number of sound projection instruments that could be adjusted in different ways with myriad filters and a reverberation mechanism. All this equipment was made available to El-Dabh, and the resource became twice as large when combined with the equipment housed at the nearby studio at 125th Street, where the Columbia-Princeton Electronic Music Center was located. The bottom floors housed the massive electronic brains—with data stored in huge cylinders, not in small chips, as in modern computers—and one floor was filled with all kinds of electronic equipment. El-Dabh and the other composers worked on the fourth floor of that building, which housed an echo chamber[51] at the rear of the recording machinery. Behind the echo chamber was a small cot, so the composers could nap; when they once started a work, they usually kept at it all night long.

In his electronic compositions, El-Dabh utilized the technique of tape looping.[52] Often he created loops encompassing the entire room, by using strategically placed music stands and operating the cylindrical part of the stand like a pulley. The loop went around the room and returned approximately half a minute later, when it would appear on the tape. It could be intimidating to enter El-Dabh's studio; sometimes he had the tapes looping ten or fifteen feet apart entering the recording head before looping back out. The looping created rhythms that were then mixed with other sounds. El-Dabh had ten remote controls to operate ten machines used to record the electronic and acoustic sounds, which enabled him to have any one of the ten come in at a certain time or stop completely. He also had access to the reverberation and echo chambers. Not satisfied with the sound combinations he had produced, El-Dabh began investigating different methods of cross-wiring the tape machines. He commenced crossing the input wires in unusual, unorthodox ways. When the maintenance engineers who serviced the machines realized what he was doing, they sternly cautioned El-Dabh that he was hurting the equipment. He responded that it was his "job to compose and their job to fix the machines."[53]

While working on "Leiyla and the Poet" (1959), for electronic tape, El-Dabh began experimenting with the idea of sounds and noise and how music could be carved out from the noise. His concept was that noise was like a piece of sculpture; he began to think that perhaps he could chisel the sound out rather than building it in.[54] The creative energy behind "Leiyla and the Poet" was based on a story of classical Middle-Eastern society. Leiyla was a cousin of a poet, a man completely involved with his poetry, with the spatial words, and with his love for Leiyla. However, since they were cousins, it was taboo for them to marry. He became known as the "poet crazy about Leiyla." There are several stories based on this theme, but the most famous is "The Story of Leyla and Majnun" written by Nezami (1141–1209), considered the greatest romantic epic poet in Persian literature.

El-Dabh envisioned that story as a kind of family relationship or a societal situation in which the voice of the poet creates the unattainable Leiyla, who in turn is drawn to her cousin's poetry and to something that she must experience. She ends by dissipating, because she is unable to touch the madness of this poet. The work had special meaning for El-Dabh, because his brother Bushra had married his own cousin, which was by then no longer considered taboo by the society.

The night "Leiyla and the Poet" premiered, the audience filled the Mc-Millin Theatre to capacity; they were expecting something modern. El-Dabh had placed thirty-two audio speakers throughout the theater and figures representing the characters of Leiyla and the poet on the stage. Although the figures were stationary, light projected on them gave an illusion of action. There was light on the stage floor, on the sides of the stage, and on those figures, which were tall audio speakers covered with cloth. El-Dabh sat with a remote control in the balcony from where he could change the sound as the piece was played. Although the work was already composed, he could manipulate the tape with the remote, making each performance unique. When El-Dabh's piece was played, there was an unexpected reaction: audience members giggled, screamed, shouted, yelled, and started throwing things. Yuriko,[55] the original Iphigenia in *Clytemnestra*, and some other dancers from the Martha Graham troupe were in the audience. Following the performance, Yuriko told El-Dabh, "Your music hit my stomach. I felt it deep in my stomach, and I jumped."[56] Columbia Records featured the work on the well known, 1965 recording *Columbia-Princeton Electronic Music Center*. (Track No. 11 on the companion CD.)

The idea that noise was a physical material that El-Dabh could sculpt or chisel to create a beautiful sound sculpture also was expressed in "Meditation on White Noise" (1959), for electronic tape. He was meditating on a large noise, which evolved into the interactions of people, the world, space, and the universe. This noise resembled the sound of an airplane, a vacuum cleaner, or a heavy truck, and the composer believed that from this noise many other sounds could be sculpted. El-Dabh believed that everyone is affected by all such "noisy" sounds. Even the high-frequency tones produced by fluorescent lights, which are above the range of human hearing, can have an affect on one's health. The noise element is part of life, and when one meditates on that white noise,[57] one begins creating from it. El-Dabh felt that by meditating on noise that is physically harmful to the body, the noise could be re-created into something that enhances the health of the body. This can be likened to the pain of an arthritis sufferer, which produces something negative; when one meditates on the pain and is capable of reducing it, it turns into a positive. El-Dabh views his "Meditation on White Noise" as his own personal meditation. He likens the process to finding a huge piece of rock in the middle of the street and realizing that the rock could harm someone. Yet when an artist takes a chisel and cuts into the rock, a beautiful image is created. (Track No. 10 on the companion CD.)

El-Dabh was surrounded by the noise of New York City; he particularly enjoyed the screeching sounds emanating from the rails of the subway trains. In his electronic tape music he was able to enhance the screeching, transforming it into something creative. For his sound sources, El-Dabh used a noisemaker, bells, and metal objects that he dragged along the floor. After he collected a sound, he filtered it and added reverberation in a multitiered process. Each time he treated a sound, El-Dabh captured it on a segment of tape, which he then hung on the wall as a particular "generation." The magnetic tape, as a material, became a process in and of itself. Sometimes he scraped the tape with razor blades to eliminate the metal oxides, on which the sound is encoded; the elimination of the oxides created new and unusual sounds as well.

During his time at the studio El-Dabh was captivated by the work of Otto Luening, Vladimir Ussachevsky, and Edgard Varèse.[58] He had wonderful conversations with Varèse in French, and the two would often ride the subway to the electronic studio together. The studio provided a wonderfully creative environment in which to work, but one day El-Dabh, struck by the realization that the human range of hearing is limited, was overwhelmed by a strange and disturbing thought. Although frequencies existed outside the range of human hearing, humans were nevertheless incapable of perceiving them. He realized that if a composer combined sounds that clashed at these inaudible higher frequencies, lower audible tones would be produced, and these frequencies could be recorded by the center's sensitive equipment, seemingly out of nowhere.

In other words, El-Dabh discovered that he could play with sounds that he could not hear, and as a result he could cause new sounds to emerge. While working with this process, he began contemplating all the sounds traveling throughout the universe and galaxies. He envisioned the interconnections between these sounds and became convinced that through this force the entire building was capable of flying into space. He ran to Luening and screamed, "Hey, if you don't watch it, I know this place is going to fly . . . the whole building is going to end up in space."[59] At first Luening laughingly brushed off the younger composer, but El-Dabh insisted that this was an extremely serious matter, that someone needed to inform the government that the building could fly into space. El-Dabh declared that he would not be responsible if it did. Realizing that El-Dabh was quite serious, Luening assured El-Dabh that he would notify someone in the government or the space program and suggested that the two go out for a whiskey sour and discuss the situation. That answer seemingly appeased El-Dabh, who now conceived, from the experience of running to Luening with his fears, of the idea of the elements and beings comprising the entire universe and of the primeval sound of the cosmos. He envisioned what it must be like to inhabit that kind of space, and as a result "Element, Being and Primeval" (1959), for electronic tape, was composed entirely with electronic sounds at the Columbia-Princeton Electronic Music Center. However, El-Dabh eventually became aware that, following this incident, Luening left him alone most of the time.

While working at the Columbia-Princeton Electronic Music Center, El-Dabh learned that Mary was pregnant with their second child, and he determined that with his success with *Clytemnestra* he would be able to afford to move his growing family into a new house. Weeks before Mary gave birth, El-Dabh moved his family into a newly remodeled barn, adorned with huge Spanish columns, in Englewood, New Jersey. Mary was not certain if she really wanted to live in the expansive house; however, he delighted in the surroundings. The light from the high glass ceilings produced an atmosphere that El-Dabh found very conducive to composing. One morning while working on a composition at home, El-Dabh's friend Jonathan Bayless, from the Rockport area, came to visit, accompanied by another man. Bayless informed El-Dabh that his acquaintance was a priest who was responsible for raising money for a Catholic order in Gloucester, Massachusetts, and that he had a possible job offer for El-Dabh. Believing that "children find their own money when they come[,] . . . they don't wait on it,"[60] El-Dabh assumed this was his new baby's money. He agreed to meet with the priest to discuss this opportunity after the baby was born.

On February 1, 1959, Mary delivered a second daughter at the Presbyterian Hospital in New York City. Martha Graham was indirectly responsible for naming the baby. When the proud father announced the birth, Graham declared that he had another princess, and he immediately christened the child Amira.[61] As he had for Shadia, El-Dabh celebrated the occasion of the baby's birth with a lullaby, "Berceuse Amira" (1959), for solo piano.[62]

On the morning following Amira's birth, the priest invited El-Dabh for breakfast at the New York Athletic Club; El-Dabh went directly there after visiting Mary and Amira at the hospital. When asked what he wanted for breakfast, El-Dabh decided to celebrate the birth of his child with a double scotch. It was soon apparent that not much would be accomplished; the priest scheduled their next meeting for a luncheon date the following week at a restaurant in the Wall Street district. El-Dabh, a relatively new driver, arrived at the meeting in his 1946 Chrysler and parked directly in front of the restaurant, disregarding the No Parking—Tow Away Area sign. The priest appeared agitated and warned El-Dabh that his car would be towed. When El-Dabh made no effort to go outside to move the car, the priest pulled out a twenty-dollar bill, slammed it on the table, and stated that that would cover the cost of the tow but that he would not be responsible for any other repercussions.

He then produced six hundred dollars from his vest pocket and informed El-Dabh that he wanted to hire him to take potential clients out to dinner and pressure them to purchase a specific gold stock from Canada. The priest would pay El-Dabh six hundred dollars every two weeks for his efforts. El-Dabh had no knowledge of stocks, but he agreed to work for the priest because he needed the money for his new child. He had no difficulty in treating the potential clients to dinner; however, the genial composer was not suited to coercing them to buy the stock. After six months of enjoying the dinners and meeting new people without making a single sale, El-Dabh received a call from the priest informing him that he was terminated from his position. He assumed this meant that Amira now had all her money.

The Living Theatre presents

A Concert of New Music
Monday evening February 16
at 530 Sixth Avenue   by

ALAN HOVHANESS AND HALIM EL DABH

PROGRAM

ARABIYAAT #7 C 13 C 15 .... Halim el-Dabh
MISRIYAAT #10 C 22 C 5

IFRIKIYAAT #10 .... Halim el Dabh
MEKTA IN THE ART OF KITA .... Halim el-Dabh
  (for children and adults)
  Book 1.   Basseet, Samai, Sayera
  Book 2.   Basseet, Samai, Sayera
  Book 3.   Basseet, Samai, Nim Nawakht, Sayera, Soufiane
SONIC #7 and #10 .... Halim el Dabh
  (for Derabucca Drum)
Performed by the composer

I N T E R M I S S I O N

VIJAG OPUS 60 NO. 3 (1946) .... **Alan Hovhaness**
Alan Hovhaness and Elizabeth Whittington
DAWN AT LAONA OPUS 153 (1957) * .... **Alan Hovhaness**
  CANTATA FOR VOICE AND PIANO
  Prelude
  Vision of Dark Places
  The Hosts Flew White
  Motionless Breath
Alan Hovhaness and Jean Harper
PIANO SONATA OPUS 145 (1956) .... **Alan Hovhaness**
Elizabeth Whittington
BLACK POOL OF CAT OPUS 84 NO. 1 (1951) *........................... **Alan Hovhaness**
DESCRIBE ME OPUS 95 NO. 1 (1952)
INNISFALLEN OPUS 95 NO. 4 (1952) *
PERSEPHONE OPUS 154 (1957) *
Alan Hovhaness and Jean Harper
CHILD IN THE GARDEN OPUS 168 (December 25, 1958) * .... **Alan Hovhaness**
Alan Hovhaness and Elizabeth Whittington
MIHR OPUS 60 NO. 1 (1945) .... **Alan Hovhaness**
Alan Hovhaness and Elizabeth Whittington

* first performance anywhere

Baldwin Piano courtesy of Baldwin Piano Company

El-Dabh was not overly concerned about his financial situation, because following a joint concert with Alan Hovhaness[63] at the Living Theatre at 530 Sixth Avenue in New York City on February 16, 1959,[64] he had secured a contract with the prestigious C. F. Peters Music Publishing Company to publish his music, and he believed he was at the height of his career. For his portion of that evening's concert, El-Dabh had performed his three piano works "Arabiyaat," "Misriyaat," and "Ifriqiyaat," which he composed at Brandeis in 1954 to express sounds of various cultures and languages. With its strongly accented rhythms, "Arabiyaat" depicts the Arabic language and the Arabic dance rhythms heard throughout Egypt. "Ifriqiyaat" utilizes polyrhythms to remind one of the drumming ensembles throughout the enormous African continent. The score of "Misriyaat" instructs the performer to pluck the strings inside the piano, portraying the harplike effects of lyres, psalteries, and lutes heard specifically around the Nile area of Egypt. (Track No. 1 on the companion CD.)

In these three piano works, El-Dabh explores the components of the European manufactured piano, the strings of which are stretched, like those of a harp, over a resonating board. Treating the piano like a large percussion instrument, El-Dabh utilized a barrage of tone clusters and other unorthodox techniques in an effort to expand the instrument's capabilities. As an African, he felt a drive within to expand the boundaries of Western music and to reach for philosophies, thoughts, and ideas directly implicit in the additive nature of African influence and culture. Just as one might be a Copt, a Yoruba, or an Ashanti, retaining one's traditional identity while adding Islam or Christianity to the overall experience, El-Dabh felt that, in the same way, new elements could be added to European harmonies allowing for expansion rather than substitution of the original system.

New York Times critic Eric Salzman[65] penned a most favorable review of the concert, stating in part, "The works . . . were full of the same repetition-variation principles applied to melody as well as rhythm. The endless play of a few simple elements was fascinating."[66] Hovhaness, overwhelmed by El-Dabh's music, wanted to record the pieces and to engage El-Dabh in other projects, but because Hovhaness was very sick and frail, the projects never materialized. However, El-Dabh had enjoyed Hovhaness's company very much and had great respect for his work.

Opposite: Program for the February 16, 1959, concert featuring the music of Alan Hovhaness and Halim El-Dabh.

Following the performance, Walter Hinrichsen,[67] president of C. F. Peters Music Publishing Company, and his wife, Evelyn, approached El-Dabh to introduce themselves. Hinrichsen stated emphatically that he loved El-Dabh's music and wanted to be his publisher. El-Dabh agreed to allow *Clytemnestra* to be published by C. F. Peters. Also, believing that no one other than Martha Graham would ever perform the two-hour work in its entirety, El-Dabh requested that several sections be published separately. This is how "Bacchanalia," "House of Atreus," and "Furies in Hades" came to be extracted from the work. "House of Atreus," the most successful of the independent pieces, had received its first performance at the McMillin Theatre on January 17, 1959, with Carlos Surinach conducting, just one month prior to El-Dabh's performance at the Living Theatre with Hovhaness. Salzman reviewed that performance as well for the *New York Times*, writing that "there was a considerable array of declamatory vocal tricks, including glissando wails and moans that took the baritone from the bottom of his range to a high falsetto."[68]

From the beginning of their business arrangement, Walter Hinrichsen treated El-Dabh as his prize composer, and El-Dabh relished the star treatment. Whenever El-Dabh was in New York City and walked into the Peters office building, Hinrichsen always treated him to a smorgasbord lunch. Invariably El-Dabh would produce a sketch of a new piece to show Hinrichsen, who would praise the work and hand El-Dabh an advance of two hundred dollars. Often as the two walked together down the streets of New York City, Hinrichsen would muse that he had made a lot of money on Beethoven and Chopin but that his grandchildren would make a lot of money on El-Dabh. After Hinrichsen's death in 1969 the advances and star treatment would cease, but El-Dabh never lost his feelings of admiration and gratitude for Walter Hinrichsen, personally or professionally.

Had Hinrichsen not been at the Living Theatre and heard "Arabiyaat," "Ifriqiyaat," and "Misriyaat" that evening in 1959, El-Dabh probably would never have sought a publishing house. He still does not send new compositions immediately to be published but rather holds onto his scores as though each were a child he must lovingly nurture and protect. He does, however, continue to share the manuscripts of his newer compositions with performers with whom he feels a special closeness.

4

Egypt, New York, and Ethiopia

Halim El-Dabh's success in New York in the fall of 1959 prompted the minister of culture of the United Arab Republic (comprising Egypt and Syria, 1958–61) to extend an invitation for the composer, his wife, and children to come to Egypt indefinitely as his guests. Mary was hesitant to accept the offer; however, her husband eagerly accepted the invitation to return home as a "conquering hero," convincing his wife that it would be the most opportune time for his family to meet her and the girls. As soon as the airline tickets to Cairo arrived, however, the impetuous El-Dabh contacted the minister and requested that they be exchanged for tickets on the SS *Independence* to Alexandria, believing that travel by sea would be more luxurious and dignified; the Egyptian government consented to pay the cost of four first-class accommodations for El-Dabh, Mary, and the two girls on board the liner.

En route to Alexandria, the ship stopped at Genoa, Italy, where El-Dabh visited his old friend Raffaele Stocchino, who had left his position at the New York Public Library to return to Italy prior to the premiere of *Clytemnestra*. From Genoa they traveled on to view the famous sights of Rome before returning to the ship to continue to their final destination. Their arrival in Alexandria proved chaotic. The entire extended El-Dabh family had come to greet their famous relative and his American wife and children. Also, El-Dabh had brought along so much baggage that getting through customs was an ordeal. El-Dabh, overwhelmed by euphoria, was oblivious to the fact that Mary and the girls were experiencing great stress amidst what was for them a maddening and confusing situation. It did not help matters that the girls suffered from motion sickness as the

Photo from the *Missouri Carthaginian* of Halim and Mary El-Dabh and their daughters, Shadia and Amira, with second officer H. E. Coffman of the SS *Independence* on the way to Cairo, Egypt (1959).

family was driven back to the home of El-Dabh's parents. Mary found weaving in and out of traffic along the fields of the northern part of Egypt the entire way to Cairo extremely trying.

Shortly after El-Dabh's arrival in Cairo, the minister of culture, Tharwat Okasha, suggested that he become involved in the development of Egyptian folk music and Egyptian music studies while a guest of the government. El-Dabh, amenable to Okasha's proposal, was immediately named to the position of "consultant expert in the fine arts to the minister of culture" and was provided an office in what had been Abdeen Palace[1] (it had been turned into an office building when King Farouk was ousted from power). It did not take long, however, for El-Dabh to discover that the demands of his administrative position were stifling, and he made an appointment with Okasha to inform him of his discontent. His primary complaint was that his duties were impeding him from composition. Okasha asked what would make him happy, and El-Dabh responded that he needed a piano in his office—and he needed an office with a view of the Giza pyramids. Also, he was frustrated and annoyed by the constant telephone calls from old acquaintances, whom he had not seen for years, wanting recommendations for jobs; therefore, he requested that there be no telephone in his office. Undaunted, Okasha found a site that satisfied each of El-Dabh's stipulations—a spacious office with a huge window overlooking the pyramids. The office was inside the Institute of Filmwork, in a building that was still under construction when El-Dabh moved into it. El-Dabh was delighted to discover that indeed there was no telephone to distract him; however, that meant that whenever Okasha wished to contact the composer a motorcyclist had to be dispatched, and motorcycle escorts had to be sent to take El-Dabh to meetings in downtown Cairo.

It soon became quite well known that although the minister of culture had provided El-Dabh carte blanche to examine and to cultivate Egypt's musical development, El-Dabh refused to become involved in the bureaucratic aspects that typically accompany such a position. Jealousy quickly spread throughout the other governmental offices, creating such tension that El-Dabh's stay became increasingly problematic. Recognizing the difficulties and acknowledging that El-Dabh was first and foremost a composer, Okasha appointed El-Dabh to work on a project known as the Castles of Music, in which all the best musicians of the folk and classical traditions in each Egyptian province were to be assembled to meet and perform. People from all over the world converged for the event, and El-Dabh was excited by the cultural exchange being promoted.

In his new position, El-Dabh's primary duty was the collection of Egyptian traditional music. For this purpose, a furnished houseboat was provided to transport the El-Dabh family on the Nile all the way to the high dam at Lake Nasser and on to the Sudan; a tug with a crew of twelve sailors was assigned to tow it. He made recordings in the villages along the river on an old hand-cranked model EMI reel-to-reel tape machine from England, operated with power from long wires leading back to the boat. He collected a great deal of material from Upper Egypt and Nubia, which he later presented to the Egyptian Government Cultural Center. When he began his fieldwork in Nubia, Mary and the girls proved to be real assets. As Shadia and Amira walked down the village roads, a line of small girls and boys would follow them, and they made friends with ease. Throughout Upper Egypt, an unaccompanied man would never have been permitted to enter into a stranger's home; having his family with him facilitated El-Dabh's access into homes to conduct interviews and record music. Everyone in the villages respected his work; often he would leave all his equipment overnight, and it would be left undisturbed. At other times El-Dabh would stay on the boat, and the musicians visited him there. He appreciated the free range of travel and recording opportunities, and he was most grateful to find, when he returned to his office by the pyramids, a grand piano waiting for him.

While he was collecting his field material for the Castles of Music project, El-Dabh was chosen by President Nasser to compose the music for the Sound and Light project, a nightly outdoor show involving colored lights projected against the backdrop of the pyramids at Giza. El-Dabh learned that he would be sent to Paris to work with the premier French orchestra, and he was elated to learn that Mary and the girls would be permitted to travel with him. Mary had become disenchanted during her stay in Egypt; as an American citizen and as a woman, Mary deemed some of Egypt's rules and regulations abhorrent. She particularly objected to the fact that she was not permitted to leave Egypt without her husband's written, signed permission, so the opportunity for the family to travel to Paris was most welcome.

Still, and although El-Dabh was humbled and honored to have been chosen for such an undertaking, he was irritated to realize that, due to the prevailing belief among Egypt's ruling elite in Europe's cultural superiority, the Egyptian government was sending him to Paris to work with a French orchestra on this important Egyptian project, rather than using an Egyptian one. El-Dabh was well aware that Cairo was replete with talented and well-trained Egyptian classical musicians and orchestras who he felt could have performed as well as any European orchestra.

In France, El-Dabh, who worked with the Radiodiffusion Française[2] on the Sound and Light project, was treated as royalty; the family was furnished an apartment on the Rue de Barri, off the Champs-Élysées, paid for by the Egyptian government. El-Dabh, who enjoyed French food and wine, fully savored this experience and opportunity, though he still found New York more dynamic. He was provided with a room in Studio Seven— the very same studio that Stravinsky had once used—where El-Dabh could work undisturbed on his new score. At the end of each day, a courier would collect the composer's work and deliver it to a copyist designated to work specifically with El-Dabh, returning the next day with parts for the individual instruments. El-Dabh was impressed by the efficiency of the process, which allowed him to compose quickly, with the assurance that each day the scores of the previous day's work would be available for the musicians to rehearse. This was how the *Egyptian Series* (1960), also known as *Music of the Pharaohs*, or *Music of the Pyramids*, evolved. It was rehearsed and recorded at the Radiodiffusion Française by the department's orchestra and chorus, under the direction of Georges Delerue. Gaston Papeloux, who had designed the lighting for the Sound and Light performances at Versailles, was commissioned to illuminate the pyramids, and the Philips Company of France was hired to provide the electronics and automation.

Music from El-Dabh's *Egyptian Series (Music of the Pyramids)* has been performed in Arabic, English, German, French, Spanish, and Italian (and more recently Japanese) at the great pyramids of Giza every evening since its premiere on July 23, 1961. Unfortunately, because it was commissioned by the Egyptian government, El-Dabh has to date received no royalties for this masterpiece.

Because the Egyptian government wanted to celebrate the achievements of both ancient and Islamic Egypt, El-Dabh was commissioned to follow the *Egyptian Series* with a related, analogous work entitled the *Islamic Series* (1960), also known as *Saladin and the Citadel*. This twenty-two-movement work was also recorded with the orchestra of the Radiodiffusion Française and was intended for the light show at the site of the famous Citadel at Cairo. This work, however, never attained the status and recognition of the *Egyptian Series*. In fact, because the *Islamic Series* was to be heard in conjunction at other government-sponsored events, El-Dabh left the full score with government officials to make certain that it would continue to be performed. Unfortunately, it was his only copy of the score, and it was never returned to him. It is now presumed lost. El-Dabh, though he retained all the individual parts, never had the full score recopied and sent to C. F. Peters for publication.[3]

Following his artistic endeavors with the Radiodiffusion Française, El-Dabh and his family returned to Egypt, where he soon realized there had been a great deal of bureaucratic maneuvering involved in the Sound and Light project. He was offered a promotion to become the new minister of culture; however, Mary became distraught at the thought that he might accept the position. Adamant that she did not want to stay in Egypt with the girls, Mary was greatly relieved when her husband admitted

Shadia and Amira El-Dabh, Christmas (1959).

that he did not want to stay either. He acknowledged that it did not suit his personality to work in such a bureaucratic setting; he preferred to continue composing rather than to become constrained by administrative demands. Finding it increasingly difficult to adjust to the jealousies and bureaucratic interferences of Cairo, El-Dabh requested to be released from his responsibilities in order to relocate his family to New Jersey, to reestablish himself in New York, and apply for U.S. citizenship, which was granted in 1961.

It did not take long for El-Dabh to reacquaint himself with his contacts in New York and began to compose new works.[4] Shortly following his return, he was commissioned by choreographer Jerome Robbins[5] to compose *Yulei, the Ghost* (1960), for Yuriko to dance at the Phoenix Theater. Yuriko, who had danced for Robbins in the stage production of *The King and I*, was a strikingly beautiful woman who had greatly impressed El-Dabh with her performance as the original Iphigenia in *Clytemnestra*. He had been most captivated by the scene in which her black hair cascaded almost to the ground as she was carried off to be sacrificed. El-Dabh enjoyed his conversations with Yuriko, in which they discussed at length stories from Japanese mythology and Kabuki and Noh[6] theater.

Yulei, the Ghost—scored for soprano, oboe, clarinet, horn, trumpet, strings, and electronic tape—requires a singer who can sing between the notes (intervals smaller than a semitone) and who possesses an incredible range. Fearing he could not find a suitable singer for the performances, El-Dabh taped the voice part; however, it is preferable that the part be performed live.

Yulei, the Ghost is one of the many Japanese stories pertaining to ghosts; Yuriko provided great insight into Japanese culture and literature, which are dominated by stories of unrequited love and the working of vengeance by ghosts and spirits. In this work, subtitled *Weird Story at the Yotsuya District,* a man abandons his wife to take a new bride. Embittered, the wife commits suicide and returns to haunt the now happily united couple. She induces the man to kill his bride, and finally, having revealed the man's dark nature to himself, returns to hopeless misery— the fate of ghosts. The word *urameshiya* is heard throughout the piece; it represents the ancient chant of ghosts, which conveys in its meaningless sound hate, spite, evil, and the vindictiveness of all rejected loves.[7]

On April 25, 1960, following a two-year absence from the Martha Graham repertory, *Clytemnestra* was restaged and once again received favorable reviews. *New York Herald Tribune* critic Walter Terry praised "the fascinating score by Halim El-Dabh, the Egyptian composer, [which] had an unusually perceptive playing by the orchestra."[8] John Martin, of the *New York Times,* noted, "Halim El-Dabh's savage, archaic, unrelenting music makes a remarkable setting for the action."[9] (However, when the work was staged once again the following season, although both Terry and Martin penned favorable reviews, they were much less lavish in their praise of El-Dabh's musical composition. Terry only briefly mentioned "Mr. El-Dabh's remarkable score,"[10] and Martin made a passing reference to the "unsparing, curiously orchestrated, Oriental score by Halim El-Dabh.")[11]

In 1960, El-Dabh also reconnected personally with Martha Graham, who again gave him a key to her studio in order that he could have access to her grand piano at night. On several occasions Graham walked in while El-Dabh was playing, and one evening they began discussing the life of Cleopatra as a possible subject for a ballet. Inspired, El-Dabh began improvising a theme to represent Cleopatra's character; Graham was impressed enough to suggest that they immediately begin work on a collaboration. Their close friendship resumed, and the two visited each other on a regular basis. The result was two compositions: the ballet *One More Gaudy Night* (1961), the title a reference to Mark Antony's desire to have "one more gaudy night" with Cleopatra,[12] and *Cleopatra* (1961), a composition, based on the ballet, for orchestra alone. El-Dabh was pleased when members from the Rockefeller Foundation attended the premiere of *One More Gaudy Night*—which, though praised, was not as acclaimed or successful as *Clytemnestra.*

After El-Dabh composed the score to *One More Gaudy Night,* Graham requested that he conduct auditions for a rehearsal accompanist who could play from the orchestral score for the dancers. One pianist after another came to audition, but each struggled so painfully that El-Dabh was forced to produce a piano reduction; however, they had trouble with that as well. Finally, an energetic man named Boris Poliakin auditioned, who could play the score flawlessly. When El-Dabh inquired how he was able to perform the music so well, the young man explained that he had grown up in Egypt. He laughingly recalled how at the age of twelve he had accompanied his violinist father to the Cairo nightclubs, where the patrons would throw cigarette butts at him; El-Dabh's music reminded him of such things from his childhood. A flattered El-Dabh requested that the young man play from the score of *Mekta' in the Art of Kita'.* Poliakin's interpretation of the work deeply impressed the composer. When he finished playing, Poliakin revealed that he had felt as if he were playing all over the piano's sound spectrum but with no sense of being scattered or pulled in different directions; El-Dabh felt such a genuine connection to the young man that he hired him immediately.[13]

At the end of the year, Martha Graham commissioned El-Dabh to compose the music for the ballet *A Look at Lightning* (1961). The resulting music, which premiered in 1962, was based on the piano pieces *Mekta' in the Art of Kita',* of which Graham had become enamored. It was scored for flute, English horn, bassoon, and harp; the lightning was represented by the harp, a difficult part utilizing the technique for which Carlos Salzedo was famous. In addition to bending, scraping, and striking the strings, El-Dabh also requires the performer to use the harp as a drum. (Because the score is considered too technically challenging, the work has rarely been performed.) Following the premiere, Harold C. Schonberg, record critic for the *New York Times,* inquired of El-Dabh how he had scored the work; although there were only four musicians in the pit, it had seemed to him that there were a great many more instrumental forces behind the sound. The question amused El-Dabh, because he had fought with Graham to have the musicians appear on stage with their instruments; he had lost the argument, however, and the musicians were placed in the orchestra pit. In a review for the *New York Times*, John Martin observed that, "from the orchestra pit come gentle, unearthly sounds from Halim El-Dabh's intriguing score that serve to compound the lightly humorous air of fantasy."[14] Walter Terry, writing for the *New York Herald Tribune*, barely mentioned El-Dabh as the composer of the score, but Joseph Kaye, New York correspondent for the *Kansas City Star*, reported that the composer "did really remarkable things with this little group. El-Dabh is drawn toward combinations of sounds as a means of expression—sounds for their own worth, rather than as accessories to melody or harmony, but he achieves a unity that has an ingratiating mood and serves his purpose excellently."[15]

Although El-Dabh and his music were becoming well known in New York once again, a persistent restlessness began to permeate his every waking moment. He attempted to conquer the urge to wander by devoting long hours working at the Columbia-Princeton Electronic Music Center, while he collaborated with Graham on *One More Gaudy Night* and *A Look at Lightning*; however, the time and energy he spent composing electronic music was threatening to both Mary and to Graham. He was used to Mary's complaints about his long absences from home, but he was surprised by Graham's reaction, and as Graham tenaciously attempted to discourage him from working with electronic music, their relationship became strained. They argued a great deal about the time he spent working with Otto Luening and Vladimir Ussachevsky—time she felt would be better used working with her. El-Dabh vigorously attempted to explain that this was a new venture in terms of the expansion of sound, and he was greatly disappointed that Graham dismissed his passionate statements.

During this difficult period he spoke harshly to her, and their once close relationship suffered irreparable damage. Consequently, in her autobiography, *Blood Memory*,[16] Graham would write nothing of her friendship and collaboration with El-Dabh, not even in her recollections about *Clytemnestra*. She would never mention her musical director Eugene Lester, or her star dancer, Yuriko, either. El-Dabh opined that she did not refer to Lester because, although Graham was like a mother to him, Lester often spoke harshly to her, and he surmised that Yuriko was not mentioned because Graham was angry that Yuriko and El-Dabh had collaborated with Jerome Robbins on *Yulei, the Ghost*. Graham never completely forgave them for what she perceived as a betrayal or lack of loyalty. Although Graham's relationship with El-Dabh remained strained for the remainder of her life, she did commission him to compose the music for *Lucifer* (1975), and the two were to see each other during El-Dabh's association with Kent State University every time she came to the Blossom Music Center, near Cuyahoga Falls, Ohio.

In 1961 El-Dabh was commissioned by an anonymous benefactor to compose a work for a special benefit concert to be performed by dramatic soprano Miriam Burton, violinist Robert Brink, and pianist Allen Barker. The event was to honor the Association for the Advancement of Musicians Incorporated (AAMI), an organization founded in 1956 to recognize achievement in the field of music by awarding grants to performers and composers. El-Dabh was eager to accept the commission, because he appreciated AAMI's efforts on his behalf during the early days of his professional career. The resulting piece, "Partita Poly-Obligati in Song Cycle"[17] (1961), consisted of three movements—"Benighted Is the Night," "Oh! Vista," and "Pale in the Shadow." To his English text, El-Dabh had added two words of Arabic origin, which exploited both the texture as well as the poetic meaning of the words, and although he had written it as a song cycle El-Dabh avoided a story line, rather looking instead for dramatic continuity of a poetic nature.

It was originally scheduled for a premiere performance on December 2, 1961, in Boston's Jordan Hall; however, the premiere was postponed until January 19, 1962. The work received mixed reviews. Kevin Kelly, writing for the *Boston Globe*, wrote that the "Partita Poly-Obligati in Song Cycle" was "an [*sic*] unique work, with a fresh and compelling approach to the vocal medium. Its three short prose-poems (English with Arabic inclusions for 'sound-texture') were sung with haunting eloquence by Miss Burton over the superbly detailed music of Brink and Barker. The composer was in the Hall and, at the conclusion of the Cycle, rose to accept the enthusiastic response from the audience."[18] The critic for the *Boston Herald* offered that the "work is an ensemble of individuals. Dynamics and technique cover a wide range in an harmonic structure that is definitely tonal; at times the tonality is almost hidden by wide melodic leaps—a sort of musical pointillism."[19] However, Louis Chapin, writing for the *Christian Science Monitor*, asserted that "the question as one listens to his setting of his own cryptically pungent little verses, is whether this mixture of Western means and Eastern ends really comprises Mr. El-Dabh's most effective medium of communication. Once in a while the ensemble becomes coherent, even exciting, but most of the textural variety is purveyed by the piano, with the voice jumping from one plateau to another and the violin wanting to belong more than it does."[20] Mr. Chapin continued, "Miss Burton manipulated her voice splendidly, the duo played with its usual poised equanimity, and Mr. El-Dabh was there to receive everyone's appreciation. But perhaps his heart, these days, belongs rather more to percussion and a tape recorder."[21]

The piece was performed again on February 2, 1962, as part of New York University's Town Hall Series, and critic Eric Salzman, writing for the *New York Times*, commented, "Except in certain rhythmical-structural aspects, it is not much like some of the composer's other works. His style is generally tight, rhythmic, oriental-abstract; this work is much more diffuse, with ostinato figures that are almost neo-classical or neo-baroque rather than neo-oriental. The difficulty is that both the details and the over-all shape of the three songs seem arbitrary and contradictory, difficulties that are only partially offset by the elegant and dramatic curve and texture of some quite extended sections of the work."[22]

Unaccustomed as he was to negative criticism, the mixed reviews deeply troubled El-Dabh, who abruptly declared to his closest friends in the New York circle that he was planning to leave New York for Ethiopia for the purpose of conducting a comparative study of the Coptic church in Egypt and the Ethiopian Coptic church. Assuming the composer was suffering from a bruised ego, the majority of his friends and colleagues did not give much credence to his pronouncements, and most attempted to placate him by recounting their own less than glowing reviews. Well aware that his closest associates were not taking his comments seriously, El-Dabh began to discuss his project openly with people with whom he had limited contact—bank tellers, store clerks, dry cleaner attendants, and so forth. He eagerly engaged in detailed conversations about what he hoped to accomplish with anyone who would listen to him, and the more he verbalized the possibility of carrying out this research in Ethiopia, the stronger his desire grew to leave New York. However, he did not discuss the topic with his wife and children. Fully aware that Mary would not support uprooting the girls again, he began spending long hours away from home, contemplating how he could broach the sensitive subject with his wife and also how to obtain the necessary funds to make such a trip.

As he wandered the streets in search of answers, he frequently stopped to watch the ice skaters at Rockefeller Center. One day, while totally mesmerized by their graceful gliding on the ice, El-Dabh was approached by a man named Faz, the chief program director of the Rockefeller Foundation, who inquired why El-Dabh was not already in Ethiopia immersed in his research. The startled composer stammered that he had not yet acquired the funding to support his travel. Fully appreciating the irony of

October 30,1961

Dear Mrs. Dabh,

Thank you very much for your letter and for sharing your views with me.

If a catastrophe should happen you will not have to "justify" this horror to your children. There is nothing you can tell them if you live in a city and you are in a nuclear war because you won't have time. It will not happen, I hope, for I think at bottom our leaders and the Russians do not want a war. It is not a matter of saving face but of negotiation. So, let us have faith in our leaders.

With best wishes,

very sincerely yours,

Eleanor Roosevelt

Note to Mary El-Dabh from Eleanor Roosevelt (1961).

the situation, Faz warmly extended an invitation for El-Dabh to follow him up to his Rockefeller Center office building (on the forty-sixth floor). There he suggested the possibility of a stipend to allow the composer to travel to Ethiopia under the sponsorship of the Rockefeller Foundation. El-Dabh eagerly accepted the invitation, which produced the funding necessary to support his research.

El-Dabh was ecstatic, but he was well aware that he faced the difficult task of informing Mary; he steeled himself for her negative response. Mary, extremely upset and angry, expressed profound displeasure that the family, having returned only recently from Egypt and France, was now to be up-rooted to Ethiopia. She accused El-Dabh of being selfish and inconsiderate, and he did not deny the charges. Appealing to her strong maternal feelings, he promised that their stay in Ethiopia would not be permanent and that they would travel in a leisurely way to their destination, stopping frequently in order to provide educational opportunities for their young daughters.

Knowing that she had expressed concern about the possibility of nuclear war, he appeased her by stating that no one was building fallout shelters in Ethiopia. His arguments were convincing and the protective mother became more receptive to the thought of taking her daughters out of the country and away from danger. However, her husband's talk of nuclear war prompted Mary to write a letter expressing her apprehension to Eleanor Roosevelt. On October 30, 1961, she received a response from the former first lady. The note read:

Mrs. Franklin D. Roosevelt
55 East 74th Street
New York City 21, N. Y.

October 30, 1961

Dear Mrs. Dabh,
    Thank you very much for your letter and for sharing your views with me.
    If a catastrophe should happen you will not have to "justify" this horror to your children. There is nothing you can tell them if you live in a city and you are in a nuclear war because you won't have time. It will not happen, I hope, for I think at bottom our leaders and the Russians do not want a war. It is not a matter of saving face but of negotiation. So, let us have faith in our leaders.
With best wishes,
very sincerely yours,
[signed] Eleanor Roosevelt[23]

The family resided in Ethiopia from the end of 1961 through 1964, a time in which El-Dabh and his works were extremely well known and popular in New York. He had made a conscious decision to walk away from his opportunity for great fame. When word spread that El-Dabh was truly leaving New York to study the Coptic church in Ethiopia, his colleagues from the Columbia-Princeton Electronic Music Center advised him to purchase a high-quality tape recorder for his fieldwork. They specifically recommended a Nagra reel-to-reel from Switzerland; so the El-Dabh family's first stop on their journey to Ethiopia was Lucerne, traversing the Alps by train. There El-Dabh purchased his Nagra, an assortment of microphones, and a copious supply of blank tapes for the sum of six hundred dollars.[24] From Switzerland they traveled to Italy for another visit with Raffaele Stocchino and for an opportunity for El-Dabh to become accustomed to his new recording equipment by capturing the ambient sounds in and around the Basilica San Marco in Venice, which was then under renovation. Because St. Mark is the patron of the Coptic Orthodox Church of Egypt, having introduced Christianity to that nation in the first century C.E., the original St. Mark's Church in Alexandria is considered the most important church in Egypt. His relics, which had been stolen from Egypt[25] by the Venetians during the ninth century, were housed in San Marco during the time that El-Dabh made his recording. On the tape can be heard the majestic bells of the basilica, as well as El-Dabh's footsteps and the young voices of Shadia and Amira.

The family's next predetermined stopover before continuing on to Ethiopia was Greece, where they stayed on the island of Hydra at the home of Rallou Manou, the director and choreographer of Hellenic Choreodrama, the famous Greek dance troupe, and her architect husband, Paul Milonas. Their spectacular home, with its breathtaking view from atop the island, was approached by 330 steps deeply recessed in the rock, and Milonas had brought from Athos a vast amount of marble to cover all his terraces. During their visit, Manou persistently urged El-Dabh to compose a work similar to *Clytemnestra* for her troupe, suggesting the subject of the Byzantine empress Theodora. El-Dabh, eager to commence his research in Ethiopia, was reluctant to commit himself to such a time-consuming collaboration, but he did promise Manou that he would consider her proposal.

Following their stay on Hydra, the family traveled to Piraeus, the port of Athens, where they boarded a ship that had begun its voyage in Split, Yugoslavia (modern-day Croatia). It transported them on their journey across the Mediterranean, with stops in Crete, Cyprus, and Lebanon. Beirut (decades before its long and destructive civil war), with its plentiful fruit gardens, invoked an image of the Garden of Eden, and El-Dabh believed it the most beautiful place that he had ever seen. The family took several day-trips to experience the city's splendid sights, and Shadia and Amira delighted in picking exotic fruit right from the trees. Departing from Lebanon, the ship continued through the Suez Canal, where El-Dabh particularly enjoyed talking to the *Bambuti*[26] men, who engaged in brilliant displays dancing all along the canal. As the ship dropped anchor at the many ports, El-Dabh, to Mary's dismay, often would jump into the water for a swim. Eventually the ship arrived in Djibouti, from where the family proceeded by train to their final destination of Addis Ababa, Ethiopia.

The terrain over which the train passed, consisting of lava and unusual rock formations, appeared to be on the moon, not the earth. Warned that bandits might stop the train, Mary, Shadia, and Amira were frightened for most of the very difficult and rough trip. They were also alarmed because the conductor, who made his rounds during the middle of the night, did so by walking on top of the train, because it was very full. They were shocked the first time they saw his boots and legs coming in at them through the windows. The collector invariably appeared to be inebriated on *tej*, made from fermented honey, or on *tala*, made from fermented grain. These drinks were the main staples in that area, because the water was largely not fit for human consumption—which proved to be another difficulty for Mary and the girls.

The family encountered more problems upon entering Addis Ababa, when a customs official, intrigued by El-Dabh's Nagra and other recording equipment, demanded that it be turned over to him. El-Dabh, lying that he had been invited by the Ethiopian government to conduct research, refused and informed the official that if he were stopped from entering the country, he would return to Djibouti, which was freer and much easier to move around in. This confrontation upset Shadia and Amira, who began to sob uncontrollably. A devout Muslim standing nearby approached El-Dabh and, speaking in Arabic, asked what the problem was and offered to take El-Dabh to the customs chief, whose office was downtown. El-Dabh turned to his distraught wife and children and instructed them to wait for his return; the two men hailed a taxicab and departed. The senior official stamped all their papers and passports, allowing El-Dabh and his family to enter Addis Ababa freely. On their return to reconnect with Mary and the children, El-Dabh offered money to the Muslim for his assistance, but the man refused to accept even one cent. When El-Dabh inquired if it was his job to handle such misadventures, the man responded, "No, no. I realized you needed assistance, and I decided to take you there."[27]

Mary, furious at her husband for abandoning her with the children at the customs checkpoint, insisted that he check them into a nice hotel immediately and then take them to dinner at a fine restaurant that very evening. Recognizing the effects of his wife's stress and exhaustion, he readily agreed and proceeded to the nearby local bank to make a cash withdrawal. There he discovered that there was hardly any money in his account. Certain there was some mistake, but not wanting to agitate his wife further, El-Dabh cabled the Rockefeller Foundation for an advance to see him through while he tried to straighten out his predicament. Believing that her husband was taking an inordinate amount of time to complete a simple banking transaction, Mary left all their personal belongings at the customs office and dragged her daughters to the bank to search for him. When he realized that all his recording equipment had been left unsecured, El-Dabh became enraged and bolted from the bank to retrieve his prized possessions. When Mary and the girls caught up with him at the customs office, El-Dabh calmly explained their monetary predicament; the Rockefeller Foundation, apparently misunderstanding the gravity of his situation, had cabled back its displeasure that El-Dabh was requesting money so early.

Overwhelmed, Mary burst into tears, which induced in El-Dabh a sudden swell of compassion for his wife and children. Aware that all the hotels in Addis Ababa were expensive and that the one where they could afford to stay did not appear to be safe, El-Dabh announced, "Let's go to the Gannat Hotel. Let's not go into that rundown hotel because we have no money. Let's go to the expensive one."[28] A stunned Mary ceased her crying and quizzically stared at her husband to ascertain if he was serious. Sensing her skepticism, El-Dabh explained that *gannat* meant "paradise," which he considered a positive omen. Gathering up their belongings, El-Dabh escorted his family into the most expensive hotel in Addis Ababa and requested a suite; he would be paying for the suite, he announced, on a monthly basis. The clerk asked if he would pay up front or at the end of the month. Maintaining his bravado, El-Dabh asked him to start an account in his name; he would settle the bill at the end of the month. While frantically communicating with Manufacturer's Trust in New York trying to straighten out their financial nightmare, the family enjoyed three generous meals a day, a lavish outside garden, and all the amenities the hotel offered, as if things were as perfect as they appeared to be.

Finally, Mary communicated with her sister, who was taking care of their business in the United States. From her she learned that three canceled checks made out to a George Papioannoy had been cashed against

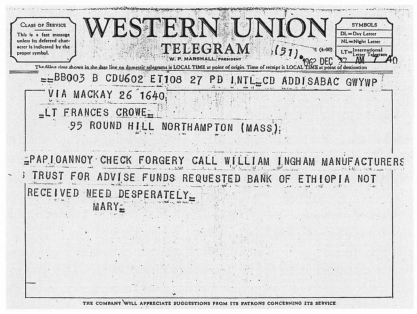

Western Union Telegram regarding George Papioannoy's forgery (1962).

their account for a total amount of $2,500. El-Dabh immediately realized who had stolen from them. He reminded Mary that when traveling from Greece the family had stopped in Delphoi, where, arriving at the end of the season, they had found no hotels available. As they were discussing where they would spend the night, a tall charismatic Greek man with a large mustache had overheard their conversation. This man, who had quite a flair about him, invited them to accompany him back to the hotel he owned, where he had some cognac ready. Throughout their stay, he had graciously offered to escort the family to various places of interest, and on one occasion he had taken El-Dabh to hear an astonishing *bouzouki*[29] performance. El-Dabh reminded Mary of another instance when the man had taken them on an excursion but then immediately excused himself and left for another engagement; it had been quite some time before he returned for them. El-Dabh surmised that this man was George Papioannoy and that he must have returned to the hotel, rummaged through their luggage, removed three checks from El-Dabh's checkbook, and forged El-Dabh's signature from the hotel registry. El-Dabh recalled that immediately following this incident Papioannoy had invited El-Dabh to Piraeus for a huge celebration, during which he had informed El-Dabh that he had received a large sum of

money and even showed him an impressive wad of cash. El-Dabh, unaware that he was enjoying a celebration at his own expense, had had a
most enjoyable time feasting on lobster and other delicacies.

Although at the time he had wondered why this man was taking such
good care of him and his family, the revelation amused El-Dabh much
more than it angered him; he greatly appreciated the man's style and flair.
El-Dabh provided a complete account to the local authorities and learned
that Papioannoy, who had perpetrated a similar scam on a millionaire, had
been caught and jailed in Athens. Though fearing that his money was irre-
trievable, El-Dabh informed the Greek embassy in Addis Ababa of his plight.
The Greek government, embarrassed, refunded all his money. Later El-
Dabh learned that Papioannoy had been the lover of the woman who actually owned the hotel that he claimed to have been his.

When the time arrived for El-Dabh to settle his bill at the Gannat Hotel, the clerk inquired if he planned to stay another month. El-Dabh can-
didly responded that since his financial situation was now more stable, he
was going to relocate his family to a less expensive hotel. Frustrated that
his financial and consular wrangling had cost him a month of research
time, El-Dabh contacted the Rockefeller Foundation to express his displeasure at the manner in which his situation had been handled. The foundation took umbrage, and after one year, their relationship ended. Mary
presumed that the severed association would precipitate their return to
the United States, but her husband announced that the family would be
staying in Addis Ababa for at least two more years; he had entered a two-
year relationship with Haile Selassie University,[30] where he had been offered a considerable salary as a professor.

El-Dabh made the switch from researcher to associate professor of
music with ease, and thus began his first official professorship. At Haile
Selassie University, El-Dabh was provided a furnished apartment, a cook,
a private car, and a Land Rover to conduct his research. It was an exciting
time for him as he learned to balance research with teaching; often he
combined the two by requiring his students to accompany him into the
villages to learn to conduct field research themselves. At first, however,
he had trouble overcoming the students' fear that if they studied the traditional music of the *azmari*,[31] they would lower their status in society
and would not be permitted to marry within their class. The students
implored El-Dabh to teach them European music, but he adamantly refused, asserting that there were thousands of Europeans who could be
invited to perform that task and that he was not in Ethiopia to teach

Halim El-Dabh with Ethiopian musicians (1963).

European music. Strangely, the curriculum at Haile Selassie University had almost nothing to do with Ethiopia, and this fact confounded El-Dabh, who eventually took the view that because he was introducing Ethiopian ideas to Ethiopians, he was leading an educational revolution.[32]

El-Dabh frequented the marketplace districts, which housed many night-clubs, known as *tej bet* (fermented honey houses) or *shai bet* (tea houses); however, the worried students warned him not to patronize such dangerous establishments. El-Dabh declared that these were the very places where the students would gain their greatest education about music and life. El-Dabh discussed the students' concerns with the university's president, Kassa Wolde-Mariam,[33] son-in-law of Haile Selassie,[34] the university's chancellor.

Wolde-Mariam, however, had his own concerns; El-Dabh was too vocal about lack of support for the university's curriculum. El-Dabh had once sent word out to the villages for local musicians to come to the city to play their music with him. Waking one morning to find thirty Ethiopian musicians standing outside his apartment, needing food and housing, El-Dabh had asked for support from Wolde-Mariam, who had laughed at the young professor. Undeterred, El-Dabh had started performing with these musicians. In his quest to educate his students, who knew so little about their own country, El-Dabh went searching for local grants and funding from the many foreign embassies located throughout the city. He met little enthusiasm until he approached the German embassy, where he received five hundred dollars for his musicians to appear on a broad-cast of the Radio of the Gospel, a major radio station located in the heart of Addis Ababa and administered from Stuttgart. The broadcast was a triumph, and El-Dabh successfully persuaded the radio station's director to pay royalties to the musicians, whom he had transformed into his "Orchestra Ethiopia."

El-Dabh had triumphantly informed President Wolde-Mariam that his new folk troupe would be traveling throughout Ethiopia to develop the culture and requested that the musicians be placed on the university pay-roll. Wolde-Mariam had been aghast, but El-Dabh had argued that be-cause they possessed knowledge no one else had, these musicians should be considered teachers. The university students were ignorant of their own culture, he maintained, and this would be a means to remedy that deplorable situation. Wolde-Mariam, impressed by El-Dabh's passion, reconsidered and agreed to place every musician on the payroll, at a re-duced salary. Nothing like this had ever occurred before in the history of Haile Selassie University. (As would be expected, when El-Dabh left the university in 1964, all the musicians were relieved of their university positions.)[35] (Track No. 14 on the companion CD.)

Although he relished his teaching responsibilities, it was visiting vari-ous monasteries throughout Ethiopia conducting fieldwork for his com-parative study of the Coptic church in Egypt and the Ethiopian Coptic church that generated El-Dabh's most memorable experiences. During one of his trips, El-Dabh visited Haïk, a monastery so isolated in the moun-tains that one had to approach it on a raft tethered to a bridge. There was a beautiful, placid lake on the monastery grounds; he was told that no mat-ter what storms or weather disturbances occurred nearby, the monastery's lake was always calm and tranquil. El-Dabh spent several days at Haïk, which housed many monks who were quite willing to share their experi-ences with the researcher. However, El-Dabh considered his stay at a mon-astery located on a small island in the middle of Lake Tana, a branch of the Blue Nile River, one of his most interesting interactions with monks. He had been traveling alone in a fiberglass boat when strong winds had hurled his boat against the rocks, leaving him stranded near the monastery. The hermit monks dwelling there rescued the battered El-Dabh and permitted him to remain with them until the weather improved enough that he could return to the mainland in a papyrus boat to bring back repairmen to fix his fiberglass boat.[36] When the time came for him to leave the monastery, he was approached by several of the monks who asked him to take them back to land; it was now time for their worldly lives. Detecting his confusion, the monks explained that although they primarily led monastic lives, after a certain number of years they had been granted permission to marry; they now divided their lives between their hermit existences and their families.

Another special visit for El-Dabh was his trip through Lalibela[37] to some of the earliest Christian shrines and churches, hewn from the rock. El-Dabh, fascinated by the sights of Lalibela, was immediately reminded of similar sights he remembered from Abu Simbel,[38] and he thought to himself, "This is what I did back in New York. I chiseled out the sound; they chiseled out the rock."[39] El-Dabh was informed that some Egyptians, indeed, had worked at Lalibela; in fact, one of the hills in the area was known as the Hill of the Egyptians—which further supported his ideas of a connection between Lalibela and Abu Simbel. The Lalibela churches were magnificent structures; however, there were no roads. One had to journey by mule over the mountain trails. It took El-Dabh, accompanied by a group of monks and five mules, four days and nights to reach the first abbey during which, despite their caution, one of the mules was lost to hyenas. Traveling down the mountain on a narrow path next to a thousand-foot drop, El-Dabh closed his eyes and hung on to his mule. He nevertheless clung to his Nagra, with which he recorded the yodeling of the people along the way. At one point the group was joined by a pregnant woman walking to the Shrine of Lalibela, where she wanted to give birth. Stopping in a mountain village, El-Dabh bought some lamb for them to eat, and one of the women in the village, who knew the monks, welcomed El-Dabh as a stranger. Before he was fed and provided a place to sleep for the night, he was instructed to remove his shoes in order for her to wash his feet, as Christ had done for his apostles at the Last Supper. He considered this to be one of the most powerful experiences of his trip.

While the family was living in Ethiopia, Amira was enrolled in a German school, and Shadia attended an American school; however, because she did not have an official connection to the U.S. embassy and was not from a military family, Shadia lacked the insurance necessary for permission to ride the school bus. El-Dabh did not want Shadia to feel that she was not good enough to ride the bus, so when he was not away conducting his research El-Dabh took his daughter to school in a horse-drawn carriage, driving alongside the school bus and Shadia's envious schoolmates. A few months later, when El-Dabh learned that the children of the U. S. ambassador to Ethiopia attended the British school, Shadia was withdrawn from the costly American school and was enrolled in the British one.

Amira's enrollment in the German school proved to be an important connection for El-Dabh, because the German school was the only one in Ethiopia that believed the traditional Ethiopian music was important for the students to learn. Wanting to provide the children with the best education, the school's administrators asked El-Dabh to bring his folk musicians to the school to perform on their traditional instruments. This interaction led to an invitation from the Goethe Institute for El-Dabh to travel to Germany later that year on a sponsored tour of Berlin, Cologne, Frankfurt, and Göttingen to lecture about his Ethiopian experience. Stopping in Cairo on the way to Germany, El-Dabh was saddened and shocked to learn that his father had died recently—and very upset that his brothers had not notified him. It was an especially difficult experience for him, because when his mother had died in 1959, his brothers had not immediately informed him of her death either. He could not believe that he was experiencing the same painful feelings of loss and exasperation all over again.

5

Greece, Germany, and Washington, D.C.

After the shock of his father's death subsided, El-Dabh felt a compulsion to complete his study of the Coptic churches of Egypt and Ethiopia, and he became obsessed with the idea of returning to Greece to visit the monasteries of Athos. Remembering that three years earlier Rallou Manou, the director and choreographer of the Hellenic Choreodrama, had urged him to compose a work similar to *Clytemnestra* for her troupe and had suggested the subject of Theodora, El-Dabh contacted her and announced that he had left Ethiopia and wanted to bring Mary and the girls with him to Greece to embark on her project. Manou, delighted, insisted that El-Dabh and his family reside at her home on Hydra until he could find suitable housing. El-Dabh eagerly accepted Manou's offer and asked her to have her husband, Paul Milonas, attempt to secure permission for him to visit the monasteries. These monasteries were like tall, heavy stone castles and fortresses, clustered in the mountainous peninsula in the northern part of Greece, close to the Turkish border. Well aware of El-Dabh's research interest and of the fact that he knew Milonas had completed a great deal of architectural work at the monasteries, the choreographer inferred that El-Dabh's primary reason for making the trip to Greece was not her troupe. Therefore, in an effort to ensure that he would begin composing immediately upon his arrival, Manou arranged for a heavy upright piano to be carried by donkey up the 330 steps to her house in anticipation of El-Dabh's arrival.

When El-Dabh informed Mary of his travel plans, she suppressed her own desire to return to the United States with her children and grudgingly packed her family's belongings to follow her husband yet again. Mary found solace in the fact that they were leaving Ethiopia, where she had never felt

comfortable, and she had enjoyed her previous visit to Hydra. Sympathiz-
ing with her husband, who was mourning the death of his father, Mary
offered little resistance and appeared genuinely supportive of his decision.
Pleasantly surprised by his wife's reaction, El-Dabh assumed that she must
finally have resigned herself to his desire for travel, and he believed this
was a good omen, promising success in researching the Greek monasteries.

Therefore he was not prepared for Rallou Manou's antagonistic reaction when, shortly after his arrival to her home, he confirmed her suspi-
cion about the primary reason he had left Ethiopia for Greece. Remorse-
ful that he had disappointed his friend, El-Dabh pledged to compose the
score for *Theodora in Byzantium* as soon as he completed his research
and promised that he would incorporate music based on what he heard at
the monasteries into his work for her, thus ensuring a truly Greek character to the piece. Manou eventually was placated and accepted his promise; however, she was smugly gratified when it became apparent El-Dabh
did not know that obtaining permission to visit the structures was a highly
bureaucratic process. He was surprised to learn that before commencing
his journey he was required to trek up a mountain to a central licensing
office, where he would be issued a certificate granting him permission to
stop overnight at the monasteries. El-Dabh, like all visitors, was warned
to arrive at each monastery prior to sundown; otherwise, he would have
to sleep outside. He learned that females were not permitted within the
boundaries of the autonomous monastic district of Athos; all the monasteries' animals, including the insects, were male. He also was instructed
in monastic customs and protocol, which included offers of food and wine
from the monks upon entering the monastery walls.

Walking over the mountains was quite arduous and harsh, and during
El-Dabh's first climb he experienced something akin to an asthma attack.
Struggling to breathe, he often wanted to rest; however, knowing that he
was required to reach the monastery before sundown, he continued to the
first monastery at Esphigmenou. When he finally arrived, El-Dabh was so
overcome with emotion that he invoked the prayers of the Greek Orthodox church, something he felt again when he later witnessed a particularly
impassioned liturgy for the Virgin Mary. At this service, after drumming
and chanting they marched in a solemn procession, some carrying torches,
others bearing huge portraits of Mary and other holy images, before throwing themselves to the ground and contorting their bodies. Impressed by
their religious zeal, El-Dabh was filled with both passion and compassion;
the monks were equally struck by El-Dabh, who stayed up until dawn
spontaneously composing and drumming in response to what he had wit-

nessed. Moved by his reaction, the monks allowed him access to the monastery's inner shrines. After viewing these most holy sites, he was informed that he would now be granted permission to stay there forever. Honored by the gesture, El-Dabh explained that he was not celibate but a married man with children. Nonetheless, the monks urged him to stay among them, and for a moment he seriously considered their invitation.[1]

Following his visits to the Greek monasteries, and much to both Mary's and Manou's consternation, El-Dabh left his wife and children in Greece while he commenced a speaking tour in Germany and Austria sponsored by the Goethe Institute. A highlight of the tour was a scholarly meeting held at the Frei Universität in Berlin with many ethnomusicologists in attendance. There Alain Daniélou[2] dogmatically stated that a composer should not be involved in ethnomusicology; ethnomusicology and composition were two completely different entities, which should remain separate from the other. El-Dabh, taking issue with Daniélou, replied that that was nonsense; a composer who studied a group of people would be stimulated creatively by the energy of the people's musical traditions. Daniélou angrily dismissed El-Dabh's comments; however, as El-Dabh was excited to see, their opposing views generated much discussion among the other participants.

Near the end of his German tour, El-Dabh stopped in Berchtesgaden to search for a man whom he had met in Ethiopia during one of his excursions with his students. El-Dabh had happened upon a Volkswagen minibus parked in the midst of a forested area; its owner had introduced himself as Mr. Kriss. He had come looking for El-Dabh because he was interested in the popular religious customs of the Ethiopian people. Kriss related his own experiences in Egypt, where he had participated in a Zaar healing procession conducted entirely by women. During the ceremony, a lamb had been sacrificed on top of his chest, and as the warm blood spilled over him, he had felt spiritually healed. At first El-Dabh was skeptical; however, Kriss stayed and talked with El-Dabh and his students for hours, and they established a solid relationship. When he left, Kriss provided El-Dabh with his name, address, and telephone number and extended an open invitation to visit him in Berchtesgaden, where he owned the local brewery.

When El-Dabh completed his lecture tour, he decided to locate Kriss. On his arrival in Berchtesgaden, he was astonished to learn that in addition to being the local brewmaster, Kriss was also the town's mayor (a town near the Austrian border where Adolf Hitler had maintained a mountain retreat). El-Dabh also was informed that because Kriss quite vocally had opposed Hitler, he had been banished from the town; however, he had later

Coronation scene of *Theodora in Byzantium* (1965).

returned and had been elected mayor by an overwhelming majority. Kriss was delighted to have El-Dabh visit him and insisted that he send for his wife and daughters to travel from Greece to enjoy a ski vacation in the Alps at his expense. It had been six months since El-Dabh had seen his family, and he eagerly accepted Kriss's generous offer. When Mary and the children flew into Germany, El-Dabh surprised them by meeting them at the airport with a used Mercedes that he had purchased in Berlin for one thousand dollars in cash—half the money he had been paid by the Goethe Institute for his lecture tour on Ethiopian music.[3] However, El-Dabh was more surprised to see Rallou Manou with Mary and the girls. Manou insisted that she would not leave until she had the completed score for *Theodora in Byzantium* in her hands to take back to Athens. El-Dabh assured her that he had been working on the piece, and he vowed he would have it finished by the end of his time in Germany. An exasperated Manou accepted his assurance but threatened that if the promised score was not produced in a timely fashion, she would track him down again.

As he was preparing to leave Berchtesgaden (Mary and the girls having returned to Greece following their fun-filled ski holiday), El-Dabh received a cable from Rallou Manou informing him that the Greek government was insisting that the composer be in attendance for the premiere of his recently completed *Theodora in Byzantium* (1965, also known as *Doxastikon*) and that arrangements had been made to fly El-Dabh to Greece

Halim El-Dabh with Rallou Manou, Dusan Trninic (as
Emperor Justinian), Yannis Moralis (set and costume
designer), and Helen McGehee (as Theodora) at the
premiere of *Theodora in Byzantium* (1965).

for the work's premiere and subsequent tour of the Greek islands. He recalled having made a commitment to conduct the orchestra but had completely forgotten about it while Mary and the girls were visiting him. He
also now remembered that he had been sent money to purchase a plane
ticket from Berchtesgaden to Athens; unfortunately he had already spent
the money on other things. He had only enough money to purchase a
train ticket on the Orient Express to Yugoslavia, from where some cars
continued on to Athens, and others were diverted to Istanbul. Shortly
after boarding the train, El-Dabh mistakenly entered the dining car tagged
for Istanbul, became engaged in conversation with another passenger, and
drifted off to sleep. When he awoke and realized his predicament, El-Dabh
made an emergency telephone call to the Symphony Orchestra of the Hellenic National Broadcasting Institute in Athens and sheepishly informed

the staff that he was not certain where he was, but that he might be in Turkey. When he finally arrived in Athens, the orchestra members, many of whom were Egyptians who had left that country for political reasons, teased him unmercifully. El-Dabh reveled in interactions with the orchestra members; however, he once again realized that he was no conductor and talked someone else into taking the podium for the performance.

Rallou Manou had required that the premiere take place be in Herodes Atticus,[4] and the magnificent walls of this beautiful ancient structure provided a spectacular backdrop for the ballet, which opened before an audience of five thousand. The ballet recounts the love of Theodora, a striptease artist in the Carthage circus, and Justinian, the emperor who takes her to Byzantium to become his queen. El-Dabh was most impressed by the coronation and marriage scene in which Theodora remembers her former life as a circus stripper and begins removing her clothing in the church. It was very effective, because though the work's basic premise is that of an intense love story, this scene captures the essence of the inter-relationship of Theodora's self-images as an empress and as a circus woman. The contrast between the coronation scene (in the context of the Orthodox church) and the conflict between Theodora's love and her memories was remarkable, and the audience's response was powerful. El-Dabh received a standing ovation from the capacity crowd, feeling deep appreciation for the tremendous amount of respect being shown to him as a composer by the Greek public. While in Greece, El-Dabh would also be introduced to the well-known Greek composers Mikis Theodorakis,[5] best known for his musical score for the 1962 film *Zorba the Greek,* and Manos Hadjidakis,[6] who won an Academy Award in 1960 for the music and lyrics of the theme-song for the film *Never on Sunday.*

Following the premiere, *Theodora in Byzantium* toured other parts of Greece as well as the islands. For El-Dabh, the most memorable event was the performance in Thebes. The energy and the excitement of that particular town was unique; nearly the entire village attended the performance. Shopkeepers opened their establishments to everyone involved in the production, and the cast and crew were provided with food and drink free of charge. El-Dabh enjoyed the interactions among the crewmembers, who utilized buckets of water to create electrical resistance for the lights. As they constructed the stage in mid-afternoon, the crewmembers screamed, shouted, and cursed at one another; the chaos ceased only for their brief respites. Each day there appeared to be nothing but confusion; each evening, however, when it was time for the eight o'clock performance, everything miraculously became orderly. El-Dabh was treated royally throughout the ballet's run, and he was very pleased with his collaboration with Manou and her company of Greek, Yugoslavian, and American dancers. Unfortunately, Greece soon experienced political turmoil, barring El-Dabh from keeping in contact with Manou and the troupe as he would have liked.

Mary and the girls were delighted to return to the United States, and when El-Dabh purchased a home in Cresskill, New Jersey, Mary was optimistic that her peripatetic husband was finally ready to settle down. Her hopefulness was short-lived, however; El-Dabh quickly grew tired of the community and announced that a change of scenery would be beneficial to his compositional creativity. Advised by an acquaintance that there was great artistic activity in Vermont, El-Dabh packed his wife and children into the family car and started driving north. When he encountered a crossroad leading in one direction to Vermont and in the other to Massachusetts, he stopped the car and stood in the highway asking himself which would be more exciting. Mary was incredulous when he returned with the announcement that the family was moving to Rockport, Massachusetts; he had remembered hearing people speak enthusiastically of the contemporary creative activity found throughout Rockport. It was late when they finally arrived and discovered that every hotel was more expensive than they could comfortably afford. Driving to the rear of a hotel, El-Dabh confidently declared that he was certain they could find a nice, reasonable place to stay.

While leaving the parking lot of the final hotel, El-Dabh noticed a nearby house and barn, and he informed his family that he was going to walk there to inquire if the owners knew of someone who had guest rooms to rent. In response to his emphatic pounding on her front door, Mrs. George Dinckel unlatched the lock and warily inquired what El-Dabh needed. Carefully scrutinizing the rumpled and disheveled composer and deciding that his story was true, she related the situation to her husband, an artist whose numerous paintings of ships and the shoreline were stored inside the barn that originally had caught El-Dabh's attention. George Dinckel insisted that El-Dabh bring his wife and children inside, and after further deliberation the Dinckels offered, at a rate of thirty-five dollars per week, to rent their furnished cottage to the El-Dabhs. The family resided at the Dinckels' cottage for three months, before renting a five-bedroom house on the ocean side of Rockport, where they lived for two years. Even after they moved away, the El-Dabhs would maintain a fifteen-year friendship with the Dinckels, stopping to visit the artist and his wife each time they passed through the region.

In light of his experience at Haile Selassie University, El-Dabh assumed that an academic career within the American university system would be a difficult adjustment and would stifle his creativity. Accordingly, he prepared to focus his energies on research and composition. To his delight, Rockport proved to be the exciting artists' haven he had hoped it would be, and El-Dabh began experimenting with teaching music by a system of color notation he had devised for the piano by which the entire spectrum of sound and rhythm was made available even to beginners. As a young child, El-Dabh had been fascinated by colors and flowers; whenever someone brought him a flower, he seemed to sense it as a sound rather than by vision. While others only looked at a rose and smelled it, he also "heard" it. Holding that his method of color notation had implications for the teaching as well as for the creation of music, he often performed lecture-demonstrations in which he discussed his concepts of musical sound and applied them to audience members—of all ages and backgrounds, with or without musical training, throughout the Rockport area. In these lecture-demonstrations El-Dabh gave examples from his own compositions for piano and for drums and played tape recordings made in the villages of Egypt and the monasteries of Ethiopia, demonstrating a rich variety of rhythm and sound.

While living in Rockport, El-Dabh was commissioned by Gelsey T. Frothingham, the manager of his old friend Allen Barker, pianist and conductor of the New Boston Percussion Ensemble, to compose for the various African, Asian, and Indian drums owned by the group. El-Dabh and Barker had met as students at the New England Conservatory, and a strong friendship had rapidly emerged as the two spent many hours walking around Walden Pond contemplating the works of Henry Thoreau.[5] "Egueypto-Yaat"[6] (1965), for two trumpets and percussion; "Hindi-Yaat No. 1" (1965), for cymbal-bells, medium-high drums, jingles, metallic discs, and woodblocks or clappers; and "Leiyla"[7] (1965), for mezzo-soprano, men's chorus, piano, timpani, cello, and xylophone—all were commissioned by Frothingham Management of Weston, Massachusetts, for an ensemble composed of Barker and percussionists James Latimer and Arnold Huberman. El-Dabh was stimulated by interacting with the group during a time when interest in percussion music among both composers and the public was mounting.[8] The experience was the impetus for his *The Derabucca: Hand Techniques in the Art of Drumming* (1965), a book in which he explains the various notation systems he created to reflect the finesse of the instrument's technique. This system, which employs a variety of unconventional symbols rather than standard staff notation, provides indications not only for the drum's major strokes, but also for a number of very subtle and delicate sounds. For El-Dabh, who had encountered literally dozens of different techniques for playing the *derabucca* in his travels throughout Egypt, the instrument was one capable of an almost infinite range of timbres. It was very stimulating for him to study and to write about these techniques. In *The Derabucca*, El-Dabh goes beyond the description of the drum's techniques and explains that the room in which the drum is played is equally important to the end product. It is vital, he argues, for the performer to sense the nammer in which the sound leaves the drum, returns, and goes back out into the room once more.

In the midst of his creative involvement with percussion instruments, John Langstaff, a great admirer of his music, invited him to become a resident composer at McLean High School in McLean, Virginia. During the summer of 1966, when it became widely known that El-Dabh was associated with McLean, Charles Franz, director of African studies, and Warner Lawson, director of choirs, at Howard University in Washington, D.C., approached El-Dabh with an offer of a faculty position in the African Studies Department. Explaining that he was a composer and wanted to concentrate on his creative work, El-Dabh declined; however, the university persisted until he acquiesced.

Although he always insisted that he did not want to have anything to do with universities and that he wanted to devote his energies toward composition, it appears that El-Dabh was born to be a teacher. Throughout his association with Howard University from 1966 to 1969, El-Dabh was invited by many universities to lecture and to perform, which provided him with opportunities to engage in creative and intellectual debates. In 1966, he performed his "Shades and Shadows" (1965), for men's chorus, drums, and jingles at Colgate University; Bruno Nettl[12] invited him to the University of Illinois at Urbana to speak to students interested in modern dance, electronic music, contemporary composition, ethnomusicology, and El-Dabh's drumming technique. Addressing a different department every day, he lectured an entire week at Urbana. There he met Igor Stravinsky's son, Sviatoslav Soulima Stravinsky,[13] whom El-Dabh found to be a very quiet, soft-spoken man, unlike his father.

In 1966, El-Dabh also became involved with the Theatre of Sound and Movement, which performed at St. Peter's Boys' High School in Gloucester, Massachusetts. Choreographer Ina Hahn created "Extensions," which was danced to El-Dabh's tape composition "Meditation on White Noise" (1959). "Extensions," a theater piece based on the direct relationship between sound and space, conceptualized an individual sound's three stages: attack, growth, and decay. El-Dabh explained to Carl P. Snyder of the *Gloucester Daily Times* that "sound generates space which is then captured by movement."[14] The composer characterized the piece as an "atmospheric disturbance in the particular area, the studio or the stage. When the sound comes into conception it has three parts, the attack, then growth, and decay. A sudden attack creates a sudden surge. The wave form created by the sound takes on a certain shape, and creates a certain space element. This is then captured during its period of growth, before it goes into decay."[15] El-Dabh's intention was for the audience to experience the progression of sound as it generated dance and finally expanded into theater. In an article for the *Boston Globe*, Margo Miller declared, "The composer feels that word generates sound which then generates movement. He has followed this sequence from New York's modern dancers to Africa's natives."[16]

Snyder's lengthy article was devoted to this new concept in theater and dance:

> For the dancer, says Ina Hahn, "it is like working in reverse. Instead of thinking of your body moving through space in a line, you think of shaping the element." "The sound is either created by the dancer or outside the dancer," adds El-Dabh. "You can use any sounds. And the space can be shaped not only by body movement, but by sculpture, color, stage design. The basic idea is how to experience the relation as sound generates dance, and how to expand this into a total theater." The process of generation is not one-sided, as the dancers reshape new spaces while preceding ones are in decay. In a kind of "feedback," as El-Dabh calls it, the new spaces call forth new sounds. "The experience is between me and them, and them and me," he says. "In the "score, certain sounds are added to the experience. But the whole composition revolves around the experience, the involvement with the thing itself." Using only a drum, El-Dabh rehearsed a piece with four dancers. In this first piece, each dancer tried to experience the space created by the music on her own, without any attempt at interrelation. In the second piece, El-Dabh "centralized" the space by playing in the area enclosed by the dancers. Then he withdrew. For a time he played his drum with one hand and the piano with the other. Then it was back to the drum. In the opening sequences, El-Dabh would prepare the atmosphere with a vibration. Then he would attack the drum and the dancer or dancers would grab the space and hold it, much as one takes a deep

breath and holds it. During the period of decay, a new space would appear. Ensuing attacks and sequences of attacks would make the space expand, contract, and move in various directions.[17]

In a review for the *Boston Herald*, Joan B. Cass observed, "Halim El-Dabh's lovely score 'Meditation of White Sound' [*sic*] was used by the dancers for a spatial study in a curiously objective fashion. The effect was of sculptured figures placed in pleasing harmonious poses and relationships, rather than of bodies moving from an inner dynamism."[18] Cass, however, was not impressed with the "Dialogue" that ensued that evening between El-Dabh and poet Vincent Fereini that concluded the evening. She referred to this portion of the performance as "an awkward half-happening, half-recital, that came off as arty rather than artistic, and could well have been omitted from the proceedings."[19]

On August 31, 1966, Hahn and her dancers performed the premiere of El-Dabh's "Wa Ka Na" ("There is, once was, a day") (1966), for dancers-singers, voice, drums, and magnetic tape. The text, music, and stage images had been composed by El-Dabh, and the choreography by Hahn. The work consists of three scenes: Breath-Creation-Birth, The All-Consuming, and The Indestructible. Twelve dancers were cast in the following roles: Being born and giving birth, All-consuming, The Unknown, Breath-Creation, Breath and Echo, Beholders, and Beings. The words used in "Wa Ka Na," chosen for their dramatic and musical content rather than for any literal meaning, had been selected by El-Dabh from the languages of the Middle East, Nubia, southern Ethiopia, and other parts of Africa in a manner that reflected the early Coptic and Byzantine church practice of fashioning phonetically structured words for use in prayers and meditations.

Again for the *Boston Herald*, Joan B. Cass wrote of "Wa Ka Na":

In a startling and effectice [*sic*] opening, a misty, luminous blue scrim revealed shadowed figures watching and participating in a birth that was poetically evocative of both human birth and creation from the void. The middle section contained a violent, exciting, physical assault on two male figures by the females, while an undulating chorus moved and muttered nearby. At the end a giant totem descended from the ceiling, and the dancers appeared to be asserting their sense of self in its presence, but this part was not as clear in intent as the other two. After the first scene, it did not seem that the largeness of concept was fully realized on the stage. Something was missing—perhaps length and development, perhaps a feeling of mass in the group relationships, perhaps a stolid [*sic*] rhythmic base. Ina Hahn's movement style and abrupt anxious phrasing may have been too neurotic or personal for Halim El-Dabh's concepts. There was a disparity between the uttered and instrumental sounds he brought from Africa and the Middle East, with their unhurried universality; and her frenetic, Western physical expressions.[20]

While employed at Howard University, El-Dabh received a second Fulbright fellowship (1967) to conduct research among the Tuareg[21] in the French-speaking African countries of Mali, Senegal, Guinea, and Niger; by now, El-Dabh thought of himself as an ethnomusicologist. He developed an interest in the connections between seventh-century Africa and eleventh-century Europe. Also, because he was interested in the creative connections between the musical materials used during the period of the troubadours and those of Bach's early career, he began exploring the lute and bowed string instrument techniques employed during that time by analyzing the musical techniques and theoretical writings found in Spain and North Africa—Egypt, Libya, Tunis, and Morocco.

While traveling in Guinea and Mali, El-Dabh received a cable from Mary that the administration of the Hawthorne School[22] in Washington, D.C., had been trying to contact him and that he should return to the United States. El-Dabh had great respect for the Hawthorne School, a much-lauded nontraditional private secondary school with an impressive record, recognized for allowing its students the freedom to choose their own curricula and make their own value judgments. Curious as to why he was being sought out, El-Dabh drove ninety miles to the airport at Bamako for a flight to Dakar, with connecting flights to Paris, New York, and Washington, D.C. The meeting was with Eleanor Orr, who, along with her husband, Alexander, was coprincipal of the Hawthorne School, and she asked him to be its resident composer. The Orrs explained that because Hawthorne made scholarships available to inner-city Washington students, it had a real diversity among its students. This integration appealed to El-Dabh, who agreed to an association that did not officially begin until 1969 but lasted for three years.

In 1967, *Clytemnestra* was restaged for another Broadway run, this time at the Mark Hellinger Theatre. Jean Battey of the *Washington Post* devoted nearly a full page to the event, recalling in great detail El-Dabh's initial encounters with Eugene Lester and Martha Graham. Of note in

Halim El-Dabh playing an African xylophone (1967). (Photo by Douglas Moore.)

the article was El-Dabh's personal reaction to the premiere and his analysis of the contributions of two singers who functioned as a Greek chorus. Battey wrote "that El-Dabh commented, 'I was overwhelmed by it. I think the staging was tremendous.'"[23] Of El-Dabh's score, she stated that it

> underlines the dance powerfully. It serves the dance, almost puritanically devoted to the emotional crisis of the story, and at the same time has flights of moving melody. The sounds are stark, shrill, haunting: a kind of sound that conjures up the searing revelations of the Delphic Oracle. The two singers often use a high, wailing sound. "The man's part has a tremendous range," El-Dabh comments. "I used a falsetto sound that has been compared to the *onnagata* voice in Kabuki. I don't work with foreground and background sounds but have an interplay, a give and take, between the elements of sound. This is a reflection of my Egyptian tradition."[24]

Guus Hoekman, Dutch basso profundo (1967).

In 1973, in an article written for the *Christian Science Monitor*, Henrietta Buckmaster would ask Graham how she had retained her original vision when obliged to divide her attention among dancers, designer, and composer. After a lengthy response, Graham singled out El-Dabh: "Halim El-Dabh wrote the music for *Clytemnestra*. This was not easy. He is Egyptian and when we were working, he would come and play the drums himself. His hand inside an Egyptian drum was an entirely different hand from anyone else's. I could never reproduce those sounds in movement but I did the best I could."[25]

In 1967, Frothingham Management commissioned El-Dabh to compose *The Eye of Horus* (1967), for bass and percussion. When the great Dutch basso profundo[26] Guus Hoekman[27] was contracted to sing the premiere, El-Dabh specifically tailored the piece to incorporate Hoekman's ability to sing with tremendous power from a low D to a G-sharp above middle C. Because Hoekman was involved in a performance with the Amsterdam Opera Company, he was unable to travel to Boston for any length of time prior to the premiere, so Allen Barker's manager, Mrs. Frothingham, sent El-Dabh to Amsterdam to work with Hoekman there. Hoekman was a large, powerful singer, and El-Dabh enjoyed taking walks with him through the villages outside Amsterdam by the sea. El-Dabh particularly relished the country scenes of farms and sheep; Hoekman would sometimes direct his booming resonant voice out to the sheep, who would react to it, much to El-Dabh's amusement.

The Eye of Horus relates the story of Osiris and Horus, examining both the rift between Osiris and his brother, Set, and a wife's vengeance for her husband's murder. Horus, often depicted in sculptures as an infant in the arms of his mother, Isis, reminds one of the baby Jesus with the Madonna. Horus is also represented, however, as a powerful eagle that circles the sky and moon. His is the story of the cycle of life. His father, Osiris, a strong Egyptian deity, is the god of resurrection and of vegetation. Osiris is always pictured with wheat growing from his dead body, but because he never really dies, he is the sign of resurrection. Osiris's brother, Set, who represents the encroaching desert, is the counterpart of Satan.

Set, jealous of his brother, tricks Osiris by showing him a sacrificial box and asking if Osiris could fit into it. Osiris enters the box, and Set locks him inside and throws the box into the Nile. Osiris's body is dismembered into fourteen pieces, which are swallowed by a crocodile. They are later collected by Isis, who works very hard to find Osiris's phallus, considered to be his most vital part. Isis reconstructs her husband and, following one last night of passion, becomes pregnant with Horus, thus vindicating Osiris by providing him with an heir.

In a review for the *Boston Herald Traveler*, Rena Fruchter stated that "employing slide projections, singing, speaking, the piano, and a percussion 'orchestra' (based on the Dutch East Indies percussion orchestra called the gamelan), Mr. El-Dabh creates the struggle between Horus and Set, representative of the balance between good and evil."[28] Fruchter continues, "Mr. El-Dabh provides some interesting percussion writing and a number of effective sections of piano and bass. Mr. Hoekman performed with spirit, understanding and fine vocal control."[29] (Track No. 16 on the companion CD.)

After a performance by the University of Akron Opera workshop, Theodore Price reviewed *The Eye of Horus* for the *Akron Beacon Journal*; he credited El-Dabh with "fusing sophisticated African devices into an essentially Western-world musical expression. 'Horus' is many things—melodically tonal one moment, pure intricate rhythn [sic] the next, episodic as a whole but highly unified, alternately sung and spoken. It is, like Schonberg's [sic] *Ewartung* [sic], a monodrama, with two exceptions. El-Dabh uses a sparse chamber ensemble of three percussionists and a pianist, and chanting chorus, instead of Schonberg's [sic] enlarged orchestra."[30] Price praised the work as "very wonderful to hear. Its taut, intricate, momentous rhythms, its crosscurrents of piano-cymbal dialog, its speech-song declarative colorations, its dramatic momentum give it a unique intensity. When evil finally reveals itself in the presence of Horus the Infant during its final pages, the score wrings out strangely exhilarating tension, unique, empowered with staggering expression between percussion and vocal instruments."[31]

While El-Dabh was teaching at Howard University, Warner Lawson,[32] director of choruses, requested that El-Dabh compose works for his choral groups. "Born from the World" (1967), for bass, sacred drums, cymbals, and jingles, was El-Dabh's initial response. It was based on an Ethiopian concept that the infant Jesus, born from the people, is simultaneously outside the world and part of the world. El-Dabh wrote the piece in an Ethiopic language with some Arabic elements; he later rewrote it in English. "Born from the World" was premiered at Howard University. Lawson then commissioned El-Dabh to write the opera-pageant *Black Epic* (1968), a theatrical piece of a poetic nature dealing with African Americans' struggle in America. However, Lawson died before he was able to premiere it; *Black Epic* has never been performed.

Shortly before his death, Lawson informed El-Dabh that Fela Sowande[33] was coming to Washington and wondered if El-Dabh would like to interview him for a position in the African Studies Department. El-Dabh, well aware of Sowande's fame, was surprised by Lawson's suggestion. El-Dabh knew that because Sowande had too high a reputation, an interview would be insulting to the great man. However, if this was the only way to secure Sowande a position at Howard, El-Dabh would agree to interview him. During the "interview" El-Dabh deferred to Sowande and treated him with great respect, as if he were a high priest. El-Dabh was very pleased that Sowande received the position; the two would share an office in the university tower overlooking the city. Sowande rarely spoke to anyone, but he became very close to El-Dabh, who believed that just to have had the opportunity to know Sowande made his time at Howard University worthwhile.

El-Dabh flourished during his tenure at Howard University. However, the administration felt that undergraduate students were too impressionable to be allowed contact with the free-spirited composer, who thoroughly engaged his students in drama, music, and dance and encouraged them to read Nigerian plays, such as *The Palm Wine Drinkard*[34] and *The Lion and the Jewel*.[35] El-Dabh was permitted to instruct only graduate students, many of whom were becoming active in the Black Is Beautiful Movement. The students engaged Stokely Carmichael[36] to speak to them at the university, and El-Dabh was impressed with Carmichael's address.

Because he believed the movement's ideals evoked feelings of pride and dignity among all people of African descent, El-Dabh fully supported his students' involvement, and he taught them of the Negritude Movement,[37] initiated by Senghor[38] in France.

El-Dabh often returned to New York at this time, and during one visit to Harlem he saw that all the women had been transformed by fashions created from beautiful African cloth, with striking African headdresses. Walking down the street, he was impressed with the theaters, the shops selling books in Yoruba[39] and Kiswahili,[40] and the people teaching and singing African songs. When El-Dabh had been in French Africa at the Institute d'Études Africaines, he had been very much aware of the beauty of being black, and he was now glad to see the movement taking hold in the United States. Unfortunately, he was not aware that the majority of Americans did not yet embrace these conventions. Learning that a Ghanaian bishop was coming to speak at the church next to Howard University, El-Dabh composed "Kyrie for the Bishop of Ghana" (1968), for mixed choir, African percussion, and African wind instruments in honor of the visit. El-Dabh and his students received the bishop in African style, with singing and drumming. The students were thrilled to perform for him; however, El-Dabh had the impression that the bishop and the majority of those in attendance really did not appreciate the work. Although there were many involved in the Black Is Beautiful Movement, there were many more who were not interested in African traditions and were more involved with European art.

The late 1960s was a period of great unrest among the Howard University students, who felt their needs were not being met. They were hungering for courses in African history and black studies, few of which were offered at the time despite the university's historically black nature, and they were attempting to define their image of what it meant to be black. During one protest, they took over the university. Tents were erected on the lawn of the Lincoln Memorial, and El-Dabh was drafted to teach there at the "Free University." In 1968, the year of the assassinations of Martin Luther King Jr. and Robert Kennedy, El-Dabh often held his classes in a pottery shop located on 16th Street, off Georgia Avenue. On the evening of April 4, 1968, a waitress screamed, "Martin Luther King is dead!" Immediately sirens pierced the night air; the city was on fire. El-Dabh and his students dispersed into the night, and he made his way back to his office in the university tower, from where he watched the flames.

The issue of how best to handle the students' demands caused infighting among the Howard University faculty. El-Dabh, frustrated and wanting to withdraw from that volatile atmosphere, decided to take a leave of absence. It was during this time that he received a telephone call from E. Lindsey Merrill,[41] the chair of the School of Music at Kent State University. Merrill had been persistently sending El-Dabh letters inviting him to teach at Kent. However, El-Dabh, as he was prone to do, had misplaced the correspondence. An exasperated Merrill now finally telephoned and stated that he was coming to Washington, D.C., to meet with El-Dabh personally. The year before, Merrill had hired George Faddoul away from his job at WCLV radio station in Cleveland to create an electronic studio in the School of Music. Merrill was certain that the combined talents of Faddoul and El-Dabh would firmly establish Kent State's reputation in contemporary music.

During lunch, Merrill convinced El-Dabh to bring his family to Kent to evaluate the School of Music. Knowing that Mary had grown increasingly concerned for their daughters' welfare in Washington and assuming that Kent would be a much safer environment in which to rear Shadia and Amira, El-Dabh agreed to a visit. When he arrived, he was most impressed to find that a party was held at the Twin Lakes Country Club in his honor; the president, vice president, and all the music faculty attended. Dean John Flower[42] expressed delight that El-Dabh was considering coming to teach at Kent State. El-Dabh, however, was ambivalent. He wanted to return to Howard, where the students were demanding that he be named the director of the African studies program.

In an attempt to mollify the students, the administration invited El-Dabh back to Howard to discuss the position. Although the administration treated him royally, it had no intention of hiring him as the director; for his part, though disenchanted with the turmoil among the Howard faculty and not interested in an administrative position, El-Dabh did seriously contemplate returning to Howard to teach. As he considered his options, El-Dabh received a cable from Rutgers University inviting him to develop a school of music at Livingston, New Jersey. Again, the problem was that he was not suitable for administration; he knew that though he would have no difficulty in hiring a staff, he would never be able to fire anyone. He declined Rutgers's offer; however, he was informed that the position would remain open for him for three years in case he changed his mind. In 1969 El-Dabh decided to accept the offer at Kent State, because the university appeared very peaceful in comparison to Howard. No one could have predicted that the National Guard would be called there in early May 1970.

6

The Hawthorne School and
Kent State University

Shortly before moving his family to Kent, El-Dabh was invited to deliver a presentation at Baldwin-Wallace College in Berea, Ohio.[1] At a daylong session entitled "The Humanities in Africa and the Middle East," sponsored by Baldwin-Wallace and the Martha Holden Jennings Foundation, he spoke of his music and of Egyptian traditions. In an article for the *Cleveland Plain Dealer*, Robert Finn quoted El-Dabh as informing his audience that "it is not enough simply to consider all African music as something 'non-Western' and hence apart from music's mainstream. Its variations are infinite, and to understand them the listener must discard all his conventional Western notions about tuning, scales, harmony, and other matters."[2] These maxims were conspicuous in El-Dabh's collaborations with the students at the Hawthorne School as composer in residence from 1969 to 1972. In 1969 El-Dabh composed *Prometheus Bound I* (1969), on a text by Aeschylus, for singers, actors, and dancers, and *Prometheus Bound II* (1969), on a text by Robert Lowell for actors and electronic tape. Both were performed by the school seniors as a requirement for their literature class. Of these performances one critic said, "El-Dabh has surpassed Hindemith in the music he has brought to young people."[3] In 1972 the Hawthorne School applied for and received the first of two grants from the National Endowment for the Humanities to support the production of an opera trilogy, *Ptah-mose and the Magic Spell* by El-Dabh, and to meet the expense of preparing performance materials that would enable other schools to stage the work.

Ptah-mose and the Magic Spell examines the power of the world and the magic of creation. Ptah, in the ancient Egyptian tradition, was one of the creators of the world, and *E-gy-ptah* in the ancient Egyptian language means the "shrine of the soul of Ptah"—thus "Egypt," translates directly as the "land of Ptah." When El-Dabh was in Ethiopia, he had been called *E-gypts*, "man of the land of Ptah." Today the word *ptah* appears in Egyptian vernacular as a mild epithet—*ptah-ey*, "I swear! What's the matter with you?"

The first opera of the trilogy, *The Osiris Ritual* (1972), addresses the same subject matter as *The Eye of Horus* (1967). While *The Eye of Horus* depicts the story of Osiris, Isis, Set, and Horus from Horus's perspective as the son, *The Osiris Ritual* recounts the narrative from Osiris's point of view as the Egyptian god of resurrection.

The second work in the trilogy, *Aton, the Ankh, and the World* (1972), aptly depicts the historical Egyptian characterization of the god Aton, represented as the sun's disk, and of Ankh as the life force joined with Aton. When the rebel Akhenaton declared Aton to be the one and only true god and used his power as pharaoh to discredit all the other gods, he ushered in the first monotheistic movement, preceding the Hebrew concept of Yahweh. Musically, El-Dabh portrays Aton as a loving—rather than punishing, warring, jealous—god.

The third of the trilogy, *The Twelve-Hour Trip* (1972), has never been performed. It depicts the journey of a recently deceased individual coming to meet Thoth, the great scribe and initiator of the young. The deceased then encounters Anubis, the god of the dead, and Maat, the goddess of balance. Anubis and Maat take the dead person's heart and place it on a balance before a jury of twelve. If the heart is as light as two feathers, the deceased is permitted to follow a huge snake on a wild, twelve-hour trip through Duat, the underworld, and thereafter to return to life and shine symbolically again with the rising sun, Ra. *The Twelve-Hour Trip* evokes Egypt as a country of balance—the twin lands of Upper and Lower Egypt—not as one but as two united elements. The positioning of the Sphinx at Giza, one of Egypt's most ancient and representative symbols, clearly illustrates this deep-seated concept of balance within Egyptian culture. The Sphinx's head faces the North (toward Lower Egypt, where the majority of the nation's universities and houses of great intellect were built), while the Sphinx itself resides in the South (Upper Egypt, where the knowledge of building the pyramids was retained). Thus the Sphinx serves as Egypt's pivot or point of balance.

Without question, however, El-Dabh's most significant endeavor with the Hawthorne School was the creation of the ninety-minute *Opera Flies*, written in the aftermath of an anti–Vietnam War protest on the Kent State University campus on May 4, 1970, that ended in the deaths of four students and the wounding of nine others.[4] El-Dabh had moved his family to Kent in August 1969 and was deeply affected by the tragedy.

E. Lindsey Merrill, director of the School of Music, and John Flower, dean of the College of Fine and Professional Arts, had so wanted the Egyptian composer to come to Kent State University that they had acquiesced without hesitation to El-Dabh's remarkable terms. El-Dabh would join the music faculty as a tenured full professor with a commensurate salary, and he would not be required to teach any classes during his first semester, because he wanted instead to walk the campus and freely converse with students and faculty as a means of learning the campus culture. El-Dabh had declared that the responsibility of teaching classes would impede the autonomous process by which he wished to accustom himself to the environment. Understandably, the granting of this unprecedented demand was not appreciated by his colleagues, who had been expected to assume teaching duties immediately and were obliged to ascend the academic ranks through the traditional tenure and promotion process. So, while the students and administration were fascinated by the talent and gregariousness of the new music professor, most of the faculty had a difficult time relating to him without jealousy or resentment.

During his second semester on the campus, El-Dabh was invited by Edward W. Crosby, professor of German, to assist in the development of Kent State's Institute of African Affairs (which would later evolve into the Department of Pan-African Studies). Crosby's dynamic personality and dedication to the development of this program appealed to El-Dabh, and he eagerly agreed to join forces with his colleague—who also envisioned a faculty and student exchange with the University of Nigeria, a dream that unfortunately never materialized. Finding Kent State's black faculty members very congenial, El-Dabh made Kent the focus of his world.

Although Kent, Ohio, seemed very different from New York and Washington, D.C., El-Dabh's creativity flourished there as a result of the vitality, talent, and diversity of the people he encountered.[5] He was pleased with his decision to move to Kent, but he often recalled Eugene Lester's earlier comment that even Washington, D.C., was too provincial a place for El-Dabh and that he should return to New York City; El-Dabh was certain Lester would consider Kent, Ohio, ten times more provincial than the nation's capital. He had enjoyed living in New York and missed the energy of the city; however, he believed that his composing and performing did not require the validation of the publicity and large organizations of New York. The milieu may have been considered by some a provincial one, but the creative process remained dynamic, and the music was still alive and vital. He was aware, however, that by abandoning New York he had certainly surrendered much of his fame, for although his level of activity remained as high as ever, few outside his immediate environment were aware of what he was doing.

On May 4, 1970, El-Dabh was walking toward a noon class on the now-famous campus when suddenly, from a parking lot about two hundred feet away, he heard gunshots. People began running in every direction, and one horrified student rushed past him screaming, "Everybody's falling dead!"[6]

Later he was outraged to read articles and letters sent to local newspapers by parents of Kent State students asking, "Why didn't they shoot them all?"[7] During the weeks following the terrible ordeal, the town and the campus struggled to come to terms with the chaos and confusion, which had touched the lives of everyone. El-Dabh decided to leave Kent State. Several Hawthorne School students, protesting against what had happened to the Kent State students, had been arrested in Washington, D.C.; Eleanor Orr, Hawthorne's coprincipal, and several of the students had contacted El-Dabh to commission an opera about the incident. However, El-Dabh, unable to write anything due to a state of depression, declined the offer, stating that he was not interested in undertaking such a project.

Gathering Mary and the girls, El-Dabh left Kent for the refuge of Allen Barker's idyllic home in Maine, where the family spent the summer enjoying the beauty and solace of their retreat, away from the turmoil of Kent. However, El-Dabh was pursued by the Hawthorne students, who were determined to persuade him to write something for them about what had happened at Kent. He again declined their offer. Finally, during a hot August night, El-Dabh awoke with a start—his creative energies had bounced back. At three o'clock in the morning he began composing the words and melody of what would be the finale of *Opera Flies*, "In the Eye of Pathos."

Aware that he had not been able to comprehend completely the horror of the Kent State shootings, El-Dabh next composed the lyrics to the chorus, "I Strolled in Jello," evoking an image of an "undulating, diaphanous substance, to symbolize this dubious condition."[8]

In the midst of men and the child cry to move.
Immense was the field.
Jello spread and covered the town when eternity came to an end.
Riffles [*sic*] were stuck deep in jello, fired and killed.
Riffles pupped in jello.
Riffles fired and killed what was already dead.
A pinkish scum covered the town when eternity came to an end.
The riffles tore the jello to shreds, the jello wiggled again and again.
Creeks, holes, the cracks were filled once more.
I strolled in jello—ou ou a ha ha ha aa.[9]

It was the cajoling of the Hawthorne students that had persuaded him to compose *Opera Flies*, which premiered in Washington, D.C., on May 5, 1971, the day after the first anniversary of the shootings. In an interview for a Washington, D.C., newspaper two days prior to the performance, El-Dabh explained, "I didn't want to write it at all," he said. "It's still growing with me, but now I'm only the composer, and I make no big claims on it now. It's the performers' activity. Now that it's complete, I can forget what I wrote and reexperience [it] and work with them."[10] Following the premiere, Kent State bussed fifty Hawthorne students to perform the work at the Kent State University Auditorium on May 8 and 9, 1971. They traveled on from Kent to New York City for several performances in the East Village and at the Brooklyn Academy of Music, sleeping in the basements of churches and cooking their own food.

In a moving account in the *New York Herald*, K. T. Maclay detailed the students' journey from Washington to Kent, vividly describing their mounting tension prior to the first performance at the Kent State University Auditorium after visiting the site where the shootings had occurred:

It's hard to say when everything fell to bits. But suddenly grief was all over us like a tent. The girls' dressing room was completely hysterical. Tears making streaky rivers out of makeup. Girls everywhere clutching onto each other and sobbing. Mutiny was at hand. None of the leads felt they could go on. Most of them couldn't stop crying. The audience filed in. A black girl in full costume of a townswoman shrieked on her way through the audience to the stage and fell prostrate still shrieking and screaming. The Director ran, now this way, now that—trying to ease the horror of it all. The boys seemed less

overtly disturbed before performance. Subdued, glazed—on the edge
of an abyss—but not yet crying. They would cry onstage. Everybody
would.[11]

Opera Flies is the story of humanity's true emotions in the eternal
struggle between individual rights and the prevailing social order. It is the
story of human against machine, where cold, mechanized faces appear
human to those engaged in civil strife. El-Dabh declared that the tragedy is
seen "as if through a prism. . . . Time does not really matter, the elements
are basic. . . . It's all about man's rights versus the need for social control."[12]

El-Dabh pointed out the irony of the "flies" in the opera's title. "They
are the students, the insects to get rid of, to be crushed," he said.[13] Instead
of a rifle, the murder weapon is a giant flyswatter, symbolic of the opera's
title; microtonal glissandi simulate the buzzing sound of the flies' wings.
The focus was on flies because they are considered unclean, as were many
longhaired young people of the time. In an article for the *Washington
Evening Star*, El-Dabh told staff writer Joy Billington, "The conceptualization of cleanliness as a virtue can be a killing force, like bullets. If a
facade is made so that nothing but the uncleanliness is seen by the ob-
server. There's nothing wrong with cleanliness in itself, but if filth is conceptualized, then it contributes towards the alienation process."[14]

The original cast consisted of nearly fifty members, including seven
soloists, three choruses, and an orchestra consisting chiefly of winds, piano, and percussion. The style, according to El-Dabh, is

> not easy to categorize; but it definitely is not rock or pop, not serial.
> . . . It is however, African in approach because of its unusual inter-
> play between instruments and people. There is a total continent
> approach that can be recognized, for example, in the way my or-
> chestra acts like a constant fountain of sound, sometimes in the
> foreground, sometimes in the background. You are aware more of
> the sound itself as a physical thing. Only traditional European in-
> struments are used, however.[15]

El-Dabh was interviewed prior to the campus performance by the Kent
State University student newspaper, the *Daily Kent Stater*. "My work
represents no traditional form of opera, but rather is a contemporary work
which puts youth and vitality into the art."[16] He saw the work "as a new

trend in opera, which hopefully will revitalize opera companies."[17] The opera also contained some highly developed technical devices. For example, in the second act, Civil War photographs taken by Matthew Brady[18] appear on a huge screen; at the same time, video of the actors is played in "instant replay" on a television set placed in the center of the stage. El-Dabh remarked, "This is another form of destruction, as I see it, and it ends with Vekeero screaming again, and running away again."[19] The character Vekeero represents the real-life Mary Ann Vecchio, the fifteen-year-old runaway from Florida who was immortalized in John Filo's Pulitzer Prize–winning photograph, kneeling over the dead body of Jeffrey Miller. Of Vecchio El-Dabh mused, "Although everything that has happened to her since then has been very bad, she generated for me the idea of the life force, running away, meeting tragedy, bouncing back."[20] Vekeero exemplified the collective compassionate drive of the Hawthorne students. Nancy Williams, the seventeen-year-old girl who sang the part of Vekeero, said of Mary Ann Vecchio, "I feel bad about playing this part. So many things have been done to her, and I don't know how she would feel about it. But this is allegorical, and exaggerated—just one part of her life, for which she became famous."[21] The burial scene that closes Act Three ends with Vekeero, her arms outstretched in horror, kneeling over the body of one of the slain "flies." (Track No. 15 on the companion CD.)

The Hawthorne production at Kent State was met with rousing applause. However, in a review for the *Cleveland Plain Dealer*, Wilma Salisbury was critical, "The story, an allegory, concerns the killing of innocent creatures (the 'flies' of the title). Overlaid with messages about revolution and social injustice and neatly tied up with a moral about finding freedom in your own conscience, the libretto juxtaposes hip expressions, stilted English phrases, nonsense syllables and African words in a mostly incomprehensible montage."[22] Further, Salisbury declared, "The music seems to be constructed primarily from modal melodic fragments, drones and syncopated rhythms—often repeated like chanted cheers at a sporting rally."[23] She continued, "Most of the 80-minute performance was sung, although occasional parts were delivered in rhythmic speech, wails, whispers and screams. In addition, the 'eternal struggle' theme was depicted in projections, closed-circuit television, attempts at audience participation and stylized movement on and offstage and up-and-down the aisles."[24] Salisbury ended her article with the harsh assessment that "as for its artistic value, however, the work ranks about as low as opera can go."[25]

Nonetheless, *Opera Flies* provided the catharsis El-Dabh had needed to purge the bitterness that had welled up inside him following the cataclysmic events of May 4, 1970. He had been troubled since the tragedy and now keenly viewed the world from a new perspective, aware of humanity's destructive potential. He had also agonized over the turmoil and strife he encountered at home. Mary had been discontented with their marriage for several years, and his daughters had become sullen and petulant in their initial bouts of adolescent angst.

El-Dabh attempted to escape his melancholy through composition; however, the remainder of the early 1970s proved to be less than fruitful for him, and the works he produced during this time were either insignificant or subjected to mixed reviews. For example, El-Dabh was invited to become a member of the Cleveland Composers Guild and composed for it the concert play "Of Gods and Men" (1972), for singers, dancers, and chamber ensemble. Hoping to capture his many experiences in Africa, El-Dabh premiered the quasi-aleatoric,[26] quasi-improvisatory piece by singing to the performers and having them imitate what he sang. El-Dabh himself found the performance extremely rewarding; however, the musicians had great difficulty with the medium, and the Composers Guild members were puzzled by the impromptu work.

The following year El-Dabh was commissioned by the Girard Bank of Philadelphia to compose a special work for the combined Philadelphia Boys Choir and Men's Chorale under the direction of Dr. Robert G. Hamilton. The work was to be premiered in Philadelphia before the singers embarked on a concert tour to Mombasa and Belgium. The result was "Abongila's Love" (1974), for boys' choir, men's chorus, and percussion, with text in Kiswahili. However, the group found the piece much too difficult, and El-Dabh was forced to simplify the complicated rhythms and text. In a review for the *Philadelphia Inquirer,* Daniel Webster declared "Abongila's Love" a "beguiling, undulating piece. . . . The music was like the wind over an African plain, soft, quiet and without beginning or end. The metrical subtleties of the writing kept it alive and unpredictable."[27] James Felton, writing for the *Philadelphia Evening Bulletin,* labeled the performance "phenomenal."[28] The boys had accompanied the work with conga drums, three log drums from Ghana, and an African bell; Felton remarked that "the music is gentle and lilting throughout, the instruments mostly adding rhythmic spice."[29] Marsha Liston Wright, for the *Philadelphia Tribune,* asserted that "Abongila's Love" is "a poem of love . . . it tells of a man, Abongila, and his wonders and love of people and life (perhaps El-Dabh himself)."[30]

Halim El-Dabh (second from left) with the Philadelphia Boys Choir (1974).

El-Dabh remained associated during this time with the Hawthorne School and was delighted when in 1974 Eleanor Orr arranged for him to meet jazz legend Duke Ellington[31] and famed pianist Marian McPartland,[32] who were collaborating on a project with Hawthorne. Orr suggested that El-Dabh compose additional material for the undertaking; accordingly, he traveled to New York to meet McPartland at Billy Taylor's[33] jazz club. McPartland had a unique piano style that combined gospel and blues elements. Finding her charming, El-Dabh was thrilled to be invited onto the stage to play his *derabucca* while she improvised. Later, at her home, she explained the Hawthorne School project, and they began working on an initial collaboration. Unfortunately Ellington became ill and died shortly thereafter, and the project never came to fruition.

In 1975 Martha Graham, who had invited the famous Soviet ballet dancer Rudolf Nureyev[34] to study her modern-dance technique, cabled El-Dabh to come to New York to discuss a collaboration on a new work on the theme of fallen angels. El-Dabh was interested in the project, but he was torn between New York and his desire to embark on a research trip to Lagos. Finally he agreed to meet with Graham, and once more she provided him with books to read. Attempting to recapitulate their greatest success, El-Dabh and Graham collaborated as closely as they had with *Cly-temnestra*, though over a briefer period. The title of the work changed from *The Falling Angel* to *The Coming Forth of Light*; it premiered as the ballet *Lucifer* (1975), starring Nureyev and Dame Margot Fonteyn.[35] El-Dabh was disappointed that, due to scheduling conflicts, he did not have a chance to meet Fonteyn, but he was pleasantly surprised to learn that Nureyev (whose name contained the Arabic prefix *nur-*, meaning "light") spoke some Arabic. El-Dabh found the dancer very polite but reserved, which he attributed to the fact that Nureyev had recently defected; presumably he did not want to reveal too much.

Of her choice of Lucifer as a subject for her work, Graham stated, "Lucifer, to me, is not what he means to many people. He is not Satan. He was made Satan in the Middle Ages. Lucifer is the Promethean figure that brought light, fire. When he fell [from heaven] through his own pride, which every man and woman endures, he ceased to be a god, to be untroubled, and he became half-man. He became a creative being, a being in the process of creation, who suffered all the terrors a man suffers. And I felt that curious explosive self-mockery, that lament for the piece of nothingness that was part of Lucifer and part of my life."[36]

Nureyev adapted effectively to the techniques of Martha Graham's modern dance, and El-Dabh was quite impressed by the Russian's abilities. However, El-Dabh felt that for his own part it was difficult to understand the dynamics of the interaction between the classical Russian and the contemporary American. He was not able to discern how the process solidified between Graham and Nureyev, yet he relished watching it happen.

Graham had great expectations for *Lucifer*, which premiered on June 19, 1975, at the Uris Theater on Broadway.[37] Its set had been designed by Filipino architect Leandro V. Locsin,[38] and costumes had been created by the famed designer Halston.[39] The work was staged as a gala to celebrate the fiftieth anniversary of the Martha Graham Dance Company and School at 316 East 63rd Street and also to eliminate the seventy-five-thousand-dollar debt her company had accumulated, as well as generate enough money to finance her coming season.

Tickets ranged in price from fifty dollars to ten thousand. There was only one ten-thousand-dollar seat, paid for by a twelve-thousand-dollar contribution by the Lincoln Savings Bank, of which ten thousand was applied to the ticket. The seat, in Row C, was made available to Covington Hardes, board chairman of the bank. Most of the 1,873 seats sold for $125, and Graham set aside a small number of seats at twenty-five dollars each for her students. The event ultimately took in a record two hundred thousand dollars.[40]

The list of donors—and the fact that honorary leaders of the drive included Jacqueline Kennedy Onassis and Alice Tully—guaranteed a glamorous event. First Lady Betty Ford, who was a former Graham student, had been an honorary chair of the sponsoring committee; Mrs. Marvin Traub, whose husband was president of Bloomingdale's, was the chair. The gala was attended by many celebrities including Paul Newman, Joanne Woodward, Lauren Bacall, Paulette Goddard, Andy Warhol, Polly Bergen, Dick Cavett, Carrie Nye, Patricia Kennedy Lawford, Jean Kennedy Smith, Diane Keaton, and Woody Allen (who elicited criticism for wearing tennis shoes with his tuxedo). An account in the *New York Times* noted that Mrs. Ford's presence had prompted Secret Service men as well as the police to patrol "the block of West 51st Street from Broadway to Eighth Avenue, as limousines snarled traffic in the theater rush. The presence of so many security persons cramped a special business that usually takes over along 51st Street, down the street, near Eighth Avenue. For that stretch of sidewalk to the west of the theater—and often directly across from it—is a promenade for flashy prostitutes and their pimps."[41]

In a review of the opening-night gala for the *New York Post*, Frances Herridge said, "*Lucifer* is not one of Miss Graham's major works, nor is its psychological drama as eloquent as it might be."[42] Herridge, however, praised the contributions of Locsin, Halston, and El-Dabh, all in one paragraph: "It has two beautiful set pieces by Leandro Locsin—crumpled golden wings and a partly melted throne. Halston has provided magnificent cape costumes (worth $250,000 according to the program notes). And the Halim El-Dabh score is immensely evocative."[43] In contrast, Alan M. Kriegsman, writing for the *Washington Post*, disparagingly stated, "There was, however, a curious discordance between the primitive austerity of Graham's choreography and the almost belligerently flamboyant decor—Leandro Locsin's craggily volcanic set pieces, and Halston's grossly iconic capes and loincloths. The acerbic music score by Halim El-Dabh is serviceably atmospheric rather than distinguished."[44] *New York Times* critic Clive Barnes agreed with Kriegsman: "Margot Fonteyn seemed to have some trouble in relating to the atmospheric but not notable music that had been provided by Halim El-Dabh."[45] Eight days later, again in the *New York Times*, Barnes was even more dismissive of the score: "The ballet—with its sculptural setting by Leandro Locsin, handsome lighting by Ronald Bates and costumes by Halston—looks good. Graham has invented some fine things for Nureyev, as a half-god, half-man uncertainly exploring a new world of human passion, but the score by Halim El-Dabh is more humdrum than hummable."[46]

Incredibly, having decided that he could no longer postpone his trip to Africa, El-Dabh missed the premiere and the subsequent criticism of *Lucifer*. However, Mary, Shadia, Amira, and several of their friends attended the gala performance as the invited guests of music publisher Walter Hinrichsen's widow, Evelyn, for which El-Dabh would remain grateful. El-Dabh had been under a great deal of stress while composing the music for *Lucifer*—pressure about neglecting his research in Nigeria, and mounting tension at home that eventually resulted in the demise of his marriage.

7

Kent, Ohio

After twenty-three years of marriage to the peripatetic Halim, Mary filed for divorce. She was awarded a generous monetary settlement that allowed her to remain in the house in Kent until Amira graduated from high school. Although she was financially secure, the divorce took a tremendous psychological toll on Mary, whose mounting frustration and resentment toward her former husband was shared by her two daughters, whose loyalties were firmly with their mother. Both Shadia and Amira felt abandoned and betrayed by their father, and his decision to travel to Africa and Egypt in the midst of the divorce proceedings augmented their emotional turmoil.

El-Dabh, absorbed in his own disappointments stemming from the failed marriage and the rather lackluster responses to his recent compositions, once more felt compelled to interrupt his compositional life and immerse himself in ethnomusicological research. Desperately wanting to conduct fieldwork but lacking funds, El-Dabh applied to the Smithsonian Institution for a research grant. Within weeks of his application, El-Dabh was selected to serve as a research consultant for the Smithsonian Institution, the National Museum of the United States. Believing that his study would make an invaluable contribution to the graduate program in ethnomusicology at Kent State, El-Dabh approached the university's president, Glenn A. Olds,[1] and asked to be released from his teaching responsibilities for the fall semester of 1975. Olds, who had been the U.S. representative to the United Nations Economic and Social Council from 1969 to 1971, was supportive of this endeavor and promised that, depending on the academic calendar, he would grant permission. Between

1975 and 1981 El-Dabh would be employed periodically as a research consultant to the Smithsonian Institution.

During his first trip under the sponsorship of the Smithsonian, El-Dabh traveled for forty days throughout central and western Africa—to Dakar, Senegal; Lagos, Nigeria; and Kinshasa, Zaire—to discover cultural links between Americans of African descent and their ancestors. Initially he had planned to include Turkey as part of this study; however, Turkey was experiencing unrest at the time, and he was advised to eliminate it from his itinerary. His work was primarily an examination of the connections between the cultures of Africa and the African diaspora in the Caribbean and North America. Prior to his trip, El-Dabh reported in an article for the *Ravenna* (Ohio) *Record-Courier*, "I am one of a team looking for the parallels of expression in the church, the home or the market place."[2] He would be "looking for the commonalities in food, music, dance, crafts and religious expression."[3]

The next phase of the research after his return from Africa would be to examine black communities in the United States to look for parallels. El-Dabh hoped to "search for the cultural links with the motherland. . . . What we are documenting is what is happening in the United States today and how that relates to the rest of the world. This is a long-range educational project which will help us to understand ourselves."[4] During the university's spring break and on weekends, El-Dabh traveled for another forty days, this time within the United States, investigating the retention of Egyptian culture in the United States. His travels revealed that Egyptian enclaves existed in, to name only a few places, Los Angeles, Milwaukee, Jersey City (New Jersey), and in New York City.

While in Zaire, El-Dabh lectured at the Kinshasa Institute for Music. There he was introduced to a Zairean scholar, Kazadi wa Mukuna, who later, in 1989, would assume a teaching position in the School of Music at Kent State University and become El-Dabh's colleague. El-Dabh's lectures at the Kinshasa Institute for Music, as well as at the Royal Museum for Central Africa, afforded him access to official papers. Also, a trip into the forest to research the Zebola people proved memorable for El-Dabh—in fact, more than he had bargained for. El-Dabh was provided an assistant to drive him around in a government-owned Land Rover near the Angolan border. The assistant was from the Mongo people, and his wife was a Bakongo woman. El-Dabh asked his new friend and assistant why he had married outside his tribe; the man responded that Mongo women are not required to be virgins when they wed; a Bakongo woman, in contrast, must prove her virtue on the wedding night. El-Dabh was greatly amused.[5]

The Mongo assistant drove El-Dabh to the sacred ground to document the dancing and ceremony. They entered the sacred ground, where beautiful young Bakongo women were seated very closely together, as still as statues. Their hair had been meticulously styled, and their makeup had been applied with great care; however, the women were stark naked. Directly before the women a fire was burning next to a large altar erected entirely of tree branches. El-Dabh and his assistant watched in silent wonderment as priestesses escorted the naked women one by one up to the altar and placed them on top. Arranged inside the altar were smoldering leaves; the smoke wafted up through the branches, creating the impression that the smoke was rising through each woman's body. As each woman was healed, or purified, she was escorted from the altar and returned to the group.

The priestesses encircled the altar and began dancing while a group of men drummed rhythmic patterns. El-Dabh, his tape recorder precariously slung over his shoulder, declared to his companion that he wanted to dance with the women. Impulsively he ran into the sacred ground, entered the circle, and began dancing with great enthusiasm. Suddenly a priestess grabbed him by his shoulders and spun him around; another approached him from behind and began marking signs on his back with her fingers. Immediately the drumming intensified, and the priestesses began dancing more fiercely; El-Dabh was frenetically whirled around and around. The moment was broken by shouts of his Mongo assistant; shrieking in French, the man begged El-Dabh to come out—he feared the priestesses were engaging in magic. El-Dabh asked what he meant; one of the priestesses informed him that he had just been married to the woman then lying on the altar. She had been healed and had been permitted to make a request to the spirit of the crocodile; her request had been to be married to the stranger. First, however, she wanted him to shave off his bushy, black beard.

Protesting that he did not want to be married or remain with these people and become a "Zebola," El-Dabh was escorted with his "bride" into a house to wait as preparations were made for their wedding night together. Terrified, El-Dabh quietly awaited an opportunity to escape. At two o'clock in the morning he stole away from the woman and made his way out of the compound and back to the Land Rover. He was delighted to find it still there; his faithful assistant had hoped that El-Dabh would be able to elude his "bride." The assistant's wife was anxiously standing beside her husband. El-Dabh was amused to learn that the only time his friend had left the area was to return to his own home to retrieve his wife; he had thought that perhaps another woman could help resolve the situation.

They drove away from the compound, and El-Dabh was certain he was well out of the unwelcome situation; however, when the Land Rover approached a major highway, their good fortune ceased. They were stopped by a barricade of armed soldiers who demanded their identification papers. El-Dabh quickly produced his papers, which stated that he was a researcher under the auspices of the Kinshasa Institute for Music and the Royal Museum for Central Africa. Unfortunately in her haste to assist her husband, the wife of his companion had neglected to bring her papers with her. The soldiers brandished their machine guns and announced that the two men were free to leave but the woman had to remain with them. Enraged, the woman's husband began cursing and threatening the guards; the terrified El-Dabh begged his friend to offer them money for her release. His irate assistant would not listen.

Angrily yelling to El-Dabh to protect his wife while he sought the authorities, the assistant promptly sped off in the Land Rover, leaving his wife and the bewildered El-Dabh standing in the middle of the road with the armed men. No sooner had his companion driven off than a truck approached with more guards. Apprised of the situation, they insisted on taking the woman with them, but El-Dabh, remembering his friend's injunction upon him, began arguing with them. His impassioned entreaties not to take the woman prompted the guards to push them both into the back of the truck and drive them to an encampment surrounded by barbed wire. As they were unceremoniously forced from the vehicle, the woman was ordered into a building. Grabbing his friend's wife by the wrist and drawing her close to him, El-Dabh implored the guards not to separate him from his "wife." Baffled, the men put the "husband and wife" together in a large room. There they stayed until daybreak, during which time the disheartened El-Dabh decided that the women's crocodile spell was keeping him from leaving the area.

As the morning sun shone into the barrack room, the camp commander sauntered in demanding to see the new prisoners. Sizing up the couple, he ordered El-Dabh to come with him and to leave his wife behind. El-Dabh firmly stood his ground and insisted that they be permitted to speak to the general. His request was granted. El-Dabh, brought before the general, immediately began to shout in French that he was an American researcher and to demand that he be taken to the chargé d'affaires (there was no U.S. embassy in Zaire). The general slyly smiled at the frustrated man and simply responded, "Go." El-Dabh, fully aware how dangerous the border between Zaire and Angola was, instantly realized that as soon as he and the woman left the encampment they would be killed—no one would ever know that Zairean troops had done it. So he began another line of argument, which was quickly interrupted by a commotion outside. To El-Dabh's delight and surprise, there in the camp stood his assistant beside the Land Rover. His friend had returned, accompanied by several officials who could rectify the situation. Finally, when everyone had been appeased, El-Dabh and his assistant's wife were released.

After this ordeal El-Dabh decided to discontinue this part of his investigation. Not wanting to be anywhere near the women and their Zebola ceremonies, he arranged to fly to Bangui, the capital of the Central African Republic. No sooner had his plane lifted off the runway when an announcement was made that the plane had suffered a mechanical problem necessitating their landing. To his horror, El-Dabh realized that they had landed very near the village from which he had made his escape; he was distraught until the plane was serviced and airborne once again. He did not fully relax until he touched down in Bangui; only then was he certain that the spell of the crocodile had been broken. He was thankful that his "bride" had foolishly made two requests of the crocodile; El-Dabh was convinced that her second wish—that his beard be shaved— had diminished the power of her first request, to marry the stranger.

During these years, despite his arduous traveling schedule, El-Dabh found time to compose. "Isis and the Seven Scorpions" (1975), for soprano, flute, harpsichord, and *derabucca,* commissioned by Kent State's English department, was premiered by soprano Margaret Palmieri, a part-time voice instructor in the School of Music and the wife of a music faculty member, Robert Palmieri; flutist Raymond DeMattia, of the School of Music faculty; harpsichordist Ruth Nurmi, wife of the English department chair, Martin Nurmi; and El-Dabh, playing *derabucca.* When El-Dabh realized that his old friend from Howard University, Fela Sowande, was in the audience, he cajoled Sowande into joining the group for the performance, during which he improvised on the *atumpan.*[6] The complex story of "Isis and the Seven Scorpions" operates on many levels. In order to protect her son, Isis sought out seven magical scorpions, each possessing a different energy. The scorpions' names, when recited, generated great power, which surrounded the boy whenever he was in danger. In the work, DeMattia was required to speak through his flute, reciting the scorpions' names: Tefen, Befen, Mystet, Mestatef, Phetet, Patet, and Maatet. Following the premiere, a group from Amsterdam asked El-Dabh for permission to perform the work; he rescored it for them for tenor, recorder, harpsichord, and marimba. He also received an invitation to perform the work himself at the Egyptian Mystery School, near San Francisco, whose members frequently recited the names of the scorpions during their ceremonies, which drew on elements of ancient Egyptian mysticism and American Indian chants; however, his schedule with the Smithsonian prevented him from accepting the invitation.

El-Dabh's *Black Genesis* (1975), scored for chorus and instrumental ensemble, combined the biblical story of creation with African American folklore; it was written for and premiered at the Hawthorne School. Because the students who performed it were required to act, sing, and dance, El-Dabh classified the work as a pageant-play. El-Dabh consciously took advantage of the fact that the Hawthorne School had awarded numerous scholarships to inner-city students, many of whom were familiar with black English. El-Dabh used their original dialect in his text and had those who could speak it teach the others. *Black Genesis*, based on Southern folk material, examines the relationship between a mouthless dog and God. Every time God eats, chitlins fall to the floor, but the poor mouthless dog can only sniff the spilled food; he cannot eat. God, pitying the dog, decides to give him a mouth, which proves problematic because the dog never ceases eating and barking. Eventually, the dog convinces God that all the other animals are in need too; he brings them one by one to God to receive mouths. However, God's benevolence creates a greater problem for the world; from that moment every animal eats and speaks endlessly.

In 1976 the Hawthorne School celebrated the twentieth anniversary of its founding. One of the printed announcements commemorating the event stated that "capturing the complex rhythms and the unpredictable tonal combinations of El-Dabh's scores, and understanding the historical context in which all these scores are rooted have caused faculty and students to discover facts of themselves they never knew. Hawthorne is proud to have helped bring these operas into existence."[7] Hawthorne also recognized its association with El-Dabh during a benefit performance of *Opera Flies* on June 5 and 6, 1976, at the Baird Auditorium of the Smithsonian in the natural history building. On that occasion Eleanor Orr introduced the composer to the African American poet Sterling Brown.[8] The result was

El-Dabh's pageant *Memphis Blues, Long Gone* (1976), which was inspired by Brown's poems and combined jazz and African musical idioms.

Orr had hoped that El-Dabh would also create several other compositions in observance of Hawthorne's twenty years; however, in 1976 El-Dabh was more focused on his association with the Smithsonian Institution and preparations for the American bicentennial celebration. The Smithsonian Institution brought performers from around the world to Washington to participate in the event, and El-Dabh was delegated to select the representatives from Zaire and Egypt. He was provided with a written statement from the secretary (that is, director) of the Smithsonian, S. Dillon Ripley, asserting that anyone assisting El-Dabh in this endeavor would be assisting the U.S. government. That letter was to prove invaluable on several occasions.

Returning to Zaire in search of musicians to represent the country, El-Dabh was presented to the traditional king of the Congo, who was conveyed on an elaborately decorated cart, his thirty wives fanning him and dancing for him. El-Dabh, who had never witnessed such exuberant dancing and celebrating, noticed that the wives appeared to be equally intrigued by him. El-Dabh still sported a beard, and the wives approached giggling and playfully tugged on it. Their husband was also fascinated by the foreigner and quickly granted El-Dabh total access to his people and their music.

From the Ekonda Forest region of Zaire, El-Dabh selected fifteen women singers; from the eastern lower section of Goma he chose nine men, who played wooden horns. When he returned to the Smithsonian to make arrangements for the groups' travel, however, El-Dabh was informed that Zaire's headstrong political dictator, Mobutu Sese Seko,[9] had his own ideas concerning which groups should travel to the United States. Mobutu wanted Zaire's colorful national music and dance group, a sixty-strong, government-sanctioned extravaganza, to represent the country in the bicentennial; it had performed for Secretary of State Henry Kissinger[10] during his visit to Zaire. Outraged, El-Dabh argued to Smithsonian administrators that the institution's guidelines clearly stipulated that performers be representative of the character of a society, not those who performed in an official capacity. The Smithsonian was not looking for a professionally choreographed exhibition; the two groups El-Dabh had designated represented the basic foundation of the culture itself. The Ekonda women were all mothers with children, and their musical expression was an everyday matter, a way of life, for them, not a performance. Likewise, the nine

Nine musicians from the eastern lower section of Goma, Zaire, selected by
Halim El-Dabh to perform on wooden horns in Washington, D.C., for the U.S.
bicentennial (1976).

men chosen performed in ceremonies—such as the crucial election ceremony of a chief, in which the chief-designate faces the four directions of
the universe and the people either claim or reject him as their leader. If
Zaire's government sent another group in place of his appointed performers, El-Dabh would not cooperate and would not meet the airplane. The
Smithsonian cabled President Mobutu stating that, in light of the guidelines, if he did not follow El-Dabh's recommendation, Zaire would not be
represented at the bicentennial. El-Dabh was gratified that Mobutu was
overruled, and he was proud that the Smithsonian, a cultural institution,
had demonstrated that its decisions would not be influenced by politics—
which sent a very powerful message.

For the bicentennial celebration, the Smithsonian erected a chapel in
the middle of the Mall near the Lincoln Memorial for performances of a
religious or otherwise spiritual character. The fifteen Ekonda women, whose
ceremonies were most dignified and reflected African womanhood, performed at that venue. Dancing as they sang, their decorated bodies drama-
tized their music in a devout manner. When a group from Suriname approached El-Dabh to request permission to pray with the Ekonda women
on the performing grounds, he was struck by the Ekonda women's re-

sponse—they had already prayed in the morning and did not want to bother God too much. They were afraid that if they prayed again, it would be too much for God's ears. El-Dabh truly appreciated these proud and dignified women, whose strength was best reflected in the lyrics of one of their songs: "If Zaire falls apart, we, the women, will create a raft, and our bodies will float. Nothing will destroy us, and we will hold the country together."[11]

Because none of the nine men El-Dabh had selected had ever been to a city, their tribal chief insisted on accompanying them to Washington. El-Dabh was relieved to have the chief there, because during their first performance one of the older men collapsed and had to be admitted to Georgetown University Hospital. When El-Dabh and the chief arrived at the hospital, the medical staff was stunned to see the imposing chief in his full tribal regalia, complete with animal skins, horns, and feathers. Since the chief and the patient spoke only French and Lingala, El-Dabh assumed the role of translator for the doctors, who quickly determined that the man had suffered a collapsed lung and internal problems, and he would be forced to remain in the hospital for at least a month. When the rest of the troupe and the chief returned to Zaire, El-Dabh faithfully visited his recovering musician each day. He soon found the patient sitting up in his hospital bed, grinning from ear to ear as he watched color television as if this was a normal, everyday activity for him. Near the end of his hospital stay, the man professed to El-Dabh that he had known he was ill back home in his village. He confessed that he had telepathically ordered El-Dabh to select him to travel to the United States so that he would receive the best medical attention and return to Zaire in perfect health. El-Dabh agreed that he must not have chosen this man by accident.

El-Dabh collaborated during the bicentennial with eleven other artists, including his good friend Fela Sowande on a project entitled "African Diaspora." For his part of the project, El-Dabh traveled to Egypt and selected twenty-eight performers to travel to the United States, but he was appalled to encounter the same difficulty with the Egyptian government as with that of Zaire. For years, Egypt had sponsored large national groups of professional performers trained in the traditional folklore; though impressive, these groups did not meet the criteria of the Smithsonian. El-Dabh was indignant when high-ranking cultural officials in Cairo asked if he was "going to take the people with their dirt on them";[12] that, he responded, was precisely the way he wanted them. Only one of the cultural ministers supported El-Dabh's choices: "The only person I would bow my head to the ground to is a villager, the one with the dirt on him.

I would not bow to anyone else."[13] Because he felt most government officials believed they were superior to the people, El-Dabh was quite touched and impressed by these words. It seemed to him that most officials forgot the people with "dirt on their backs"; he viewed this lack of respect for the villagers as in fact a lack of self-respect.

When the Egyptian government pressed El-Dabh to accept "clean" troupes, tailored to represent the country, he insisted on following the Smithsonian guidelines and requested authentic village performers, who made music for themselves, not for staged exhibitions. He visited many villages throughout the country and selected performers from Upper Egypt, Nubia, Port Said, the eastern and western parts of the Nile Delta, and Alexandria, representing various aspects of Egyptian music and tradition.

El-Dabh returned to Washington, where Secretary Ripley informed him that the Egyptian officials might send a different, more professional group. Enraged as before, El-Dabh responded as he had before—that if the Egyptian government sent a different group, he would not meet it at the airport. This word was cabled back to the ministers in Cairo, who agreed that El-Dabh's choice was probably for the best. However, they insisted on purchasing new clothes for all the performers before they traveled to the United States. Among the twenty-eight performers was a fourteen-year-old girl, a gifted traditional dancer. However, because of her age, another performer, a man who would demonstrate the traditional Egyptian marriage-ceremony stick dance,[14] was assigned as her guardian to ensure that she was not accosted in the United States. One fateful day this girl could not be found, and her guardian was frantic. When El-Dabh asked why he was so upset, the man responded that he was responsible for her for life; if anything happened to her, the government would have him killed. The two men were most relieved when the girl reappeared unharmed.

El-Dabh believed that bringing performers from all over the world to the American bicentennial was one of the greatest endeavors the Smithsonian had ever sponsored, and the experiences of that time would remain with him for years. For El-Dabh, encouraging African Americans to compare traditions with Africans was very exciting. He most enjoyed watching the interaction of people from the Mississippi Delta with people from West Africa. There was also an Islamic group from Ghana that connected with Islamic groups from other parts of the world. The sharing of these traditions and musical experiences made for a fascinating ethnomusicological and sociological study.

El-Dabh's contribution to the Smithsonian during the bicentennial celebration led to an invitation to participate in a most significant event in the history of the Coptic Orthodox church. In a letter dated February 28, 1977, Fr. Mikhail E. Mikhail, the parish priest at St. Mark Coptic Orthodox Church, a Cleveland parish of the Orthodox diocese of North America, informed El-Dabh of a "great historic event that will be a source of spiritual joy and happiness not only to the Coptic Orthodox congregations but also to all Christians in the United States and Canada."[15] Fr. Mikhail requested that El-Dabh serve as a member of the advisory committee to assist in planning the arrival of Pope Shenouda III. His Holiness, considered the 117th successor of St. Mark—author of the oldest canonical gospel and the founder of the Coptic Orthodox church—would be visiting the United States and Canada from April 14 to May 23, 1977.

In the history of the Coptic Orthodox church, this auspicious occasion marked the first time a Coptic pope had ever visited North America, and El-Dabh was thrilled to participate. El-Dabh was equally delighted that following a series of rather disappointing romantic encounters, he was beginning to find happiness with a young woman named Deborah Jaken, whom he had met in Kent.

Deborah had been working on a master's degree in art when she was introduced to the charismatic El-Dabh, and the two had soon become inseparable. With interests in both theology and art, Deborah aspired to study primitive Christian communities located throughout Brazil, and the opportunity for the couple to conduct research together was very promising. El-Dabh's first wife, Mary, still living in Kent when he and Deborah were married in 1978, was stunned to learn that her former husband had married a woman young enough to be his daughter; she immediately hired an attorney to ensure that her own financial security would not be compromised. Wanting to spare Deborah any unpleasant repercussions of Mary's legal action, El-Dabh suggested that his new bride accompany him on a trip to Egypt to visit with friends and family; Deborah, eager to escape the gossip her marriage to one of the university's best-known personalities had generated, readily agreed.

Unity at the Crossroad (1978), for full orchestra, was composed and premiered in Cairo during this trip to Egypt.[16] In the piece El-Dabh addressed the concept of various cultures meeting and unifying over their commonalities; he envisioned world peace being achieved through this kind of unity. Inspired by Deborah's interest in Brazil, the work also is a reference to the Afro-Brazilian concept of the crossroads, which are believed to be very dangerous. Eshu, the trickster god, is believed to be present at crossroads, ready always to play tricks on the unsuspecting; if one's house is built at a crossroads, one must always be on guard. For El-Dabh, crossroads mean that one must make a conscious choice, and that when people meet at crossroads they must make an active, conscious effort to achieve and maintain unity. The piece expressed El-Dabh's desire that Mary and his daughters would accept, or at the very least tolerate, his new wife and his remarriage.

Following their return to Kent, Deborah completed her master's degree and began working on a Ph.D. in sociology. However, the stress brought on by Mary's legal proceedings to secure a greater alimony settlement gave Deborah severe back problems, which, when combined with her pregnancy, prevented her from continuing with her doctoral studies, and instead she completed a master of fine arts degree, which at that time was the terminal degree in the School of Art.

On March 8, 1979, El-Dabh received a letter from Cynthia Parker, general manager of the Martha Graham Center of Contemporary Dance, informing him that *Clytemnestra* was to be filmed for the PBS presentation "Dance in America," which would be televised nationwide. The letter continued that C. F. Peters had been contacted regarding the rights to the score; however, the work had to be cut to fit the time allotted for the production. Parker indicated that Graham and conductor Stanley Sussman had begun to look for places where the work could be cut choreographically; El-Dabh was invited to provide his input into the project. Remembering a rather awkward moment the previous year when El-Dabh and Graham had been briefly reunited, however, he opted to have Graham and Sussman work out the logistics alone.

In 1978, El-Dabh and Graham had been invited to give separate lecture-performances and to conduct master classes at the University of Michigan at Ann Arbor. When El-Dabh appeared at her class unannounced, Graham became extremely uneasy and finally exclaimed, "El-Dabh, I can't face your eyes when I'm giving my master class."[17] She later informed him that his being there had confused her. Although they were cordial, it was evident to both that their relationship was strained.

Habeeb El-Dabh[18] was born March 24, 1979, twenty days following his father's fifty-eighth birthday, and El-Dabh was thrilled that he had finally become the father of a son. However, the occasion was bittersweet; to El-Dabh's deep regret, his relationship with his first wife and

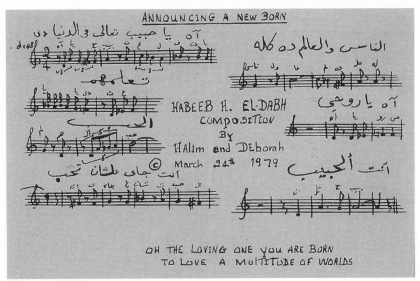

Habeeb El-Dabh's birth announcement (1979).

two daughters was terribly strained. In an effort to express his conflicted emotions, he composed "Hajer" (1979), for soprano and piano, which conveys the universality of Islamic thought.

Hajer (Arabic for Hagar), the second wife of Abraham, is depicted as a black woman, thereby making the mother of the Arabs a black woman. Abraham is considered by Muslims to be the father of all prophets; thus, every time Abraham's name or any of the major Islamic prophets' names are mentioned, one must invoke God and his blessing upon Abraham—that is, "And God's blessing and peace be bestowed upon him." Accordingly, one must automatically invoke God's blessings on anyone descended from Abraham.

El-Dabh's version of the biblical story is that Abraham walked from Ur to Egypt to meet the pharaoh, because Abraham, in need of manpower and transportation, wished Pharaoh to give him men and donkeys to help build Canaan. Before the two met, Abraham was warned that Pharaoh might desire Abraham's beautiful wife Sarah and would kill Abraham in order to have her. When Abraham arrived in Egypt and Pharaoh asked who this beautiful woman was, Abraham falsely replied that she was his sister. Believing that Sarah was indeed Abraham's sister, Pharaoh had her taken to his palace, where he engaged in sexual intercourse with her. God was greatly angered with Pharaoh, who upon learning the truth beseeched God's forgiveness, stating that he was ignorant of the true nature of Sarah's relationship to Abraham. Because Abraham had lied to him, Pharaoh believed he should not be punished; promising to make amends, he invoked God's blessing upon Abraham. Pharaoh pledged that he would give Abraham all the men, donkeys, and goods he needed for his journey. He also promised to give Abraham a beautiful woman from his court, and so Hajer, a highly educated and beautiful black woman, was presented to Abraham.

The piece emphasizes the beauty of this woman and her importance as Abraham's second wife. Hajer bore Abraham a son named Ishmael. When a jealous Sarah insisted Hajer leave them, Hajer traveled with her infant son to what is now called the Kaaba. Hajer and Ishmael almost died of thirst, but at the Kaaba a well sprang forth in front of them, and the water came out plentifully. Today the Kaaba, located in Mecca, is the central place of worship for all Muslims of the world.

"Salma Ya Salama" (1979), for chorus, was written for a group from Ann Arbor that had commissioned El-Dabh to write a choral work for it before it traveled to Egypt. "Salma Ya Salama," based on a village folk song, describes the women of Egypt. Frequently, the men in the villages leave their homes to construct buildings for others, and upon returning they sing of their warm feelings toward the awaiting women. *Salma* is the word for home; *salama* means peace and prosperity. The essence of the song is, "We have gone, and we came back. We return in good health, and we return to beautiful women who will meet us in the garden."[19]

In "Tonography" (1980), for clarinet, bassoon, marimba, and percussion, El-Dabh explored sound and its movement. El-Dabh spoke of the inspiration he found in looking back on his roots and in Ethiopian chants. He addressed the relationship between color and music in "Tonography," whose title refers to the choreography of tone. The work consists of three movements: "Serenity," "Joy," and "Equinox." It was composed for David Harris (clarinet), Sue Schrier (bassoon), Richard Moore (marimba and percussion), and dancers Pam Farer and Geneva Norman. On the title page of his handwritten manuscript, El-Dabh wrote, "Tonography explores new dimensions for the performing artist to experience his body in relation to tone and space. Movement-gesture in the process of generating sound, help shape the production of tone. Sound tones after inception shape up the space. The musician follows the tone in gesture movements to delineate the action of his tones in space by the guidance of a language of symbols and designs."[20] El-Dabh later revised the piece as "A Moroccan Fantasy: Tonography III" (1984), for five wind instruments. This version

Sketch of the third movement of "Tonography" (1980).

bears little similarity to the earlier incarnation. In 1991 a member of the Kent State University faculty, Dennis Nygren, would perform a third revision of the work for solo clarinet during El-Dabh's retirement concert.

In 1981 El-Dabh, through the auspices of the Smithsonian Institution, became involved with the Fifty-Five Nations Meeting held that year in Washington, D.C. Once every two years, the Organization for Security and Cooperation in Europe (OSCE) has a meeting in a different location to evaluate security, democratic principles, and human rights conditions around the world. This is followed by a summit of the heads of states (including the U.S. and other nations). In preparation for his presentation at this meeting, El-Dabh was also granted a leave of absence from Kent State to study the puppetry traditions in Egypt, Guinea, and France. El-Dabh, wishing to research the correlations between the traditional and the more refined puppetry practices of these countries, first traveled to Upper Egypt looking for surviving puppetry traditions, which had been performed as a part of ceremonies and rituals of resurrection associated with Osiris. In ancient Egypt, threads were attached to the puppets' bodies in the manner of marionettes. The tradition can be traced back thousands of years, so El-Dabh felt it was important that Egypt be represented at the Fifty-Five Nations Meeting through the presentation of these findings. El-Dabh hoped to bring a group of street puppeteers to participate, but he had little chance of obtaining the appropriate papers and visas required. He appealed to the U.S. embassy but was informed that he would need affidavits for the puppeteers; since they were essentially homeless and did not have jobs, there would be a six-month wait. Because they were street people and had no history, Egyptian officials threatened to arrest them. Filled with a sense of hopelessness, El-Dabh wondered how he would be able to get all the paperwork completed in time.

One evening, El-Dabh was invited to attend a large party outside Cairo. As he sat on the floor in the corner of the room, a man attired in a *jallabiyah*[21] approached him and commented that El-Dabh did not look as though he was enjoying himself. Responding that indeed everything was bothering him, El-Dabh commenced to relate the history of Egyptian puppetry. The man sat down beside the forlorn researcher and expressed his amazement that the country had such a rich tradition. El-Dabh complained that the government did not understand this treasure. El-Dabh's new acquaintance finally instructed him to come to his office in the Octagon, a large area in the middle of Cairo that was almost a city in itself. The man directed El-Dabh to bring the puppeteers along and promised to see to it that they all received their visas and passports. Although El-Dabh was skeptical, the next day he gathered his six puppeteers, put them in a taxicab, and headed to the Octagon as instructed. Before they arrived, El-Dabh had the cab stop at a large nearby park where vendors and photographers were open for business. Lining up his puppeteers, El-Dabh had their pictures taken just in case they really would be acquiring passports that day. Next they proceeded to the man's office, and within ninety minutes El-Dabh was handed six stamped and signed passports. El-Dabh was to escort the puppeteers to the U.S. embassy, where the visas would be ready. Smiling, the man finally identified himself as the head of the passport agency office and informed the dumbstruck El-Dabh that he had used his power in this manner for one reason only—he was impressed by the important history of Egyptian puppetry traditions that El-Dabh had taught him, and he was convinced that these puppeteers were going to be fine representatives of Egypt in the United States.

The puppeteers were not quite convinced that they were really going to America, and when they arrived at the American embassy, El-Dabh was not certain either. In the early 1980s it seemed as though everyone wanted to travel to the United States, and the line forming outside the embassy was inordinately long. Disheartened, El-Dabh decided to cut ahead of the others in the line. Amid demands that he wait his turn, El-Dabh announced at the window that he had urgent business and needed to see the consul general immediately. When the woman behind the counter began to question El-Dabh's authority, he suddenly remembered that he was carrying Secretary Ripley's official statement, left over from his work with the bicentennial five years earlier, specifying that anyone who assisted Halim El-Dabh was assisting the U.S. government. El-Dabh instructed the woman to take his card and the letter to the consul general. Shortly thereafter, the consul general himself appeared and personally handled El-Dabh's request. Immediately, and rather astonishingly, all the puppeteers received visas valid for an entire year.

There was a fear, however, among the Egyptian officials that the puppeteers were going to take advantage of their situation and disappear into the streets of Washington and never return to Egypt. El-Dabh had the responsibility of ensuring that this would not be the case. He also had the responsibility of explaining to customs that in addition to their triptychs, wood, and all their performance equipment, the puppeteers also were traveling with marijuana. At the airport in Washington El-Dabh approached the U.S. customs officials and informed them straightforwardly that they would find the illegal substance, which was there for cultural reasons. It was nothing dangerous and strictly for their own use on the stage; because the drug aided them in their transformation into their performance mode,

Halim El-Dabh playing the *derabucca* (1980).

they could not be puppeteers without it. Remarkably, the customs officials allowed the puppeteers to come through without incident, and they
expressed to El-Dabh their appreciation of his candor.

Adjusting immediately to their new surroundings, the puppeteers were
a sensation throughout Washington. Although they did not comprehend
the language, they instantly began making jokes and puns about both
Presidents Jimmy Carter and Gerald Ford. For Egyptians, puppetry is an
art of displacement of thoughts; the humor comes not from hating, ridi-
culing, or belittling someone else (often authority figures) but rather from
the ability to substitute one idea with another in an unexpected way.
The puppeteers created great enthusiasm in Washington, and many of
the more sophisticated American puppeteers, whose craft was more highly

developed, were excited to see them with their voice-transforming *swazzle*s and their battered trumpets from the 1800s. The festival encompassed a two-week period, after which, although they had enjoyed the experience, the puppeteers were eager to return home. They explained to El-Dabh that they missed the constant activity found in Cairo, where they were able to fraternize with people on the street, in restaurants, and in cafeterias. The puppeteers observed that in Washington no one really related with or talked to anyone; because this was unpleasant for them, they did not want to stay. Remembering that the Egyptian officials were fearful the puppeteers would come to the United States, make money, and never return to Egypt, El-Dabh was amused by their reaction and desire to return home.

Following his involvement with the Fifty-Five Nations Meeting, El-Dabh was invited to perform at Georgetown University for the Arab-American Cultural Foundation in Washington, which promoted Arabic poetry. He composed *Drink of Eternity* (1981), for flutes, ceramic pots, shakers, bells, narrator, and dancers, for the occasion. He was thrilled to learn that Hamza El-Din,[22] internationally known for his ability to play the *ud*, was scheduled to appear in the first half of the program. *Drink of Eternity* involved the recitation of one of El-Dabh's poems in an avant-garde setting. At the time, El-Dabh was engaged in experimentation with dance movement, using some African American students from Kent State University and the University of Akron; he had brought four dancers along to accompany him. Dressed in a flowing gown embroidered with gold, El-Dabh looked ethereal as he sat at the side of the stage, reciting his poetry and playing original traditional instruments, ceramic pots, flutes, and gourds, while the dancers expressed the interrelationship between dance and sound. The work reflected, in an abstract sense, the transfer of power in the rising and the falling of empires. It likened culture to a massive building that, lacking a foundation, tumbles to the ground. Tracing history from ancient Egypt to the decline of modern powers, it was an impressive piece.

Although the performance engaged the audience, *Drink of Eternity* shocked many who had believed they were going to be entertained in a traditional manner. Instead, they had been involved in a clash of thoughts regarding philosophies, empires, power, and human failings. The organizer of the event became angry that El-Dabh had performed something that he considered too avant-garde. There were several representatives from the Smithsonian Institution in attendance that evening, including

Bernice Johnson Reagon,[23] director of the Africa Diaspora Program. Following the performance she acknowledged to El-Dabh that she had been overwhelmed by the experience and that she "didn't know he had it in him."[24] She had not been prepared to see El-Dabh challenge the audience in that manner, nor had she been prepared for the audience's rather shocked and insulted reaction. El-Dabh's attempt to bring life onto the stage had been threatening to those who were not ready to be awakened to new modes of thought. The Arab-American Cultural Foundation had planned to collaborate with El-Dabh on another work, which was to be performed at the Kennedy Center for the Performing Arts. However, the collapse of the relationship that evening was the demise of that effort, and the project was abandoned.

In 1983 El-Dabh became involved in an ongoing project with Middletown, Ohio, through his acquaintance with William Appling, the music department chair at the Western Reserve Academy in Hudson, Ohio. Appling conducted a group that had performed in Middletown's annual international festival, known as Middfest, which highlighted a different country every year. Egypt was selected to be the featured country in 1983, and for the event a small pyramid was built. El-Dabh created new renditions of *Music of the Pyramids*, for narrator, orchestra, and chorus, and *One More Gaudy Night*, for orchestra and dancers. Middfest was concentrated into four days; however, prior to the event El-Dabh lectured throughout the community and spent several months visiting the schools and teaching both elementary and high school students drumming and songs about Ra, the Egyptian god of the sun. Performing in public libraries, El-Dabh introduced Middletown's inhabitants to Egypt by presenting papers on the history of Egyptian religion. He also brought Egyptian horns and flutes to Middletown and trained local musicians to play them.[25] It was an exciting experience for El-Dabh, and he was delighted to be sent to Egypt to find musicians and puppeteers for the festival. El-Dabh traveled first class on Pan Am Airways and received twenty-five free tickets for travel between Cairo and Cincinnati. He brought an entire troupe of dancers and musicians from Egypt that performed in the square in nearby Cincinnati, in hospitals in Cincinnati and Dayton, in front of grocery stores, and in every other conceivable venue.

Every year the Middletown City Hall provided space for the festival, and the city government made every possible accommodation for the event. In 1983 the four floors of the city hall were filled with Egyptian artifacts, the walls were covered with artwork and tapestry, and a huge portrait of El-Dabh was hung. In the center of the first floor Egyptian puppeteers enacted puppet shows, while the dancers performed outside the building. El-Dabh was impressed with the organization and the dedication of the volunteers, who wanted to bring culture to their community and who were truly involved with the experience. El-Dabh would work with Middletown for subsequent festivals as well, and each time he would be invited to speak about music and to give performances; he enjoyed these experiences immensely. The year India was featured was especially memorable for El-Dabh, because he had the opportunity to discuss music with the nephew of Ravi Shankar.[25]

In 1984 Martha Graham revived *Clytemnestra* to superlative reviews. In a review for the *New York Times,* Anna Kisselgoff wrote that "John Ostendorf and Johanna Albrecht, as the spine-chilling singers, were in the pit rather than onstage for technical reasons. Halim El-Dabh's fragmented oriental and insistent modern melodies, conducted by Stanley Sussman, resonated with real power."[26] El-Dabh, however, paid little attention to this revival of his masterful composition. From 1984 to 1986 El-Dabh had become completely involved with Brazilian thought as he sought greater understanding of the African-Brazilian culture and the survival of the Yoruba culture in Brazil. To further his understanding of Brazil's African-derived beliefs and practices, he obtained a research grant from the American Philosophical Society for studies in Afro-Brazilian music and religion.

With that grant he traveled to Brazil, where he had the opportunity to attend many *candomblé* ceremonies, in which he learned about the *orisha*s. *Candomblé,* practiced in Bahia, is considered the most African of the Macumba (Afro-Brazilian) sects. It is an Afro-Brazilian religion characterized by a marked syncretism, or combination, of traditional African religions, Brazilian spiritualism, and Roman Catholicism. The *orisha*s are the powerful spirits present in the *candomblé* houses, each personifying a force of nature and a set of humanlike behavioral characteristics. Adherents believe that an *orisha* can intervene on one's behalf or enter into one's being and, through possession, become part of one's personality. El-Dabh was also involved in attending performances of *capoeira,* a folk dance popular in the Brazilian northeast. Originally a deadly sport or martial art developed in Brazil by slaves from Angola, the *capoeira* is now a dance in which two men face each other and emulate the blows of the "fight" to the rhythms of the *berimbau,* or musical bow; the *caxixi,* a woven wicker basket shaker; the *atabaque,* a drum; the *pandeiro,* a tambourine; the *agogo,* an iron bell; and the *reco reco,* a hollow, round wooden object with a grating on which a thin stick is rubbed back and forth.

While El-Dabh engaged in his fieldwork in Bahia, Deborah conducted her own research on the Franciscan orders in Rio de Janeiro, and he enjoyed the opportunity to travel between the two regions. Outside Rio he found what he referred to as "different strata of culture," an intermingling of African and European traditions. El-Dabh found this inseparable fusion of Africa and Europe fascinating and stimulating. *Rhapsodia Egyptia-Brasileira* (1985), for orchestra, was performed in a version for piano by El-Dabh in a concert at the Cultural Center of Petropolis, adjacent to the Villa-Lobos[27] Institute outside Rio de Janeiro. During one six-month period in Brazil, El-Dabh was invited to lecture about music at the University of Bahia and to participate in lectures at the Brazilian Cultural Center. Unfortunately, having had only basic lessons in the language, El-Dabh spoke very little Portuguese; Deborah, who spoke it fluently, did not have time to teach him. She informed her husband she was confident he would find his way, and he did. Needing to communicate, he began practicing the language and soon found himself speaking Portugese without thinking about it.

One of the most impressive of all the *candomblé* ceremonies was for the trickster god Eshu (Ixú) and his wife Pombajera, and El-Dabh was excited to learn of an opportunity to attend one of these ceremonies. A Brazilian friend who had participated in a seven-month initiation ceremony had been granted permission to have El-Dabh accompany him. With his tape recorder hanging suspended on his back, El-Dabh entered the darkened *candomblé* house and was quickly reminded that Ixú is partial to red and black; in the darkened space the only light was red. El-Dabh was fascinated by the participants, who smoked large cigars and appeared to be in trances with their eyes wide open. Suddenly El-Dabh and his companion were dragged into the middle of the crowd, and El-Dabh was overwhelmed at the sight of a woman who had been transformed into Pombajera. She started speaking in a frenetic manner and suddenly threw a bowl of *cachaça,*[28] a popular drink, in El-Dabh's face. As she refilled the bowl, El-Dabh was dragged farther into the midst of the participants, who were dancing and moving in trances. His recorder was on, and he was able to capture the voices and sounds of the participants. He was most pleased to have captured the transformed voice of Pombajera on tape.

A few days following this *candomblé* ceremony, El-Dabh was invited by a "sanctified" drummer to attend a special party in the central part of

Bahia. Divine, or sanctified, drummers in Bahia are those who have been initiated, or baptized, in a special ceremony; all such musicians were to attend the event. At the last minute El-Dabh decided to take his small Egyptian flute with him. The gathering of such musicians was so remarkable that when El-Dabh played his flute he felt "the flute was playing itself. It was fantastic. I have never played it so well. It was as if I had played that flute forever, and the ceremony was incredible."[29]

The next day at nine o'clock in the morning, as El-Dabh was preparing to leave to visit Deborah over seven hundred miles away in Rio, someone knocked on his door. The person was calling his name, but the *m* in his first name was nasalized as an *n*. Without thinking, El-Dabh opened the door; there stood a man pointing a gun at him. As he was walked backward into his apartment, he noticed a second man at the door holding a knife. El-Dabh recalled that he had been warned never to open his door in Brazil to anyone—not even to his own mother—without first looking through the peephole. However, after the pleasant experience of the evening before, as he waited for his landlord to settle his account for his absence and for his friend Broderic from Sierra Leone to give him a ride to the airport, his preoccupation had caused him to forget the warnings. The shock of the intruders induced an out-of-body experience—El-Dabh saw the two men and himself walking back inside the apartment. He wondered if he would see himself be shot or stabbed.

Speaking in Portuguese, El-Dabh asked them what they wanted. The response was *dinheiro*. El-Dabh felt relief, because his pockets were full of money for his trip to Rio. He began pulling the money from his pockets and throwing it at them. The bandits looked at each other in disbelief, and one ordered the other to bind him. He was thrown down on his bed, and his mouth, arms, and legs were secured with strong tape, following which the men searched the apartment. After an hour, El-Dabh heard them unlock the door and leave. Hoping to obtain the attention of passersby, he made his way to the window. An elderly man noticed El-Dabh; however, the sight of him caused the old man to scream and run away. El-Dabh stumbled over to the doorjamb and attempted to undo his bindings. Eventually he freed himself, opened the door, and went into the hallway. He began knocking on the doors of all the other apartments, but no door was opened to him; everyone had apparently remembered and heeded the warnings. Finally Broderic and the landlord arrived, and they were shocked at El-Dabh's appearance. Although he had no proof, El-Dabh suspected that the landlord had plotted the attack, because he always had cautioned

El-Dabh against attending the *candomblé* sites, which he declared were dirty places. El-Dabh was grateful that the men had not hurt him. However, they had stolen not only his money but also his tape recorder and most of his research tapes from the *candomblé* houses, including his prized tape of Pombajera. Some of his research materials remained, but his most important tape was gone. Additionally, they had stolen all his new leather bags. Because leather in Brazil was very inexpensive and beautiful, El-Dabh had gathered a huge collection of leather bags and sandals he was planning to take to Deborah in Rio.

El-Dabh was relieved when he realized that he still had the tape of his recording of the spirits from Itaparica,[30] an island off the coast of Bahia. There he had attended the *Egungun* ceremony, which occurs in the middle of the night and is known as the "masquerades of spirits."[31] During *Egungun* ceremonies, in a tradition coming from Nigeria, all the women hide from the spirits, because it is harmful for a woman, especially a pregnant one, to see the *Egungun;* when women hear the ceremony beginning, they lock themselves away.

El-Dabh had arrived on the island at six-thirty in the evening and found the women cooking. He had been invited into their compound for the evening meal, and he had felt as though he were in a village in Nigeria, not in Brazil. He was still with the women when they heard the sound of the *Egungun.* They told him he had to be locked in with them; instead, El-Dabh left the women and was invited by a high priest to interact with the spirits. As he entered the sacred hall where the ceremony was to take place, the chanting, singing, and ritual circle dancing was already beginning. Captivated by the exceptional playing of the drummers, he had watched the sheep and chickens being prepared for the sacrifice. After several hours El-Dabh became exhausted, and by two o'clock in the morning he felt as though he were hallucinating. By three o'clock several cloths in vibrant African colors had been brought into the hall and placed around the floor. The heightened drama of the whole situation was nearly unbearable as he watched in amazement as the cloths began to rise. Hanging all the way to the ground, they had risen without any visible means to have allowed this to occur. The "keeper of the two sides" had hit the ground hard with his stick to prevent El-Dabh and the others from touching the cloth; to have done so would have ensured that the participant would be transported into the other world. As he struck the floor, the high priest had instructed El-Dabh to ask questions of the spirit. When he spoke, the spirit answered back. El-Dabh felt that every time the ground was struck, it was a reminder that here were two worlds, present together. He had had the feeling that he was on one side, and the spirits were on the other. The intersection of these two worlds had been a powerful moment.[33]

While in Brazil, El-Dabh spent time in both the poorest and the wealthiest areas, experiencing many types of religious ceremonies. While in the richest area of Rio, he stayed with a very wealthy family. When their son became ill, they went to the Father of the Orishas to consult him. Despite the fact that the family was Catholic, the contact was made because, although Brazil is a predominantly Catholic society, the African-derived religions are prevalent throughout all levels of society regardless of color, race, or class. El-Dabh realized that the mixture, or syncretism,[33] of Catholicism and West-African religion was quite strong throughout the country. El-Dabh felt that he had experienced an intensely vital energy in Brazil; when he returned to the United States he realized that he wanted to compose something drawing on that experience.

On his return El-Dabh composed the trombone concerto *Bahia: Father of the Orisha* (1986), which was premiered by Elliot Chasanov at Kent State University on December 7, 1986, during a concert honoring El-Dabh's sixty-fifth birthday. The program consisted of Franz Schubert's *Symphony No. 2* in B-flat major, D. 125; and El-Dabh's "Fantasia-Tahmeel" in a version for timpani and strings (Michael Burritt, timpanist), *Vision at the Crossroads* (a variant title for *Unity at the Crossroads*), and *Bahia for Trombone and Orchestra* (an alternate title for *Bahia: Father of the Orisha*). As the program notes for the concert explained, "Bahia, the first state in Brazil, means a port of lights and also the port of All Saints. It has a similar meaning in Egyptian. By coincidence, 'Bahia' is also the name of Halim El-Dabh's grandmother."[34]

Although "Bahia" is considered a feminine place name, the people refer to it as the "father," and El-Dabh's work deals with the power of Bahia, or "Trombo," the father of saints. In Bahia, El-Dabh had attended a ceremony led by a woman who referred to herself as a "father." Calling herself "Pie José," she had informed El-Dabh that even though she was a woman, she could function as a spiritual father. A very wise woman, she executed the ceremony in the role of a father, guiding El-Dabh in many of the *umbanda*[35] and *candomblé* ceremonies. She was later very helpful to El-Dabh in explaining what had occurred. Taking her hand at their first meeting, El-Dabh had sensed strange electrical vibrations emanating from her. He told her that he desired to learn more about how one becomes possessed during trance. She refused to pursue that point, because, as he had previously participated in *candomblé* rituals, he already held that knowledge. He only needed to delve deeper for a better understanding of himself.

Because Bahia is also called Trombo, the trombone seemed the natural instrument for this piece. In the work, El-Dabh envisions the voice of the trombone speaking to the people in the manner of a *condomblé* priest representing God as father and mother. The piece recounts El-Dabh's experiences in the *candomblé* ceremonies, in which the *orisha* is called to enter into a person who is in trance. That person is known as a *cavallo*, or a horse, a "vehicle" that allows the deity to enter his or her body to speak. In Brazil these events happen all over the country; some are real, and some are staged for tourists. The Brazilian government has attempted to make tourist attractions of the ceremonies to undermine their worth, devalue their power, and lessen their energy.

El-Dabh also composed two other significant works during the year following his return from Brazil. "Tahmeela, Concerto Grosso" (1986), for derabucca, or timpani, and small orchestra, is a piece that may really be considered a continuation of a 1958 work, the "Fantasia-Tahmeel." In this piece, El-Dabh interprets the word *tahmeela* to be as a concerto grosso, or a juxtaposition of different instrumental groups, and this connection is emphasized by the work's title, which combines both the Arabic and Italian terms *tahmeela* and concerto grosso. Similarly, the major themes of the piece are juxtaposed among the various instruments.

Unnatural Acts (1986), a play by David Henry Hwang,[36] was presented to El-Dabh by director Lou Salerni, who commissioned El-Dabh to compose incidental music for the production at the Porthouse Theater, next to the Blossom Music Center near Cuyahoga Falls, Ohio. For his score, El-Dabh utilized a chamber group consisting of flute, clarinet, violin, cello, marimba, and electronic tape; he created the music from different sources, including sounds from the underside of the marimba and his own voice, later distorted. Sculptor Giotta Fujo Tajiri of the Netherlands designed the sets for the play, which examines the interaction of natural and created (unnatural) objects, forces, and human actions. Each of the three acts is a self-contained analysis, examining a misguided man, a mother and her son wandering on a beach, and a manipulative corporate executive.

In 1987 El-Dabh was commissioned by the Memphis Symphony Orchestra to compose a work for the city's celebration of the sister cities of Memphis, Egypt, and Memphis, Tennessee. *Ramesses the Great: Symphony No. 9* (1987), for large orchestra, was the result. Egypt lent the city in Tennessee a huge bust of Ramesses III, which arrived by boat for display in the Memphis Convention Hall. Visitors were taken to Mud Island to witness demonstrations of the similarities between the Mississippi and Nile Rivers. They were shown that certain fish, such as catfish, are common to both rivers. The similarities between the two cities were emphasized as well, strengthening their ties to one another. Memphis, Tennessee, was teeming with excitement. The city constructed a huge pyramid for the event, and before returning the original bust of Ramesses to Egypt, it had a replica constructed. El-Dabh was engaged to compose a three-movement symphony, which required him to spend a great deal of time traveling between Memphis and Kent; often he would copy the parts during his flights. El-Dabh was booked into the Crown Hotel in the exclusive section of downtown, overlooking the Mississippi River. In the lounge he met Bill Theiss, who was working with music technology, which fascinated El-Dabh. (Soon after, he purchased his first computer with music-writing software and learned how to use it.)

El-Dabh thrived on the atmosphere of the city. He enjoyed watching the Elvis Presley impersonators as much as he enjoyed spending time with local musicians. Following the rehearsals, El-Dabh would often stop to eat in one of the restaurants along Beale Street. Once he entered an Italian restaurant very late at night. The owner was in the midst of closing for the evening but grudgingly agreed to serve El-Dabh. Scrutinizing El-Dabh, he finally recognized the composer from the newspaper items on the upcoming performance. His demeanor changed drastically. He telephoned some of his friends, family, and even newspaper photographers to come over to the restaurant, and he began serving El-Dabh everything he wanted, at no charge. People began entering the restaurant, and the owner invited the bemused composer to come to the restaurant any time he wanted and to bring his friends—everything would be "on the house." El-Dabh was exhausted, and the sudden friendliness of the restaurant owner had surprised him. However, he was pleased to see that this man was excited to have a composer in his restaurant, and El-Dabh delighted in sharing drinks with the owner's friends and in having his photograph taken for publication in the local newspapers.

Alan Balter conducted *Ramesses the Great,* which premiered on May 1, 1987, in the Vincent de Frank Music Hall in the city's Exhibition Center. The score is subtitled *Symphony No. 9,* not because El-Dabh had composed eight previous symphonies but because it makes reference to the Ennead, the nine religious forces that dominated the daily lives of the ancient Egyptians. *Ramesses the Great* represents the energy and the life

Sketch for *Ramesses the Great: Symphony No. 9* (1987).

force of Pharaoh Ramesses II while depicting him as the lover of Nefertari. Ramesses was the great builder of Egypt, and the symphony contains elements of architecture, power and energy, and love. Ramesses was considered a great lover because he had a hundred wives; however, he loved Nefertari best. A man of power, he was capable also of great, tender love for his wife. Also, El-Dabh incorporated elements revealing Ramesses's relationship with his father, Seti. It was because of this strong relationship between father and son that the gods blessed Ramesses, who lived to be ninety-two years old.

In the program notes by Leonard Burkat one learns that *Ramesses the Great: Symphony No. 9* is written in three movements, to be performed without interruption:

The first movement, *Allegro Moderato: Moderato—Piu mosso Ma non Troppo—Maestoso—Con Bravura*, depicts Ramesses, a great leader of his people, as architect, builder, and sculptor. It depicts his victories and achievements. The second movement is an intercession with the nine divine life forces including animal divinities. These nine life forces have been presented towards the end of the first movement when nine heartbeats mark the beginning of the *Adagio Mysterioso*. The third movement, *Allegro Vivo*, depicts Ramesses as a simple man, enjoying daily life, in love with his wife Nefertari and protected by the Goddess Isis. In this composition, traditional Egyptian musical instruments are expressed through the use of contemporary counterparts. These are the *buq* for trumpets and horns, *rebaba* for strings, *derabucca* for drums, *nay* for flutes, *zamr* for single and double reed instruments, *arghoul* for bassoons, *systrum* for cymbals of different sizes.[37]

Burkat also suggests that the composition "represents a wealth of experiences with a universal scope bearing the strong stamp of his heritage: the instruments, the textures, the folk melodies and the philosophies of Egypt."[38]

Five months after the premiere of *Ramesses the Great*, the Third International Musicological Symposium at Samarkand, in the Soviet republic of Uzbekistan, was held October 1–9, 1987. El-Dabh was one of three participants from the United States, among leading composers from more than twenty countries invited to present insights. The meeting was sponsored by the Union of Soviet Composers, the Music Council of the Soviet Ministry of Culture, and UNESCO's International Council of Music. Its focus was on the link between the life and traditions of the people of the Middle East and East Asia and modern musical cultures. El-Dabh presented a paper entitled "The Maqam[39] in the Oral Traditions of the Peoples of Sharqiyya, Egypt." Because Samarkand had used Arabic as an official language until 1927, El-Dabh delivered this paper in Arabic. He had also chosen to conduct his research in Sharqiyya, the province considered the seat of intellectual thought in ancient Egypt. It is the site of that country's oldest university of theoretical study, dating back at least to 1,000 B.C.

On his return from the USSR, El-Dabh spontaneously decided to make a surprise visit to Martha Graham in New York. Arriving at her studio, he was informed that she was attending an afternoon rehearsal at the City Center. Approaching the backstage guard at the center, El-Dabh forthrightly announced that he was there to see Martha, and the guard let him pass. As soon as he was backstage he recognized a dancer with whom he had worked, and he instinctively prepared to jump onto the stage to give the dancer a hug. As he was about to leap, he heard a voice announce, "Hello, darling."[40] Forgetting about the dancer, El-Dabh turned toward the voice and spied the famed choreographer, now in her nineties, seated in a wheelchair. They embraced, and after engaging in small talk Graham suggested that perhaps he would be more comfortable watching the performance from a seat in the hall. El-Dabh was stunned; he had been moments from leaping onto the stage in the midst of a matinee, not just interrupting a dress rehearsal.

He was also surprised to learn that later that month, after a three-year absence from the stage, Graham was to revive *Clytemnestra* yet again. In a review of the revival for the *New York Times*, Anna Kisselgoff would report that a "transparent black curtain to symbolize the underworld—contrasts with the recent colors added by Miss Graham and Halston to costumes that once focused on black."[41] This was not the only change, however, that Kisselgoff would mention, as "one sour note, *Clytemnestra* is a theater piece in the purest sense. For the first time, it is accompanied by tape in New York rather than a live orchestra. The sound of the singers and music is wrongly muffled, detracting from the liveness it should have."[42] El-Dabh's score is mentioned in the review as "both sinuous in its Oriental motif and modernist in its clear droplike percussion."[43]

In 1988 El-Dabh was commissioned by the Theater Department of Youngstown State University in Youngstown, Ohio, to compose a work based Aristophanes's *The Birds*. El-Dabh's music was scored for an ensemble composed of piano, synthesizer, flute, percussion, choruses, and singers. The production also featured actors and dancers. It was his first composition created with computer software. El-Dabh employed an IBM personal computer with a Sony keyboard and a MIDI[44] processor to teach the actors, dancers, and singers. In 1988 this was a novel approach, and occasionally El-Dabh became frustrated when the computer, incapable of handling some of his harmonies, would only approximate the pitches. El-Dabh had to make frequent adjustments, which annoyed him and stifled his creativity. However, by providing an efficient method for instructing the performers, it served its purpose well.

El-Dabh was delighted, during the creation of this work, to become involved with the choreographic areas of the dance. Evoking some Greek movements he recalled from working with Rallou Manou, El-Dabh conducted workshops in which he described Greek movements how one should stand and hold the body in the manner of a specific bird. *The Birds* transported El-Dabh back to the era of Aristophanes and Aeschylus and to his time with Martha Graham exploring the colorful story of Clytemnestra. He also reflected on his time in Ethiopia, where he had lived amid rare, exotic, and multicolored birds of many types and species. It was very stimulating and enriching for El-Dabh to return to Greek thought, and he enjoyed working with the Aristophanes play and with the actors, dancers, and singers. However, he was surprised that no one from Youngstown State's music department was involved in the project. It seemed as if the music and theater departments were divorced from one another, and he felt it strange that they were so territorial with their personnel. After this singular experience, El-Dabh preferred to work with theater groups outside the university setting.

On December 2, 1988, El-Dabh collaborated with his dear friend Art Wohl in a performance sponsored by DanceCleveland and the Cleveland Music School Settlement. This was a benefit concert for the Jenny Oppenheim Dance Therapy Scholarship Fund to assist deserving students. Jenny Oppenheim, a dancer, choreographer, and dance and movement therapist, worked with the elderly and with mentally challenged adults and was active in promoting the study of dance and dance and movement therapy in Cleveland. El-Dabh and Wohl's collaboration resulted in "Journey through the Centers of Being" (1988). Wohl, a performer, composer, artist, and dancer, played viola and violin with Tutare, a New Age group from California. His interest was in exploring the effects of movement, sound, and music on the healing and transformation of the mind and body, incorporating principles of dance and *t'ai chi ch'uan.*[45]

"Journey through the Centers of Being" consisted of four sections: Eshu (greeting to the Protector of the Space); Ogum (the Warrior Spirit, Protector of Life); The Seven Scorpions (from ancient Egyptian teachings); and Centers of Being. The seven Centers of Being represented the following: the base of the spine—Earth; the lower belly—Water; the solar plexus—Fire; the heart—Fire and Water; the neck—Air; the center of the forehead—Akasha (spirit); and the crown of the head—Life Force. The work was warmly received but drew little attention following its first and only performance.

In 1989 El-Dabh was honored with the status of University Professor at Kent State. Since its inception on May 23, 1968, only eleven professors have achieved this special academic rank, and his nomination was the first for the School of Music in the College of Fine and Professional Arts. El-Dabh was deeply appreciative when he was notified of his nomination; however, when he learned that he would be required to submit a file chronicling and enumerating his academic and professional achievements, he quickly became less enamored of the idea. Having not been required

Habeeb El-Dabh, age five (1984).

to ascend the academic ranks through the tenure and promotion process, El-Dabh felt that if the members of the university community sincerely wished to award him this honor, they should do so without his input. He believed his record spoke for itself and that if those determining whether or not he would receive the honor did not know of his accomplishments, it was not his responsibility to enlighten them. El-Dabh's colleagues in the School of Music—well aware that awards of this level of prestige are not typically awarded to professors in the fine and professional arts but rather to colleagues in the "hard sciences"—were aghast. They believed that El-Dabh's unwillingness to complete the required paperwork might cause him to lose this recognition, which they perceived as something from which they would benefit vicariously. In a rare showing of solidarity, several members of the School of Music urged El-Dabh to reconsider and agreed to help him compile his curriculum vitae and the supplemental materials required. As a result of his colleagues' supportive efforts, El-Dabh was awarded this high honor.

Five Etudes (1989), for concert band, was also composed on the computer during a time in which El-Dabh was absorbed with the thought that American high school bands could be vital forces in fostering cultural experiences. Because a high school band is an institution that involves students, parents, and the community, El-Dabh believed that they could enhance an entire musical curriculum. As his own son, Habeeb, was learning to play the saxophone, El-Dabh became discouraged that the school bands had a tendency to use the same material over and over. El-Dabh believed that the music was simply rehashed each year, and the experience was not creative. He said that the young musicians would be more inspired if the music education programs were more innovative.

Unfortunately, Habeeb became bored with the band and eventually gave up the saxophone. It was discouraging to El-Dabh that with all the energy and enthusiasm he saw on the part of the students, there was little interest in doing more than the regular and routine. El-Dabh wanted to create something new for Habeeb and his peers by strengthening the concept of the marching band. He believed strongly that it could be an exciting experience, one that could open the minds of the high school musicians and encourage them to continue with their instruments in college. It was a very noble idea on El-Dabh's part; however, because it was easier for everyone to continue with their routines, he was met with resistance, and his dreams of creating an invigorating learning environment went unfulfilled.

"The Jade Flute" (1989), for soprano, trumpet, and piano, was commissioned by soprano Joanne Couch, trumpeter Charles Couch, and pianist Laura Silverman. On March 4, 1990, the trio premiered the work at Kent State University. El-Dabh believed this to be his most significant work since his *Ramesses the Great: Symphony No. 9.* Consisting of four movements—"When the Swallow Returned," "Contentment," "The Girl at Home," and "Eternity"—the piece is based on four ancient Chinese poems (in English translation) to which El-Dabh added phonetic syllables of his own. Pointing out that "'The Jade Flute' [is a] curious title for a piece in which no flute is heard and jade is never mentioned,"[46] Robert Finn, music critic for the *Cleveland Plain Dealer,* wrote that "El-Dabh had his trumpet line sometimes echoing the voice, sometimes playing in counterpoint to it, sometimes commenting in between vocal phrases. The cycle begins with a kind of impressionist expressiveness in the first poem; the second and fourth poems are more linear in the language, and the third is a solo for unaccompanied fluegelhorn."[47] Finn further states that

the piece is attractive and expressive in a conservative way—but one felt when it was over that the main issue had not been resolved. El-Dabh uses some picturesque musical devices in this piece. He

Halim El-Dabh playing African harp (1990).

establishes a short motive and then repeats it often enough so that
it sticks in the memory—the opening line for the soprano, for example. His vocal writing sometimes echoes the sense of the words—
on the word "laugh," for example. And the final movement unfolds
slowly over a steady two-note ostinato pulse in the piano—a device
familiar from the famous mock-scherzo in Mahler's first symphony.
. . . Despite its central technical problem, this is an attractive and
listenable piece.[48]

As a continuation of his desire to create exciting works for band students, El-Dabh began composing *Conversations with Shu* (1990), for wind

ensemble. The work had a reading under the direction of Wayne Gorder, Kent State's director of bands; however, as Habeeb lost interest in the saxophone, El-Dabh consequently lost interest in this piece. It remains unfinished; only one movement of the three-movement work was completed. Shu, the Egyptian god of air and wind, was one of the Egyptian members of the Ennead, the nine forces of ancient Egypt, which El-Dabh had used in *Ramesses the Great: Symphony No. 9*. Gorder found the work challenging and encouraged his colleague to complete the other two movements; however, quite uncharacteristically, El-Dabh has no desire to resurrect it.

In 1990 El-Dabh was designated one of three recipients of the Cleveland Arts Prize. The prize had been established under the auspices of the Women's City Club by Martha Joseph and Klaus Roy.[47] Although award winners might have achieved national fame, they had to have a Cleveland-area connection to be eligible for the award. By 1990 the prize had been given to over ninety recipients in thirty years. The other two recipients in 1990 were Adrianne Kennedy, a writer, and Judith Solomon, a visual artist. This prestigious honor was fitting for a man who had made the greater Cleveland area his home for two decades. It also marked the beginning of a new phase in El-Dabh's life. He was about to enter his seventieth year and announce his retirement from Kent State University.

8

Retirement

In 1991 El-Dabh announced his intention to retire from the Kent State University School of Music; however, he emphatically expressed his desire not to "retire" in the traditional sense but to remain active as an adjunct professor in the Department of Pan-African Studies. He also promised his colleagues in the ethnomusicology division of the School of Music that he would be available to assist them any time they desired. Almost immediately, preparations were initiated for a concert honoring his tenure at Kent State. Quite characteristically, instead of programming works written previously, El-Dabh chose to compose several new pieces for this special event. He also attempted to write works for a variety of instrumentalists and ensembles with which he felt particularly close bonds. One very unusual work premiered at that concert was "Habeeb's Lullaby and Rebuttal" (1991), for solo alto saxophone and bassoon ensemble. El-Dabh, who wrote the saxophone part for his twelve-year-old son to perform, was exploring the connection between band and symphonic wind instruments in the piece. However, to the members of the audience, the young Habeeb seemed to suffer from either a severe case of stage fright or lack of practice. The members of the bassoon ensemble seemed quite distressed until the final cadence, and the piece was not the best-received work of the evening.

By contrast, "Kalabsha on River Nile" (1991), for *zheng* (a twenty-one string Chinese zither), was performed on the harp by Alissa Pesavento and was greatly appreciated by the audience. The effects of the harp, by turns meditative and virtuosic, assuaged the listeners' senses; they sat mesmerized by El-Dabh's musical reflection of a town along the Nile where he had once lived. Egypt is composed of areas with distinctive musical influences. For example, Nubi is the southernmost part of Egypt, bordering Sudan, and its inhabitants are known as "Nubians." The town of Kalabsha is a part of the Nubian culture, where all the inhabitants, in addition to any of seven other local languages, speak Arabic, and the lyre is an important traditional instrument. In this work, El-Dabh depicts various aspects of Nubian daily life, exploring the complete sound spectrum of the stringed instrument.

"Ceremonial Fattening for Death and Resurrection" (1991), for bassoon ensemble, displayed the true capabilities and talents of the individuals in the Kent Bassoon Ensemble. El-Dabh seemed to be deliberately providing a vehicle by which to showcase the ensemble's technical skill and ability; understandably, the members of the ensemble, under the capable leadership of David DeBolt, conveyed greater enthusiasm while performing it than they had while playing "Habeeb's Lullaby and Rebuttal." The piece required all the musicians to exercise command over the entire range of their instruments. The piece consists of three movements: "Procession Victorious," "Dance of Condemnation," and "Lament and Resurrection." Composed during the Persian Gulf War, it contemplated in a darkly humorous fashion the American government's role in having assisted foreign political and military leaders such as Manuel Noriega[1] and Saddam Hussein[2] in their rise to power only to see the leaders later use that power against the United States. In the work, El-Dabh attempted to expose what he perceived to be the superpower's foolishness throughout its history of figuratively "fattening" and then "slaughtering" foreign leaders; the irony is that quite often the deposed leaders are replaced by others who are exactly the same. Although the composition involves a tragic situation, there is also a comedic quality to it, and El-Dabh briefly considered expanding the concept behind this work into an opera. Believing that the larger-than-life characters on the world stage conveyed the complexities of all human beings, he felt the subject matter would translate well into a dramatic medium.

The most poignant work during the retirement concert was "Go Down Moses: The Planet Earth Is the Promised Land" (1991), for soprano, baritone, and piano. Based on the well-known African American spiritual "Go Down, Moses," its reference to Moses commanding the pharaoh to "let my people go" had great personal meaning to the composer. El-Dabh's music has always been a consequence of interaction—of people, ideas, and incidents in his life. Throughout his academic career, El-Dabh never could have been accused of living in an "ivory tower," isolated from the world around him; his music was not conceived in a sterile environment. In this piece, El-Dabh contemplated the world, and he expressed the ideas that oppression is universal and that Moses was not the leader of just one particular race but rather of all.

"Dragons and Floating Lilies" (1991) was composed for Kent State University graduate student Lu Guang, who performed the piece on the *zheng*. El-Dabh and Lu had spent many evenings discussing Chinese musical composition, and El-Dabh had hoped to compose a work that reflected both the essence of the Chinese *zheng* and the philosophical conversations the two had shared. Lu, a masterful performer on several traditional Chinese instruments and the director of Kent State's Chinese Ensemble, contributed greatly to ensuring that the composition reflected the *zheng*'s musical characteristics with authenticity and integrity. The audience responded positively to the technique of the personable Chinese virtuoso. Wisely, El-Dabh had allowed Lu's skill to be highlighted in several improvisatory passages, and the musician ably met the challenge.

"Dialogue for Double Bass and Ceramic Egyptian Drum" (1991) was composed for an unassuming undergraduate student, Bryan Thomas, whose remarkable talent had found him places in virtually every ensemble in the School of Music. El-Dabh, who considered Thomas's musicianship superb, astonished Thomas with the announcement that he planned to write a piece for the two of them to perform at his retirement concert. The work utilized several advanced double-bass techniques, including upper-register playing and high harmonics. Thomas was also to vocalize and to strike various parts of the body of the instrument. "Dialogue for Double Bass and Ceramic Egyptian Drum" paid homage to Aswan, a six-thousand-year-old city at an intersection of routes between the west and east coasts of Africa and home to numerous tribes and languages over the millennia. Aswan has long been considered a major cultural center, and it was there that the treasures of Upper Egypt and Nubia converged. Impressed by the manner in which African culture had dispersed—from beyond the Niger River to the Nile; on the Nile to Punt (ancient Ethiopia); south to the rivers of Kenya, Uganda, and Tanzania; and back again to the Nile—El-Dabh reflected this cultural exchange in this piece. Just as elements of all the African tribes that engaged in trading activities remain within Aswan, El-Dabh explored and exploited the various timbres and textures of the double bass and the ceramic drum.

Perhaps the most enjoyable performance of the retirement concert was that of clarinet professor Dennis Nygren in El-Dabh's "Tonography," for solo clarinet (originally composed in 1980; revised in 1984; and revised again for this concert in 1991). The work combines standard musical notation with graphic symbols and other enigmatic shapes. Additionally, the soloist must shift among a B-flat, A, and E-flat clarinet, as well as dance and sing. Nygren's performance delighted the audience as he demonstrated his skill in switching back and forth among the three clarinets with a facility that was matched by the ease with which he danced, sang, and moved about the stage.

Invigorated by the success of his retirement concert, El-Dabh entered a very active period of composing and performing music. "Theme Song: The New Renaissance" (1991), for flute, cello, and piano, was inspired by Joann Lattavo, a visual artist from Canton, Ohio, who had created a series of paintings pertaining to the concept of a reawakening or rebirth; El-Dabh felt compelled to transform this wonderful art into sound. The result was the musical score for a modern ballet; Lattavo worked vigorously to secure the famous dancer Mikhail Baryshnikov[3] for the work's first performance. Baryshnikov showed interest, but his fee could not be settled. Undaunted, Lattavo was instrumental in arranging for the Tom Evert Dance Company to premiere the piece at the Bolton Theater of the Cleveland Play House on June 6, 1991.

The following month El-Dabh collaborated in a large-scale enameling workshop at Kent State University initiated by Mel Someroski and led by Cathy Taylor and Deanna Robb. Earlier in the year El-Dabh had traveled to Columbus, Ohio, with these three colleagues from Kent State's School of Art to attend an exhibit featuring the works of Barbara Shabazz. El-Dabh, moved by the exhibit, had asked the gallery staff to unlock the grand piano so he could play his response to the art. The three art professors had been captivated by El-Dabh's aural reaction to the visual stimulus and began discussing various methods and avenues by which to engage students in a collaborative process involving art and music. The idea produced the enameling workshop, which proved quite successful. It was supported by the Ferro Corporation, which donated a Pereny flatbed furnace measuring nineteen and a half feet to the university. During the course of the workshop, students designed, fashioned, and performed on their own enameled metal instruments. When the event came to a close, El-Dabh led the students in a parade around the campus in an impromptu "graduation" performance.

On the tenth anniversary of the Middletown, Ohio, Middfest international festival, the previously featured nations (Brazil, Egypt, Italy, Mexico,
Japan, Switzerland, Ireland, India, Luxembourg, and Canada) were recognized. El-Dabh composed *Harmonies of the Spheres: Ten Nations Rejoice* (1991), for wind symphony, for this commemorative occasion. Recalling an ancient Egyptian musical notation system utilizing color, for
Harmonies of the Spheres El-Dabh created his own color notation system in which different colors appeared in circles of various sizes. Small
cards depicting El-Dabh's color notation system were printed and distributed as part of the festival's advertisement and marketing campaign. Because ten nations were highlighted, the event was a particularly exciting
celebration, and a large wind ensemble orchestra was assembled. The
work's first part, "Harmonies of the Spheres," symbolized the relationship of the planets in alignment and embodied a feeling of the unity and
universality of the concept of harmony among the world's peoples. The
festival drew a wide variety of participants from around the globe, and El-
Dabh flourished in the exchange of musical ideas that were presented at
the various workshops. He appreciated the opportunity to converse with
people and reflect at these gatherings.[4] Thousands gathered for the performance of "Harmonies of the Spheres." A light show, with slides and
designs representing the relationship of color and sound, was projected in
one blaze of light on the exterior walls of the city hall, in synchroniza-
tion with the music. During the final performance El-Dabh began singing euphorically and persuaded the audience to join in an impromptu
finale with the orchestra, as if they were all "rejoicing." Following the
larger work was a series of ten smaller, separate works, each of which
focused on an individual country—such as "Jangada," which explored
Brazilian folk materials; "Baladi," which was based on a popular Egyptian folk song; and "Adriatica," which captured the spirit of Italy's eastern coast. (Track No. 19 on the companion CD.)

Near the end of 1991 El-Dabh received an unexpected telephone call
from a former student, Larry Losier, who was employed as a limousine
driver in New York City. Losier reported that he had been serving as the
driver for pop icon Madonna,[5] and on this particular day Madonna was
being accompanied by a woman whom he recognized to be Martha Graham. Losier had been surprised to overhear Graham refer to El-Dabh and
their collaborations. Breaking the company rule of not engaging in conversation with a client, Losier interrupted the women to announce that
El-Dabh was his former teacher at Kent State University; Graham, who

had been rather frosty with Losier, became polite and cordial. Now, at his first opportunity, Losier was informing his former teacher that Graham had been educating Madonna about their work together. El-Dabh was both amused and pleased at the news.[6]

The following summer El-Dabh was commissioned by the city of Cleveland to write a children's opera for the Cleveland Museum of Art's Egyptian exhibit and for a city festival honoring Amenhotep III, whose reign was considered one of the most artistically creative periods in Egyptian history at a time of great cultural development throughout Egypt and neighboring areas. At that time, Egypt had been a vast country, encompassing large parts of Asia Minor and the Near East. Egypt had been prosperous, and its focus on art and creativity had been considerable. El-Dabh's *Sobek, the Crocodile* (1992) depicts the crocodile in Egyptian history and mythology as a figure representing the Nile; the piece considers the crocodile in its multifarious nature and its significance to the Egyptian people. Ancient Egyptians used animals to portray various aspects of the universe. They viewed the world not only from a human perspective but also through the eye of the crocodile. It would have been egotistical to presume that humans were the only ones who could see; one had to consider what the crocodile saw as well. Throughout Egyptian history, the crocodile has been perceived as both an animal and as a god and was believed to have a special relationship to children—their innocence, their growth, and their power combined. In that sense, Egyptians still believe that it is possible to embody the energy of the crocodile.

For the work El-Dabh united children from both the inner city and the suburbs of Cleveland. He wrote a simple text with simple musical ideas, mainly songs and drumming patterns. El-Dabh worked with the children on all creative aspects of the work. They made their own Egyptian-style jewelry, costumes, and headwear, and they painted the sets themselves. El-Dabh often traveled to the west side of Cleveland to rehearse with the students. He also created tapes for adult leaders and trained them to work with the students when he could not be there. There was a great deal of collaboration and cooperation in this community project, and it was quite invigorating for El-Dabh, who relished interacting with the young people and teaching them African rhythms. In addition to the two scheduled performances of the opera, there was a preperformance pageant and a celebration at Cleveland's City Hall. The pageant occurred in the park next to the museum; the students were costumed as small pharaonic figures, and huge, colorful flags were displayed. Rockefeller Park Lagoon, with an

Egyptian-style boat and a camel nearby for the children to ride, served as the backdrop for the festivities. The Iroko Drum and Dance Society, led by Baba David Coleman, joined in the celebration, dancing on tall stilts in African style. El-Dabh relished the great spirit of cooperation and participation evoked by this opera.

In October 1992 El-Dabh received the dreadful news that a catastrophic earthquake had struck Cairo. Grief-stricken, El-Dabh immediately telephoned several friends and family members to learn the extent of the damage. Never imagining that there would be an earthquake in Cairo, he was stunned that this one had proved to be most unusual and devastating. Unfortunately, it was determined, some contractors had not properly followed building codes, and several buildings had been constructed too high; these structures toppled readily during the earthquake.

The Society of Heliopolis Musicians invited El-Dabh to travel to Egypt to compose and perform a new work as a tribute to the earthquake victims. When he learned that all of the proceeds of the performance would be donated to the victims, he readily agreed and composed *Eulogy to Cairo's Earthquake Victims and Their Families* (1992), for piano, consisting of three movements: "The City of Cairo," "The Planet and the Earthquake," and "Lament, Love, and Hope." When El-Dabh and Deborah traveled to Egypt for the performance, they experienced a powerful aftershock but were unharmed. The work premiered at a downtown hotel in Heliopolis, which had been built as an extension of an old cultural palace. Never meant to serve as a palace for kings, this building was a palace for the myriad cultural celebrations and activities of Heliopolis. When the palace became somewhat dilapidated, a hotel was built across the street; the palace, though disused, was preserved as a relic. El-Dabh recalled that in his youth he had spent many happy hours there; this return to Cairo was indeed bittersweet.

In these early years of his retirement El-Dabh frequently composed new pieces for his students to perform in various venues throughout Kent State University. He also often wrote pieces for particular music students who showed an interest in his compositional style. Two such examples are *Lucy, Come Back* (1993), for singers, dancers, drummers, and multimedia; and *Global Order for Two Tubas and Egyptian Drum* (1993). *Lucy, Come Back* is based on the 1974 findings of the anthropologist Donald Johanson[7] and his team in Ethiopia. El-Dabh involved the students from his African music and dance class in the work to create a dramatic event combining light, costumes, masks, drumming, and singing, involving much improvisation. Building on the premise that "Lucy" (as the original owner of a prehistoric skull found by Johanson was popularly known) had been the first black woman and that she had been brought back to life through Johanson's research, the piece depicted a skeleton returning to life. It emphasized El-Dabh's speculation that 3.5 million years ago a black woman had been born and that she was the ancestor of everyone living today. *Global Order for Two Tubas and Egyptian Drum* was composed for two Kent State University undergraduate students, Michael Foster[8] and Robert Munson. Three movements—"The Pendulum," "The Shiver," and "The Balance"—make up the work, which was commissioned by the university's Delta Omicron Honorary Music Fraternity for the dedication of the Elizabeth Ludwig Fennell Green Room in the School of Music. El-Dabh joined Foster and Munson in the work's premiere, playing the *derabucca*.

During this period El-Dabh also composed "To the Letter of His Name" (1993), for flute, which was premiered in Stow, Ohio, at a birthday party for Kent State University professor emeritus and good friend Raymond DeMattia. The piece was fashioned in the manner in which Robert Schumann and other composers created pieces based on the names of friends and patrons, using the letters of their names to represent musical notes.[9] DeMattia had been the flutist for El-Dabh's "Isis and the Seven Scorpions," and he had been a great champion of El-Dabh's compositions for several years; he had assisted El-Dabh by creating computer-engraved scores for his compositionss, using a music-writing software program. DeMattia and his wife, Kathy, had gathered weekly with El-Dabh and a select group of friends since the mid-1980s for breakfast meetings to discuss current events and books. The circle of friends, which was quite close, included a podiatrist and specialist in parapsychology and biofeedback, Francis Rogers and his wife, Joan; and a Kent State professor of ethnomusicology, Terry E. Miller, and his wife, ethnomusicologist Sara Stone Miller. In the beginning, these breakfast meetings were highly structured, with members determining in advance which topics they would discuss. However, over time the gatherings became more spontaneous, and occasionally Deborah participated when the events were of a more social nature. These weekly gatherings proved to be a source of inspiration and satisfaction for El-Dabh, who also participated in weekly assemblies led by Rogers on Tuesday evenings. The latter group, numbering from six to twenty on any given evening, considered itself to be an informal spiritual and meditation organization; its purpose was to discuss the works of such authors as Neale Donald

Walsch and James Redfield.[10] El-Dabh found his intellectual interactions with this group to be most stimulating.

In the 1990s El-Dabh became interested in a group known as ACE (Association for Consciousness Exploration), a national organization headquartered at in Cleveland Heights, Ohio. This interest led him to become associated with similar groups that discussed and explored consciousness raising and related topics. During one meeting, in Sherman, New York, El-Dabh was introduced to Timothy Leary;[11] the two became fast friends. Leary referred to El-Dabh as "my favorite younger brother"[12] and invited him, with Deborah and Habeeb, to visit him and to stay overnight in his California home, which they did. Teenaged Habeeb liked Leary very much, but Deborah found the house—which Leary had wired with sound, video, and light installations that turned on and off at random intervals throughout the day and night—quite unnerving. She was relieved when their four-day visit concluded.[13]

During their visit with Leary, the El-Dabh family was treated to two very memorable parties. During the first, held in Leary's home, El-Dabh at one point was handed a double bass and asked to perform. Rather than playing the instrument in the traditional manner, El-Dabh laid the bass on the floor and assembled a group of party guests around it. He instructed selected individuals to play the bass as if it were a hand drum. Each performer was given an area on the instrument and taught a separate rhythm to play. By the time the performance ended, El-Dabh had charmed everyone. The second party occurred at the Beverly Hills mansion of Ringo Starr[14] on the occasion of Starr's birthday; there were many celebrities in attendance. El-Dabh was amused when Leary introduced El-Dabh to Starr by laughingly declaring to the famous Beatle, "Ringo, I want you to meet a real drummer!"[15] El-Dabh invited Starr to participate in an avant-garde event in Cleveland in which El-Dabh was to perform with Kent State University student Mike Hovancsek.[16] Starr promised to check his schedule, and that was enough encouragement for El-Dabh to announce to Hovancsek that Ringo Starr would perform in Cleveland with them. Hovancsek was convinced that El-Dabh was genuinely surprised when Starr failed to appear for the performance.[17]

El-Dabh and Leary often discussed such topics as astral travel and Leary's advocacy of LSD. El-Dabh shared with Leary the story of his only experience with the drug, which had been slipped to him in a beverage without his knowledge in 1961 while he was living in Demarest, New Jersey. That year, at a party at the United Nations, a beautiful young woman had approached El-Dabh and requested that he take her into the city on his way home. She had then offered him a drink "for the road." El-Dabh accepted the drink and escorted her to his automobile. Fortunately, it was four o'clock in the morning, and the city was almost deserted. As he was driving, El-Dabh began experiencing visions—the skyscrapers were growing and swaying in the wind, and the faces of passersby seemed to glow and contort hideously. Realizing that the woman had drugged him, he stopped at a traffic light and turned toward her. Apparently the look on his face frightened the mysterious woman, who leapt from his car and ran down the sidewalk.

Feverishly, El-Dabh attempted to find his way to the George Washington Bridge and the security of his home in Demarest. As if guided by divine intervention, the dazed El-Dabh safely got on the bridge, but when he saw the red light at the toll booth, his mind played tricks on him. Disoriented, El-Dabh assumed that New Jersey must be closed for the night. Intending to return to the United Nations to spend the night, he put the car into reverse and began backing across the George Washington Bridge for New York. He traveled a few yards and noticed that the light at the toll booth was now green. Pleased that New Jersey must now be open, he drove back to the booth. "Have you been drinking? What's the matter with you?" the irate attendant barked. El-Dabh shot the man a glaring look, paid his toll, and drove on to his home. He was greeted by a very angry wife, who demanded to know where he had been. Looking past her as he stumbled into the house, he immediately fell ill from the effects of the drug. He was sick for two days. Although El-Dabh was now able to find some humor in the incident, Leary was aghast. Although Leary was a great champion of the use of LSD, he was adamantly against tricking another into taking it.[18]

In 1995, in honor of the twenty-fifth anniversary May 4, 1970, El-Dabh transformed *Opera Flies* for three different public performances at Kent State. The first was a rescoring of the opera for soprano, narrator, and piano. The second was an open "pageant" in which local artists of various music disciplines would improvise on elements from the original work. That event included drumming, art, poetry, and individual personal reflections on the tragedy. The third, and the most involved of the three transformations, was a restaging of the original opera, minus most of the original choruses but adding elaborate montages of light and video projections, atmospheric sound sources, and tapes of the actual newscasters' reports remixed to produce a collage of sound and narrative about current topics that reflected on the twenty-five years since the shootings. In the notes for the first of these programs, dated March 22, 1995, one learns that "The burial scene, composed as an African Ritual, projects the cycles of life and death, making real man's experience of his eternal struggle between his individual rights and social order."[19] El-Dabh wrote, "The entire opera is created and seen through a prism, whereby the multifacets of life are interacted. Man with machine and civil strife. Man the particular through all his generations with Comedy, Tragedy and Pathos."[20] In an article by Marc Vincent for the *Daily Kent Stater*, El-Dabh is quoted reflecting on the twenty-fifth anniversary: "A kind of healing is needed now. This is the best aspect to bring it about."[21] El-Dabh invited a panel of young musicians and artists to help breathe new life into the revised performance slated for May 4, 1995: "We don't necessarily need people with an extensive background in this sort of production. What we do need is a large group of creative active people who are willing to work hard and devote a lot of time to this project."[22]

The revival of *Opera Flies* was the result of the efforts of a small committee of dedicated students who were attached to El-Dabh and his compositional style. The more active members of the group included David Badagnani, Blake Tyson, Mike Foster, John Kuegeler, Mike Hovancsek, and Daniel Ryan. When El-Dabh first decided to restage his work, he contacted the School of Music and the School of Theatre and Dance at Kent State University; however, both thought his work was too large and too controversial to perform on campus, even though the university's upper administration had granted its official recognition and support, and they discouraged El-Dabh from pursuing the project, the deadline of which was only ten months away. Hovancsek recalled the negative feeling the production team felt when El-Dabh received a fax from the School of Theatre and Dance—"Not only would they not help us with the opera, they also would not allow us to use any of their students, equipment, or performance spaces."[23] Because the School of Theatre and Dance's complex was close to El-Dabh's office in the Music and Speech Building, the fact that the reply was sent via fax rather than delivered in person or by telephone was perceived by the groups as exceedingly disrespectful.

Undeterred, the students sought permission from the university's Scheduling Board for a performance venue. They were delighted to be granted the use of the E. Turner Stump Theater in the Music and Speech Building for several dates leading up to the May 4 event. Fortified by this news, the group rallied and determined to increase its collective efforts. The committee members seriously began examining the work's libretto as well as audio tapes of past performances; however, they soon realized they did not have a complete score. El-Dabh apparently had misplaced the work. Hovancsek kept a journal of his personal involvement with the project, and from his account one learns: "Most of what we had was pieced together from a rather illegible version of the piano score and parts of a chamber music arrangement that had some serious flaws in its structure (e.g., the number of measures didn't line up between the various parts). We also had tapes from the extremely different versions of the 1971 version of the opera, all of which were incomplete and which differed substantially from the scores we had."[24]

In another entry, Hovancsek paints a detailed scene of the attempt to locate the score:

We dug around Halim's office in a futile attempt to find more pieces of the score. Unfortunately, his office looked like someone dumped the contents from a dozen yard sales into a recycling bin. The search turned up several odd bits from the carnival that is Halim's life. We found uncashed checks, letters that he forgot to send twenty years earlier, hundreds of unraveling reel-to-reel tapes, dozens of illegible notes that he wrote to himself, letters from Otto Luening, slides, stacks and stacks of scores, drawings, technical notes from Martha Graham. . . . We also found numerous "To Do" lists that read like this:

Call Edgard Varèse
Spark of Light
bread
cheese
onion soup
man against machine
Finish Martha Graham piece
wash car
oil change.[25]

Eventually the group prepared for the first of the three incarnations, which was performed in Ludwig Recital Hall at Kent State University on March 22, 1995. Per Enflo (piano), Annika Enflo (soprano), and Calvin A.

McClinton (narrator) brought the work to life, as Hovancsek and Ryan handled video and slide projections for the performance. The second event occurred in Kent State's Student Center Kiva. This rendering consisted of a series of performances involving musicians who had been committed to the project in one manner or another. Mark Allender (double bass), Kuegeler (trumpet), El-Dabh (piano), and Hovancsek (koto) played improvisations over some of the projected artwork that Hovancsek had assembled for the May 4 performance. Tyson, Allender, and Chad Mossholder performed improvisations for dancers, who later appeared in the final version of the opera. Jayce Renner recited excerpts from the opera's text while Tyson played piano. To conclude the event, El-Dabh led the audience in a version of the opera's finale, "I Strolled in Jello," and an African percussion group paraded the audience out of the hall. The final incarnation met great resistance up to its scheduled performance time. The greatest opposition came from Raynette Halvorsen Smith, director of the School of Theatre and Dance, who expressed concern that a student-generated program might not be perceived as professional and would reflect poorly on her program. Meetings were scheduled and canceled. Sadly El-Dabh and Smith became more confrontational than collegial when the meetings did occur, until the frustrations of both led to a total failure of communication.

Because reporters had learned of the opposition, the local media became interested in the event, and their coverage brought attention to the restaging. Kuegeler and Hovancsek were interviewed by the university's radio station, WKSU (a copy of that broadcast remains in the May 4 collection). However, the press involvement and the mounting antagonism caused several of the committee members to withdraw. Eventually Hovancsek and Kuegeler emerged as the leaders behind the project, and the two determined that involving Timothy Leary in the project could be a powerful statement to any dissenters. They were thrilled when Leary agreed to participate in the performance. Hovancsek had envisioned Leary joining the ensemble during the symbolic killing scene; he wanted Leary to "step over the bodies, into a lone spotlight. From there, I wanted him to do an improvisational rant about protest, technology, and the changing role of activism in society."[26]

Everything appeared to be progressing smoothly until two days before the final performance, when Hovancsek contacted Leary with final details for his arrival and participation. A disheartened Leary announced that he did not think he would be able to perform after all and handed the telephone to his business manager, who informed Hovancsek that earlier in the day Leary had been diagnosed with inoperable cancer. Stunned, Hovancsek offered his sympathy and quietly hung up the telephone.

The day prior to the performance was a jumble of setting the stage and juggling the fifty-piece wind orchestra, the vocalists, the dancers, the lights, and the video and slide projections. Eventually, after a fourteen-hour day of preparation and rehearsal, the performance was ready. Without question, the production would not have been successful without the monumental efforts of Wayne Gorder, who directed the Kent State University wind ensemble for the performance. Gorder spent hours reorchestrating for his musicians the score the students had pieced together. "It was a difficult task," Gorder commented about the experience, "however, it was well worth it for the students to have the opportunity of working with someone of Halim's genius."[27]

Hovancsek engaged two artists, known as Artbrats Union Local 12:21, to construct a totem pole from television sets on which video images would be displayed out toward the lobby. The two also designed a rear-projection video setup with a four-image video loop and four plastic tommy guns, with pictures of the four slain students on them.

Hovancsek, assisted by Ryan, amassed a sound collage, complete with the sound of buzzing flies that greeted the audience as it assembled for the performance. Slides of Hovancsek's artwork were projected across the length of the stage. Hovancsek and Ryan had painted panes of glass with green and yellow shades to represent springtime colors, which they then shot on video. They had also placed a television set on its back and positioned candles atop the screen. On film, the flickering of the flames appeared to be floating in space. They also videotaped superimposed images of crystals and lace to create an ethereal effect. As the vocalists and dancers interacted with the ensemble, Ryan and Hovancsek manipulated the slide and video projections from the floor. For Ryan, the experience was a "spontaneous happening full of energy which had such great possibility and potential for healing within the community."[28]

Unfortunately the scars caused by the negativity earlier in the production process were evident on the back of the printed program: "We would like to thank all of the people who tried to sabotage this event. Your attempts to ruin *Opera Flies* turned out to be the best promotion that we could ever have hoped for."[29] As the opera concluded, the capacity audience gave a lengthy standing ovation, and all the participants spontaneously ascended the stage to congratulate one another. El-Dabh joined the group onstage, and in an exhilarating moment grabbed a microphone to

Halim El-Dabh with Mary Ann Vecchio, on whom the
lead female character, Vekeero, in *Opera Flies* is based. In
1996 Vecchio returned to Kent State University (for the
first time since 1970) and spoke about her experiences.

announce (erroneously) that there would be "several more performances
of *Opera Flies* in the next few days." Fortunately, the microphone was
already dead.[30]

As soon as Habeeb had completed his sophomore year of high school,
El-Dabh, Deborah, and Habeeb prepared the family van to serve as both
transportation and lodging for an extensive family vacation, traveling
across the United States from Ohio to California during the summer of
1995. After the arduous *Opera Flies* production and the news of Timothy
Leary's terminal illness, the trip provided a much-needed respite for El-
Dabh. The warmer climate also was therapeutic for Deborah, a longtime

arthritis sufferer, who hoped that her family might relocate to the Southwest, preferably Arizona. For years following El-Dabh's retirement, she had attempted to convince her husband and son that the time was right for them to leave Kent, and she strongly believed that this trip would be her best opportunity to persuade them to move.

Although Deborah found relief in the Southwest, El-Dabh and Habeeb were adamant that they had no interest in relocating. For El-Dabh the trip was merely a diversion, and he soon grew eager to return to his life in Kent. He did admit, however, that the family grew closer during that vacation, and he and Habeeb found a special bond working as extras on Hollywood sound stages for television programs. On the return trip, El-Dabh drove his family to Colorado to visit the area where he had lived in the 1950s. It was there that he had first become passionate about the beautiful Aspen trees located throughout the scenic landscape. Now, following a forty-year lapse, he was inspired to compose *Big Tooth Aspen* (1995), for flute and *derabucca*, to immortalize his intense feelings toward these trees, so named for the large, irregular "teeth" on their leaf edges. His feelings were so strong that he presented a copy of the score to the Aspen City Hall and another to the Aspen School of Music. The work, dedicated to Blake and Liana Tyson, consists of three movements—"Twigs," "Drooping Flowers," and "Hairy Seeds in the Wind"—which represent life, death, and rebirth in the life cycle of the tree and the evolution of its numerous flowers and seeds, which are dispersed vast distances by the wind.

In 1996 Blake Tyson, who had been accepted as a graduate percussion major at the Eastman School of Music, contacted the composer with a request to write a piece for him to premiere at Eastman. "Secrets of the Sky and Earth" (1996), for marimba, depicts Nut, the Egyptian goddess of the sky, and Geb, the Egyptian earth god. The title of the composition refers to the mythological secret that Geb and Nut originally had been one but had been separated because humans needed to have the sky overhead and the earth below. Most depictions of Geb and Nut are quite sensual, showing Geb returning to Nut with his phallus coming toward her solar plexus, before Ra is born through her body. In this depiction it is as if the solar plexus is the center of the cosmic magnetism between the earth and sky. The piece also reflects the importance of the *chakras*[31] of the body, which El-Dabh was investigating in his weekly meetings with Francis Rogers. The work, which premiered April 14, 1996, at the Eastman School, is based on the composer's concept of expanding or increasing the vibration of the entire range of the marimba as the chords employed throughout the work are played. El-Dabh considered this chordal relationship another secret of the universe, and he contemplated arranging a version for four marimbas, in order to emphasize this point further.

That same year El-Dabh was commissioned to compose *The New Pharaohs Suite* (1996), a collection of twelve movements for ten wind instruments, in conjunction with the opening of the Cleveland Museum of Art's exhibit of the Louvre's Egyptian collection "Pharaohs." Some of the work's movements are: "King Tut," "Isis, Mother Goddess, Mistress of Mankind," "Passion," "Village Gatherings," "The Garden," and "The Spirit of the Sphinx." The festive piece, based on Egyptian folklore and El-Dabh's immediate contact with the people in the villages, employed actual Egyptian village tunes. *The New Pharaohs Suite* created a sonic link between ancient and modern times, providing a setting in which ancient Egypt was reborn.[32]

For a preperformance party at the museum, a replica of Akhenaton's tomb was built,[33] and El-Dabh dressed his dancers and musicians in pharaonic garb. Guests entered into "ancient Egypt" underneath draperies and skylines with studded stars and were greeted by an exquisite display of canapés, papyruses, and flowers. El-Dabh's musicians, dubbed the Hook and Flail Orchestra, treated him as though he were a pharaoh, and the dancers placed flowers before him. The piece premiered on March 8, 1996, and El-Dabh considered it a most appropriate celebration for his seventy-fifth birthday.

Following the success of his Hook and Flail Orchestra, El-Dabh was commissioned by Jerry Freedman, the director of Cleveland's Great Lakes Theater Festival, to compose original incidental music for Shakespeare's *Antony and Cleopatra*. El-Dabh composed copious amounts of music for the work, from which Freedman selected the few pieces that he felt would best accent the play, which was presented in January and February of 1997 at Cleveland's Ohio Theater. For El-Dabh, the primary function of his music was to engage the actors. He felt it was the music's role to assist them in creating their characters by enabling them to speak the words energetically, which he believed would in turn be conveyed to the audience. David Birney,[34] who was cast in the role of Antony, later revealed to El-Dabh that his experience was exactly what El-Dabh had hoped for.[35] Annalee Jefferies,[36] as Cleopatra, informed El-Dabh that his music had made the actors feel very alive[37] during the grueling rehearsals. El-Dabh appreciated their positive feedback.

This experience was quite different from composing for a modern play or musical. In those situations, El-Dabh would follow the play carefully while combining sound and words in the modern sense. The difficulty in this work was that during the dance sequences, because dialogue was also being delivered, the sound level of the music, which was actually a taped version played back for the performance in lieu of a live orchestra, was decreased for the audience but was kept high backstage for the dancers. Otherwise, the balance would have been off in a segment such as "Bacchanal"; if the music were too loud the audience would have concentrated only on the dance and not on the dialogue.

There was a touch of contemporary thinking in this production of Shakespeare, evidenced in the manner in which the characters were dressed. The army was costumed in Desert Storm uniforms, and a general was dressed as Saddam Hussein. At one point Caesar and his ambassador, Lepidus, were attired as businessmen, while Pompey and his men were dressed as pirates. The close collaboration that characterized the production's development, El-Dabh felt, created a very special relationship among the creative designers. He believed Masha Archer,[38] the jewelry designer for the production, was capable, if allowed, of upstaging everyone with her jewelry creations. However, she made pieces that served the presentation as a whole. The individual components—the jewelry, the costumes, the music, and the words—were tied together in a truly collaborative effort. El-Dabh was thoroughly impressed with Freedman's fresh approach in directing the play.[39]

Throughout the spring and summer of 1996 El-Dabh took advantage of several opportunities to compose new works for young musicians. "Multicolored Sonata" (1996), for two trumpets, was composed under the auspices of the Cleveland Composers Guild. Asked if he would be interested in participating in an upcoming program in which composers would write music especially for young performers, El-Dabh enthusiastically agreed. The pairings were done by chance; two ten-year-old boys, Davis McKinney and Brian Kleve, who studied trumpet with Dale Kleve at the Cleveland Music School Settlement, drew El-Dabh's name, and he composed this work for them. The boys enjoyed the titles of the three movements: "Red," "Blue," "Sky," and "Purple Plus." In contrast, *The Untold* (1996), a pageant for singers and dancers, combined African song, dance, stories, and folktales. El-Dabh composed the work for his African cultural expressions class at Kent State, whose students constructed papier-mâché masks that represented the different tribes they had studied. Unlike the two talented boys who had performed "Multicolored Sonata," the students in El-Dabh's class represented a range of musical skills and talent; the majority could not read music. In an interview for the campus newspaper, El-Dabh explained, "After the creation of the experience, you are ready to express it."[40] This was what he was trying to share with his students: "The students learn a lot about their own culture in relation to the culture they already know."[41] The improvisational and participatory nature of *The Untold* is typical of the works he has written for students throughout his career.

In 1998 El-Dabh composed a fourth "book" for his seminal piano work *Mekta' in the Art of Kita'* (1955), for his friend, talented pianist and composer Felipe Hall, an American of Panamanian origin who had graduated from the Manhattan School of Music. Hall's graduate studies at the University of Michigan in piano, composition, and philosophy had led to performances at the Lincoln Center Library and the Carnegie Recital Hall. For years Hall, a staunch admirer and advocate of El-Dabh's music, had pleaded with the composer to write something for him, and El-Dabh opted to expand his successful 1955 work for his young friend. Book IV consists of only two sections, "Nawakht" and "Soufiane." Hall has actively performed these and other El-Dabh pieces in concert.

In 1999 El-Dabh was drawn back into collaborating with major talents in the realm of modern dance and choreography when he agreed to work with the Cleo Parker Robinson Dance Company in Denver, Colorado. El-Dabh had first met Robinson at her dance conference in January of that year, and she invited him to return to participate in her international summer dance institute in July. The two began speaking about a collaboration, and initially Robinson envisioned a ballet on the subject of Cleopatra. However, following a trip to Egypt in April, an enthusiastic and inspired Robinson decided that she wanted to create a piece about the power of the Egyptian women who had nurtured the great kings and were major figures in Egyptian history. The result was the thirty-minute score *In the Valley of the Nile*, which premiered in September 1999, with an ensemble including flute, clarinet, saxophone, two trumpets, piano, double bass, and percussion. There are also four singers, representing Nefertari (favorite wife of Ramesses the Great), Nefertiti (wife of Akhenaton, thought to have been a major force behind his declaration of monotheism), Hatshepsut (an eighteenth-dynasty queen who ruled as a pharaoh), and Cleopatra. When asked how difficult it was to compose the music, El-Dabh asserted, "For me it's easier to write this music than to write a letter."[42]

As the dance developed, it evolved into five major sections: "The Manifestation of Ptah" (considered the creator god of Egypt), "Prayer to Re" (the sun god), "Temple of Ramesses" (including Re, Osiris, Horus, and Thoth), "Valley of the Queens," and "Reclaiming Isis." In an article by Glenn Giffin for the *Denver Post,* El-Dabh spoke of his interpretation of Robinson's thoughts on the project:

Cleo is focusing on the aspect of queens and how they created their pharaohs. Each has a different presence. Nefertiti was at a time of transition and in the music I have the sense of transition to a new age, so I have a little jazz feeling there. I first heard jazz in the '30s in Alexandria. Cleopatra was a lush woman, very powerful, but always calling on the goddess Isis. Hatshepsut is one of the biggest sections. She was a beautiful woman and made connection to the Land of Punt in Africa and the healing herbs and spices from there. She seems to have recognized herself as an African woman.[43]

Working with Robinson and the troupe, during the creation of the work El-Dabh utilized a great deal of improvisation. "I set up rhythms of 11 beats or seven beats, and having the class interact which kind of generates an image. . . . I know when I'm writing, I feel each one [of the dancers] has a different sound and I hear that as I write the music. I conceive music almost visually. I 'see' the sound in my own mind. [The music] is formulating. I write a lot, whether I use it or not."[44] One of El-Dabh's hallmarks is his rhythmic sense; though he has admitted, "I come out with complicated rhythms, not practical. I have to pull myself back." (Track No. 17 on the companion CD.)

In 2000 El-Dabh was approached by Vietnamese-born pianist Tuyen Tonnu, who wished to perform his piano works in a recital in the Ludwig Recital Hall at Kent State University's School of Music. Tonnu, a graduate of both the Eastman School of Music and the Cleveland Institute of Music, had programmed El-Dabh's "Osmo-Symbiotic" (1952), for two pianos, in a performance for the Cleveland Composers Guild (November 7, 1999) with her former professor at the Cleveland Institute Daniel Shapiro. The performance had been well received, and Tonnu, wishing to learn more of El-Dabh's piano pieces, worked closely with the composer in an attempt to capture the proper nuances of the works in performance. Continued collaboration between El-Dabh and Tonnu led to a February 5, 2000, concert of El-Dabh's piano, chamber, and percussion music. With the assistance of graduate student David Badagnani, who wrote the program notes for the concert, Tonnu actively advertised the event, which drew a capacity crowd. In typical fashion, El-Dabh composed several new works for the event, which fit well with pieces from earlier decades. Tonnu performed *Mekta' in the Art of Kita'* (1955) and "It Is Dark and Damp on the Front" (1949). During the intermission, a portion of the recording El-Dabh had made in the Basilica San Marco during his trip to Venice in 1961 was played over loudspeakers; however, this appeared to produce confusion for many members of the audience who seemed uncertain if they should leave the hall during the intermission.

Immediately after the intermission Tonnu and Shapiro performed "Osmo-Symbiotic" (1952), which was followed by a composition composed expressly for the event, "É Certo" (2000), premiered by Ted Rounds, Kent State University percussion professor, on marimba, and his wife, Tyler Rounds, voice. According to the program notes, the work was "composed between January 31 and February 1, 2000,"[46] and although that obviously meant that El-Dabh had composed the work in a two-day period, some members of the audience mused aloud whether El-Dabh had created another day, "January 32." In his notes, Badagnani revealed that the "text, in Brazilian Portuguese, was written by the composer. . . . The contrast between the polytonal nature of the accompaniment and the tonal, diatonic lyricism of the vocal line is meant to represent the dichotomy in the song's text between the elite of society, who drink their coffee with fine sugar, and the marginalized people who 'live in the bar' drinking their cachaça (sugar cane liquor)."[47]

Next Badagnani (oboe), graduate student Jacob Murphy (violin), and Tonnu (piano) performed the trio "Thulathiya" (1955), which was followed by "Tabla-Dance" (1952) with Ted Rounds (conga, *tumbadora*, and *djembe*) and graduate student N. Scott Robinson (*riq, derabucca*, and cymbals) joining Tonnu (piano). To close the program, Rounds, performing on marimba, was joined by El-Dabh, playing a West African marimba, in the debut of "Duo for African and Contemporary Marimbas" (2000). Again quoting from the program notes, "'Duo for African and Contemporary Marimbas' was composed in February 2000. The piece represents a creative outgrowth of the composer's researches into the traditional marimbas of various African nations, which are tuned to many different scale systems. The composition represents an encounter between the sonorities of two similar, yet unique instruments, and this juxtaposition can represent a metaphor for the dynamic interplay between the traditional and the modern within contemporary African society."[48]

Those who know El-Dabh well will not be surprised to learn that the composer first handed the score of "Duo for African and Contemporary Marimbas" to the talented and unflappable Rounds moments before the performance began. The concert was an enormous success and proved to be quite a testimony to a man who had touched the lives of so many. The variety of people in the capacity crowd was impressive. Representatives of all ages and races, from all ethnic, economic, and social groups had converged in that recital hall. People who normally would never come in contact with one another had been brought together to pay tribute to and experience the music of Halim El-Dabh.

In March of 2000, just days following his seventy-ninth birthday, El-Dabh was introduced to a man named Jimi Kola (also known as Jimi Imij) at an art exhibit held at the North Water Street Gallery in Kent. Kola had in his large collection of audio recordings a 1961 release of El-Dabh's music for the pyramids, *Here History Began.* Elated to learn of the record's existence, El-Dabh agreed to meet with Kola to autograph the jacket. Kola believed the record had probably been sold as a souvenir at the gift shop near the pyramids in the 1960s. El-Dabh was amused to see his name written as "el Dabe" on the jacket, which also stated, "The music was composed by Mr. Georges Delraux [*sic*]. Two musical themes, added by Mr. Halim el Dabe, infuse the whole with a truly pharaonic tinge."[49] Hearing the recording, which brings to mind the soundtracks of such Hollywood films as *Ben Hur* and *Samson and Delilah,* was equally amusing for the composer, because although *Lamentation de Pharaon* and *Pyramide pierre jusqu'au ciel* had not been altered, none of the other pieces he had originally composed remained. Although most of the record's music had been composed by French film composer Georges Delerue, El-Dabh's joy in meeting Jimi Kola and making a new friend far outweighed his disappointment with the recording.

"Ogún: Let Him, Let Her Have the Iron" (2000), for dramatic soprano, flute, clarinet, trumpet, violin, percussion and piano, was commissioned by the Fortnightly Musical Club in Cleveland, Ohio. El-Dabh, who also wrote the poem serving as the work's text, completed the score on October 31, 2000. The score contains detailed instructions for the placement of the singer and musicians on the stage, and the singer is instructed to read the poem in a dramatic fashion before the piece begins. The impetus for the creation of the work, which examines Yoruba traditional religious beliefs, was El-Dabh's continuing interest in the transfer of Yoruba religion to the New World via the trans-Atlantic slave trade. The work is named for the warrior Ogún, the *orisha* of iron. Only the love of Oshún, the *orisha* of fresh waters, is capable of reaching inside Ogún's iron heart. In his synopsis, included in the score, El-Dabh explains that:

> Guns and everything manufactured of iron are regarded as sacred. Iron will abuse those who abuse the iron. Thus, holding a gun is a scared act not to be abused. Ogún is both creation and destruction while his body is surrounded with fire that transforms iron into steel, he has reached the gate and is the balance in the midst of all deities.[50] (Track No. 18 on the companion CD.)

Meanwhile, Tonnu had mastered nearly El-Dabh's entire output for solo piano, and in the early spring of 2000 she approached the composer with a request that he write a piano concerto for her. El-Dabh, pleased with how well Tonnu played his music, readily agreed; receiving word of a small grant from the Ohio Arts Council, El-Dabh commenced working on the score in June. Although the piano had always been his primary instrument, he had never before completed a concerto for piano. He completed the work in October, and *Surrr-Rah: Concerto for Piano and Orchestra* (2000) was premiered on November 17, 2000, for a student preview concert and then officially on November 19, 2000, at Kent State's Ludwig Recital Hall.

The concerto's Arabic title has at least three distinct meanings. In the first, the word *Surrr-Rah* refers to the human navel, which in Arabic culture is believed to be the center of the human body. In its second meaning, *Surrr-Rah* refers to a nearly imperceptible sound that is heard each morning immediately before the appearance of the sun. The third meaning, often spelled *sura* or *surah*, is one of the 114 individual segments, or chapters, of the Islamic holy book, the Qur'an. In the composer's view, the first two meanings exhibit the similarity between the solar plexus, the human body's center of gravity, and the sun, the solar system's center of gravity, around which the planets revolve. The work expresses the composer's belief in the interrelationship between humanity and the cosmos.

The concerto is in two movements. The first subtitled, "The Belly amidst the Satellites," bears the performance indication "With vigor, detachment, and engagement." The second movement, subtitled "It Is What

It Is," bears the performance indication "Lively, with ecstasy." In the program notes by David Badagnani, the composer recommends that "listeners not attempt to over analyze the music, but instead simply sit back and enjoy a new musical experience, becoming a part of the music's brilliant sound."[51] The concerto is scored for solo piano, with a large orchestra including three flutes (the third doubling piccolo), two oboes (the second doubling English horn), two clarinets, bass clarinet, alto saxophone, two bassoons, contrabassoon, four horns, three trumpets in C, three trombones, tuba, harp, strings, and four percussionists playing the following instruments: three timpani, snare drum, tenor drum, three tom-toms, bass drum, large tambourine, two suspended cymbals, crash cymbals, triangle, bell plate, mark tree, two crotales, *riq*[52] (small Arabic tambourine), *bendir* (Arabic frame drum with snares), *djembe* (Senegalese drum with tin jingles), xylophone, and marimba. Shortly thereafter, in order that the piece might receive more performances, El-Dabh prepared a second version for piano, oboe, English horn, violin, and percussion, which has been performed several times.

The excitement generated by the premiere of the piano concerto continued throughout 2001 as El-Dabh prepared to celebrate his eightieth birthday. Badagnani, a doctoral candidate in ethnomusicology, worked tirelessly to organize a series of nearly twenty concerts and other events commemorating the milestone. March 4, 2001, fell on a Sunday. A reception honoring El-Dabh's eightieth birthday was held at the North Water Street Gallery, which exhibited photographs of the composer as well as the title pages of many of his scores. The afternoon was filled with impromptu performances by several well-wishers, and El-Dabh regaled those in attendance with many stories of the colorful events of his life. The revelers did not adjourn until almost midnight, and the honored guest, who had been one of the first to arrive, was the last to leave the party.

The culminating event of El-Dabh's birthday celebration was a concert entitled *Halim El-Dabh 80th Birthday Gala Concert* held in Ludwig Recital Hall on April 17, 2001. Thirteen pieces, representative of El-Dabh's sixty-year compositional career, were programmed for the occasion, which almost seemed to be a continuation of his retirement concert ten years before. Interspersed between the musical selections were honors presented by Kappa Kappa Psi, the National Honorary Band Fraternity, and by the Department of Pan-African Studies. Several statements of congratulations from El-Dabh's famous colleagues worldwide were read as well. Although the concert lasted well over three hours, the majority of the audience

Halim and Deborah El-Dabh at the brunch prior to his receiving an Honorary
Doctorate of Music from Kent State University (2001).

remained to attend a reception, complete with two birthday cakes decorated with Egyptian symbols and designs.

Only one of the thirteen works heard on this gala concert was newly
composed. El-Dabh wrote "I Touched a Single Ray," for tenor voice and
viola (2001), for Peter Laki and Adrienne Elisha, husband and wife, who
performed it at the concert. Laki, born in Budapest, Hungary, has served
as the program annotator for the Cleveland Orchestra since 1990. Elisha
is a violinist, violist, and composer and had earned a professional studies
performance diploma in viola at the Cleveland Institute of Music. El-
Dabh says of the work, "Watching the sun come out, I had a peaceful
feeling of nostalgia for its rays. I also reflected on the Egyptian pharaoh
Akhenaton, who received the rays of the sun in his hand."[53] The piece
had been begun in January 2001, after El-Dabh learned of Peter Laki's
birthday, and he had completed it in a single afternoon.

In addition to "I Touched a Single Ray," the second work heard that
evening, the program consisted of "Sonic No. 7" (1955);[54] "Dialogue for
Double Bass and Ceramic Egyptian Drum" (1991);[55] "Tonography"[56] (1980,
revised 1984 and 1991); *Big Tooth Aspen* (1995); *A Look at Lightning*

(1961); "Ceremonial Fattening for Death and Resurrection" (1991); "Osmo-Symbiotic" (1952); "Secrets of the Sky and Earth" (1996); "Ifriqiyaat" (1954) and "Misriyaat"[57] (1954), performed by El-Dabh; and "Electronic Fanfare"[58] (1959). The program concluded with the electronic tape piece "Leiyla and the Poet" (1959), following which El-Dabh delighted the audience with an impromptu Arabic-language "rap," accompanied by several of the evening's performers.

The highlight of the year for El-Dabh occurred on May 13, 2001, when he was honored during Kent State University's afternoon commencement exercises with the presentation of an honorary degree of doctor of music. As stated in the program, El-Dabh received the award "in recognition of his contributions to the world of music and education."[59] An area had been reserved for his close friends, who earlier had been the guests of the president of Kent State University, Carol A. Cartwright, at a brunch in honor of award recipients and special graduates. El-Dabh's guests included his wife, Deborah; his colleague Terry E. Miller and his wife, Sara Stone Miller; his friend Francis Rogers and his wife, Joan Rogers; pianist Tuyen Tonnu and her husband, Phong Nguyen; and his colleague and biographer Denise Seachrist and her husband, Charlie Wentz, as well as her mother, Eloise Seachrist. During the ceremony, as soon as his degree and been conferred and he was hooded, El-Dabh startled the ever-poised and self-possessed Cartwright by approaching the podium and launching into an exuberant Yoruba chant to celebrate his joy. The audience responded with warmth and enthusiasm; however, President Cartwright appeared relieved when the ebullient composer returned to his seat.

In early August 2001 an international symposium and festival entitled *Composition in Africa and the Diaspora* was held at Churchill College of University of Cambridge in England. As announced in the symposium's program, the event was "dedicated to Professor J. H. Kwabena Nketia, Ghanaian scholar and composer and to Professor Halim El-Dabh, Egyptian composer, in celebration of their 80th birthdays."[60] The symposium commenced with an eloquent speech by Akin Euba, a Nigerian composer and Andrew W. Mellon Professor of Music at the University of Pittsburgh (and the symposium's organizer), which focused on Nketia and El-Dabh and their contributions to music. He presented the two with citations, beautifully hand-decorated with fine calligraphy, commending them for their many achievements. The moving award was followed by two keynote addresses by the respective biographers of the honored men. Denise Seachrist spoke of El-Dabh's experiences at the Columbia-Princeton

Electronic Music Center, and Euba addressed Nketia's relationship to the African avant-garde.

During the symposium and festival, Books I and II of El-Dabh's *Mekta' in the Art of Kita'* were performed by Yasser Mokhtar, an Egyptian-born pianist living in Berlin who had performed with several German orchestras. Maxine Franklin, born in Kingston, Jamaica, and an active teacher and recitalist in London, played Book III on another program. El-Dabh was very pleased with both renditions of his work; however, he was truly elated to hear violinist Roger Zahab and pianist Robert Frankenberry premiere a work he had composed expressly for them in honor of this African diaspora conference. "Rivers in Confluence," for violin and piano (2001), a work in three movements, had been composed "in the sense of a confluence of streams and rivers of American culture flowing together to meet in Cambridge and then join other rivers of the world."[61]

For El-Dabh, the climax of the symposium was meeting for the first time the twenty-five-year-old twin grandsons of his brother Bushra. When El-Dabh learned that he would be traveling to Cambridge, he contacted Bushra's son, Fatthi, who had replied that he would send his sons, Damien and Luke, who were living near London, to meet their great-uncle at the conference. The meeting was a wonderful moment for all the conference attendees to witness, and the two young men displayed a genuine pride in and affection for the famous uncle of whom they had heard so much but whom they had never had the opportunity to know. On the evening of their meeting, long after the other conference participants had retired for the night, the eighty-year-old composer sat in the bar with the young men, drinking beer, laughing, and sharing family stories. Later the twins admitted that their uncle had exhausted them. They had traveled all day to meet him in Cambridge, but although both were weary, they felt compelled to stay up with this energetic and revered member of the family, who showed no signs of fatigue.

One month following the euphoria of meeting his brother's grandsons in Cambridge, El-Dabh was anguished by the devastation that occurred in the United States on September 11, 2001. The unspeakable horror paralyzed him; he had not fully experienced such emotional turmoil since May 4, 1970. Without much conscious thought, he began composing a piece to speak to the victims of the tragedy—that is, all human beings alive on September 11, 2001. He reflected on the composition that had first brought him prominence, and once more he was convinced that "war truly does begin in the heart of mankind. . . . [I]t is dark and damp on the front." "Spiral Spirit," for *dàn bâu* (Vietnamese monochord) and piano (2001), was El-Dabh's musical reaction to the hijacked U.S. airliners' crashing into the World Trade Center's twin towers in New York City, into the Pentagon in Washington, D.C., and into a field in a rural area of Pennsylvania. He felt a personal relationship to the events of September 11. New York had been where he lived at the height of his fame. The city had always seemed alive to him; now he could think only of death. Washington was where he thrived, teaching students at Howard University and the Hawthorne School. There he had been thoroughly caught up in activities under the auspices of the Smithsonian Institution. Now he was overwhelmed with thoughts of the destruction, and he was alarmed that this horrible act had been brought about by the hatred of a Muslim religious fanatic and his followers.

"Spiral Spirit" envisions the spirits of the victims ascending to a better place, to embrace freely and unfettered in true harmony. It also represents the tenacious spirits of the rescue workers who labored tirelessly to save them. El-Dabh wrote the work for Vietnamese master musician (and husband of Tuyen Tonnu) Phong Nguyen, to perform on the *dàn bâu* while El-Dabh improvised on predetermined themes on the piano. They premiered the work on the Artists Series at Kent State University Trumbull Campus in Warren, Ohio, on October 8, 2001. Prior to the performance, El-Dabh addressed the audience, explaining his thoughts and emotions as he created this piece. While the audience sat in still silence, Tonnu lit a solitary, white pillar candle that had been placed at the foot of the stage. As the opening tones of the piece began wafting through the recital hall, she lit a single stick of sandalwood incense and quietly left the stage. The soft, peaceful, and gentle tones of the monochord calmed the audience; however, dissonant, pounding chords from the piano were jarring and harsh, unnerving the listeners. This was, of course, El-Dabh's message. The monochord represented the innocent spirits, and the piano represented the unimaginable terror. When the piece ended, the audience remained sitting silently, each person alone in individual contemplation.

Eventually, the spell was broken by appreciative applause, but the mood remained reflective throughout the reception that followed the performance. The tenor was altered only when three young female students approached El-Dabh and began speaking in Arabic. One of the young women shyly requested that he pose for a picture with them, and he was happy to comply. In the flash of the camera his countenance brightened, as did the expressions of everyone around him. The young women expressed their gratitude to the composer for writing music that spoke to them individually. They thanked him for sharing his gift during a difficult time that they, as young Arab Muslims, faced attending college classes with American Christians. They expressed their hope that El-Dabh's music could help heal the pain and create better understanding and appreciation of cultural differences.

As others joined in the conversation, it became evident that El-Dabh had touched countless lives over the years and that he would continue to do so for as long as his music is performed. As a composer and as a man, Halim El-Dabh has witnessed many changes in the music of the twentieth century, and he has embraced opportunities that have allowed him to experience the innovations personally. Always looking toward the future, he is not one to promote the legacy of his past. This is his charm; this is his genius.

El-Dabh's genius was acknowledged on a grand scale when he received an invitation from the Egyptian government to celebrate his eighty-first birthday with a series of concerts of his music at the newly reconstructed Bibliotheca Alexandrina (the famous Library of Alexandria of antiquity). The concerts featured new pieces as well as works composed throughout the span of El-Dabh's sixty-plus-year career. El-Dabh presented one concert of his pioneering electronic and electroacoustic works from the 1940s and 1950s and two concerts of his orchestral and chamber music in collaboration with the Bibliotheca Alexandrina Chamber Orchestra, under the direction of Sherif Mohie El Din the library's music director.

For the concerts a group of nine musicians—David Badagnani (oboe and English horn), Hardin Butcher (trumpet), Charles "Al" Couch (trumpet), Kent Larmee (horn), Dennis Nygren (clarinet), Tuyen Tonnu (piano), Blake Tyson (percussion), Liana Tyson (flute), and Denise Seachrist (mezzosoprano)—was invited to accompany El-Dabh to perform in collaboration with the Egyptian string orchestra. The group was also joined by Julie Grant, a news reporter and producer at WKSU-FM, an affiliate of National Public Radio based in Kent, Ohio, and Joel Jacobson, a videographer creating a DVD documentary of the trip under the auspices of the Department of Pan-African Studies.[62]

As the travel arrangements were being finalized, Badagnani located the Internet site for Egypt's *Sound and Light* show at Giza. Knowing that the group would want to experience this spectacle in the presence of El-Dabh, Badagnani contacted the Misr Company for Sound and Light that produces the performance. It was his hope that El-Dabh would be publicly recognized during the performance and that the entire entourage would have the admission fee waived. Badagnani received the following e-mail response on March 21, 2002:

Dear Mr. Badagnani,
We're sorry, the music composer of the Sound & Light show at pyramids is the famous French composer Monsieur Georges Delerue. Any way, we agree to give Dr. Halim El-Dabh and his friends (12 persons) a discount 25% to attend the English S&L show at the pyramids on Saturday, March 23 at 6:30 p.m.

Best Regards,
Misr company for Sound & Light[63]

Badagnani immediately responded with the following e-mail:

Dear Sound and Light,

Thank you for your email and for your kind offer for a discounted admission for the Saturday show. Regarding Halim El-Dabh's participation in the Sound and Light of the Pyramids: in 1960 Halim El-Dabh was ordered by Gamal-Abdel Nasser to come to Egypt to do research on pharaonic themes in various rural locations of Egypt, and then to go to France to compose music for the Sound and Light, to be performed by the French Radio and Television Orchestra. He composed a series of 8 pieces for orchestra and chorus. Georges Delerue was the conductor of this music in Paris. Later, the Egyptian government asked Delerue to compose music based on El-Dabh's music, much of which was used in the new score for Sound and Light. Unfortunately many of the pieces El-Dabh composed were not eventually used in the Sound and Light of the Pyramids.

However, you should be aware that two sections of Halim El-Dabh's ORIGINAL score, "Lamentation de Pharaon" and "Pyamide pierre jusqu'au ciel" are used, in their original versions, in your Sound and Light today! I would think that your staff would be informed both of El-Dabh's original involvement in the creation of this music, and the fact that his music is still heard in the performance each day. Since Mr. Delerue is now deceased, and Dr. El-Dabh is still alive (and the original composer of the Pyramids music), so it will be a great pleasure for him to hear these pieces at the Pyramids, along with the American musicians accompanying him. Many thanks for your email, and we look forward to seeing you in Giza.[64]

There was no further correspondence between the Misr Company and Badagnani regarding this situation.

On March 22, 2002, Halim El-Dabh left Kent, Ohio, with his contingent of musicians to begin what would prove to be a most satisfying trip to Egypt. None of the others in the group had ever traveled to the land of the pyramids, and the opportunity to perform El-Dabh's music in his place of birth was greatly appreciated by all. During the layover between the flights from Cleveland to New York and New York to Egypt, the group was amused to witness El-Dabh's venture into the duty-free store to purchase two bottles of whiskey for his nephew Fatthi, a poet, who had beseeched his uncle to arrive at the Cairo airport with a bottle of Jack Daniels and one of Jim Beam. The elder El-Dabh was happy to comply with this request.

The American musicians assumed that they had been sufficiently mentally prepared to undergo the thorough security checks at the Cairo airport of which they had been forewarned. However, the musicians and reporters were extremely anxious about the safety of their valuable instruments and equipment, which were hand inspected time and time again. And nothing could have prepared them for the hordes of people waiting to greet loved ones at the arrival gate in Cairo. The chaos generated by the mob was overwhelming, and attempting to retrieve luggage proved nearly impossible as the swell of humanity appeared as though it would never abate. El-Dabh embraced his nephew, who immediately inquired if his dear uncle had brought the prized whiskey, and soon the two were regaling each other with family stories. The rest of the entourage were shepherded through the airport by two representatives from the Wings Travel Agency, which had been retained by officials from the Alexandria Library to accompany the group in Cairo. Engaged for the express purpose of providing security while escorting the special visitors to tourist areas, the representatives eagerly announced that they had made arrangements to transport the group to enjoy a performance of the whirling dervishes at the Citadel that evening. Aware that this would be the

The author and Halim El-Dabh before the Sphinx and Pyramids at Giza, Egypt (2002).

only opportunity for them to witness the *Sound and Light* show at the pyramids, there was an outcry, and the schedule was immediately altered to accommodate the wishes of the group. Unfortunately the party arrived at the performance venue to hear the closing minutes of the English version before acquiring tickets to be seated for the following performance, which was in Spanish. Regardless, it was truly memorable to witness the show with the composer, and El-Dabh beamed with pride as he heard his music broadcast over the immense sound system.

The following morning was devoted to touring the acclaimed Egyptian Museum of Cairo, which houses much of the famous treasure of King Tutankhamen. Plans to visit the Cairo Opera House for a performance of traditional Egyptian music were thwarted when security closed the site due to the arrival of Suzanne Mubarak, wife of Egyptian President Hosni Mubarak, and her large entourage. El-Dabh, who was preparing to address a group of Egyptian composers at a symposium in his honor under the auspices of the International Music Council of UNESCO and the Egyptian ministers of high culture later that evening, was amused that his plans had been altered by the presence of Mrs. Mubarak. However, his traveling companions were less than enthusiastic about the change of plans. The mood brightened considerably at the symposium as

El-Dabh received a most impressive plaque from Samha El-Kholy[65] and Rageh Daoud,[66] who bestowed many accolades and acknowledged El-Dabh as Egypt's greatest living composer.

The following day the group was to travel to Alexandria, and the very full day began with an excursion back to the site of the pyramids at Giza to appreciate and photograph their majesty by daylight. The giant head of the Sphinx first greeted the tourists, who were amused when Al Couch and Hardin Butcher posed with their trumpets before the mammoth lion as an homage to Louis Armstrong,[67] who had struck a similar pose as he serenaded his wife, Lucille, in 1961. For many in the group it was easy to appreciate the words of Dominique Vivant Denon, who wrote, "With a monument like this, there can be no doubt that art was at a high level of perfection."[68]

The opportunity to enter the great burial chamber of the pyramid of Khafre[69] was eagerly seized by all the members of the group; however, none was truly prepared for the arduous trek into the center of the pyramid. The eighty-one-year-old El-Dabh appeared energized by the experience, so none of his much younger comrades had the nerve to complain of the physical challenge they encountered. Although many secretly admitted to one another of sore muscles for days following the pyramid climb, several in the group were not certain if the aches and pains were truly a result of the climb into the pyramid or from the inability to fend off the persistent camel-ride touters (which rendered some of the most prized photographs from the trip).

The two-hour bus trip to Alexandria along the Desert Highway provided an opportunity for El-Dabh's musicians to rest following their visit to the pyramids, and the journey was uneventful until the bus stopped for a break at a roadside rest area. As the journey recommenced, the Americans became aware of the armed military escort accompanying the bus. It was revealed that during the rest stop the bus driver and tour guide had been asked the nationality of the occupants; upon learning that the bus contained American citizens, the guards viewed the group as a possible target for a hostage situation and insisted on the escort. El-Dabh conveyed a calm demeanor, but most of the others did not return to sleeping for the remainder of the bus trip.

When El-Dabh and the musicians first arrived in Alexandria, nicknamed the Bride of the Sea by the Egyptians, they were escorted to the famed library where they were met by Sherif Mohie El Din, the library's music director, who greeted El-Dabh warmly and deliberately introduced himself to each member of the party. Small in stature but possessing a quick and bright smile, Mohie El Din excused himself and soon returned with Ismail Serageldin, the library's first director general. The tri-lingual Serageldin (Arabic, French, and English), who earned a Ph.D. from Harvard University, was a most affable man who exuded obvious pride in the structure under his charge as he welcomed El-Dabh and his colleagues to the library.

The Bibliotheca Alexandrina, as recently reconstructed, is located on a magnificent site in the Eastern Harbor facing the sea on the north and Alexandria University complex on the south. It overlooks the Silsilah Peninsula and is very close to the location of the Old Library in the Ancient Royal Quarter.[70] Rebuilt with the assistance of UNESCO funds, the structure is a 200-million-dollar, state-of-the-art, eleven-story library, complete with planetarium and concert hall designed by Snøhetta, a Norwegian architectural firm. The design concept is a simple disc inclined toward the sea, partly submerged in a pool of water: symbolically the image of the Egyptian sun illuminating the world and human civilization. The disc deliberately was not made a complete circle, which represents the concept that knowledge is never complete. Moreover the inclined roof allows indirect daylight and a clear view of the sea. The building is surrounded by a wall of Aswan granite engraved with calligraphic letters and representative inscriptions from the writing systems of the world's civilizations. It is anticipated that the library, projected to house up to four million volumes, will become the most important storehouse of knowledge, as it had been in ancient times, for North Africa and the Arabic world as a whole. At its zenith the ancient library attracted intellectuals, scholars, and scientists such as Aristarchus, the first to proclaim that the earth revolves around the sun; Hipparchus, the first to measure the solar year within a six-and-a-half-minute accuracy; Eratosthenes, the first to measure the circumference of the earth; Euclid, who wrote the elements of geometry; Archimedes, the greatest mathematician of the ancient world; and Callimachus, a poet, the first to write a catalogue for books classified by topic and author, thereby becoming the father of library science.[71]

For three days the American musicians rehearsed on their own and together with the Bibliotheca Alexandrina String Orchestra, and despite unforeseen difficulties with the rehearsal space, insufficient chairs and music stands, and a piano that would not maintain its tuning, the experience was musically very fulfilling for everyone involved. El-Dabh, who was regularly engaged in interviews for all facets of media, generally maintained a positive attitude. However, one afternoon when several thousand students blocked the entrance to the library protesting the Israeli occupation of Yasser Arafat's compound, El-Dabh, observing hundreds of police donning full riot gear and assuming formation behind their shields, was reminded of the awful scene he had witnessed at Kent State University over thirty years before and briefly worried that the performance might not take place.[72] It was fortunately not the case.

The first concert featured a new work for string orchestra entitled *The Reappearance of the Lotus Flower* (2002), composed specifically for the occasion of the library's inauguration and dedicated to the Bibliotheca Alexandrina String Orchestra on the occasion of its inaugural performance. For the Egyptians, the lotus flower symbolizes rebirth or a reawakening, and the three movements: "Facing the Ocean Waves," "Stars under the Sea," and "The Lotus Flower" were well received at the premiere, which was broadcast live before an appreciative audience of thirty print, radio, and television reporters. (Track No. 20 on the companion CD.) The piece was heard again later that evening (March 29, 2002) at a concert of El-Dabh's orchestral and chamber works that featured: "It Is Dark and Damp on the Front" (1949); *A Look at Lightning* (1961); "Fantasia-Tahmeel" (1958); "Ogún: Let Him, Let Her Have the Iron" (2000); "Trois thèmes pharaoniques" and "Prière au Sphynx" from *Music of the Pyramids* (1960); and "Baladi—Egypt" from *Harmonies of the Spheres: Ten Nations Rejoice* (1991). The American musicians, accustomed to concerts beginning precisely on time, were not used to what they perceived to be a disregard for punctually and an overly casual approach to organizational matters. This was not, however, reflective of the talent and musicianship exhibited by the Egyptian musicians; in fact the American musicians were impressed by the Bibliotheca Alexandrina String Orchestra and were especially excited by the talented young violinist Ahmed Fahmi. However, they found it unnerving that the 8:00 P.M. concert did not start until twenty-five minutes after the hour. The performance also was lengthier than expected because El-Dabh and Mohie El Din were descended on by photographers and interviewers during the intermission.

The second concert (March 30, 2002) also featured works by other leading Egyptian composers. Pieces by Gamal Abdel Rahim, Ahmed El Henawy, Rageh Daoud, Mauna Ghoneim, Khaled Shokry, Ali Osman, Mohammed Saad, and Randa Abd El Bar were programmed for the concert, and El-Dabh's "Processional Invocation to Ptah" from *In the Valley of the Nile* (1999) was the final number performed that evening. El Bar, a former student of El-Dabh's at Kent State University, performed her piano piece, "Back to Alexandria," which she had composed and dedicated to her teacher for this occasion. The genuine affection the two shared for each other was most evident, and El Bar graciously opened her home to her mentor and his entire entourage, serving them succulent traditional foods and providing rehearsal space when necessary.

The final concert (March 31, 2002) was designated a concert of El-Dabh's electronic, electroacoustic, and acoustic compositions. The program consisted of "Venice" (1961); "Electronic Fanfare" (1959, composed with Otto Luening); "Element, Being, and Primeval," (1959); "Tonography" (1980/91); "Sonic No. 7" (1955); "Thulathiya" (1954); "Wire Recorder Piece" (1944); *Big Tooth Aspen* (1995); "Leiyla and the Poet" (1959); and "Monotone, Bitone, and Polytone" (1952). The concert, as with the previous ones, was extremely well received, and it appeared that the appreciative audience might never allow El-Dabh to return to the United States. The ovation was thunderous and continuous, but eventually Mohie El Din was able to shepherd the venerated composer and the Americans for a celebratory farewell dinner at a nearby restaurant acclaimed for its Italian and French cuisines.

During the bus ride to Heliopolis the next morning, accounts of various sightseeing experiences were shared with one another. Time had been set aside for the Americans as a group to tour Alexandria's famed archaeological museum with its Greco-Roman exhibits revealing much of the Alexandrian culture and the second-century Roman amphitheater in white and gray marble at Kom ed-Dik. However, some had ventured off individually to view the massive Citadel of Qaitbey, now a naval museum, which was built on the ruins of what was considered one of the Seven Wonders of the World, the lighthouse by Sostratus of Cnydus; the tombs and catacombs of Kom el-Shuqafa; the pink granite column of Pompey, also known as Pompey's Pillar; and the beautiful gardens and palace at Montazah.

Arrangements had been made for the group to have lunch at the exclusive Heliopolis Athletic Club as guests of Laila Lababidy and Hamed Ammar, parents of Nawal Ammar, associate dean of arts and sciences and associate professor of justice studies at Kent State University. Lababidy, who serves as a member of the Board for the Alliance for Arab Women, and her husband, who had been a regional advisor with the United Nations Economic and Social Commission of Western Asia and who is currently a professor of education at Ain-Shams University in Cairo, proved to be most gracious and charming hosts. They genuinely enjoyed meeting their daughter's colleagues, and during the bountiful meal, El-Dabh and Ammar, who had not previously met, were delighted to learn that their birthdays were only weeks apart and became so engrossed in conversation that they seemed to forget the others seated around the table.

Following the luncheon, the group was transported to a luxurious five-star hotel to rest and relax for three hours before heading to the Cairo airport and the twelve-hour flight back to the United States. During the check-in at the airport, it was discovered that only Blake and Liana Tyson, Denny Nygren, and Denise Seachrist had confirmed seats on the plane; the others would have to wait until the next flight out twenty-four hours later. For the first time during the trip El-Dabh appeared gravely concerned, and his tension was palpable; his relief, however, was undeniable when the representative from the Wings Travel Agency was able to sort out the confusion, assuring everyone a seat aboard the airplane.

The group returned to the United States on April 2, 2002. For the next few days El-Dabh was energized, and he entertained his family and friends with tales of his triumphal reception in his birthplace. His euphoria was disrupted when he received word that his former wife had died on March 30, while El-Dabh was celebrating in Egypt. On April 5 the Kent, Ohio, newspaper ran Mary's obituary, "Mary El-Dabh, 79, Former Kentite Dies in N.C." Although the article neglected to list Mary's cause of death, it did reveal that "she and her family [had] traveled throughout the world and spent time living in Egypt, Africa, and Europe studying and learning from other cultures."[73] The account named her two daughters, three sisters, and grandchildren as survivors; however, no mention was made of her former husband, who ironically had begun work on his most recent project, the large-scale opera-theater piece, *Blue Sky Transmission: A Tibetan Book of the Dead* (2002), which was commissioned by the Cleveland Public Theater.

Postscript

In the preface to this work, I asserted that because El-Dabh has never been prone to self-promotion, it is easy to understand why throughout his life many of his closest associates and faculty colleagues have not always seemed to appreciate fully the treasure they had among them. However, I do not believe, nor do I wish to suggest, that they should be criticized for this presumed lack of awareness, recognition, and respect. Although major music reference sources have acknowledged El-Dabh's success in and relevance to twentieth-century musical composition, his name is omitted from virtually all past and current general music history and literature textbooks for music majors and nonmusic majors alike. The vast majority of undergraduate music students have not heard his music nor do they know his name. Even students within the very institution of which he has been a prominent fixture for more than thirty years learn nothing of his achievements as they do of his contemporaries.

What is the explanation? Why did his career burn like a shooting star—shining ever so brightly, giving the awed spectator a moment of surprise that just as quickly disappears from sight, fading to a pleasant memory? Why was so prominent a figure in the New York City scene of the 1950s unmentioned in the autobiography of one of the world's most acclaimed choreographers, with whom he collaborated so successfully?[1] Why did electronic music pioneer Otto Luening, in his autobiography, mention the young Egyptian only as part of a list of young composers from various countries working at the Columbia-Princeton Electronic Music Center? Why did he not expand upon El-Dabh as someone with whom he collaborated?[2]

This biography chronicles the life of a man devoted to music for most of the twentieth century. Close relationships with famous composers, choreographers, and celebrities fill the work. The book details the life of an extraordinary man, living in extraordinary times, facing extraordinary circumstances, and yet the question remains—what is the lasting significance of this man, this composer whose music has been heard daily at the Great Pyramids of Giza for the past forty years?

There are a great many other questions as well, but the answers must remain speculation and educated guesses. This work has been written while the subject is still very much alive and active; the sense of perspective necessary for assessing El-Dabh's place in the history of twentieth-century musical composition is not yet available. The musical world of Halim El-Dabh presents a great paradox, and often the contradictions, incongruities, and inconsistencies cannot be fully explained, but that does not negate the importance and value of making such an attempt. I believe the paradox is vital to understanding the essence of the man and his music. As will be argued, the very ironies of the circumstances of his life have impelled El-Dabh's creative output.

Why do so many people, regardless of race, class, gender, and age, clamor to attend a retrospective concert of his works? Why is his name so well known in some circles but conspicuously absent from others? Why did he disappear from the contemporary music scene just because he had left New York City at the height of his fame? The names of others who left the glamour and fervor of New York appear notwithstanding in all the standard textbooks of music history and appreciation devoted to musical composition in the twentieth century. George Crumb[3] left the New York scene, and yet his music is always mentioned. Charles Ives,[4] who spent his life as an insurance salesman in Connecticut and did not compose a single work in the last thirty years of his life, is widely mentioned. Where is El-Dabh?

Another dilemma encountered in the attempt to place El-Dabh in context is the challenge of formulating a priori theories to explain his compositional style. I have previously described this style as "blending elements of Egyptian music with the contrapuntal and harmonic devices of the West,"[5] a quality that may also be ascribed to the work of El-Dabh's recently deceased colleague Alan Hovhaness (substituting Armenian for Egyptian music). Of Hovhaness's style, Richard Kostelanetz wrote in a 1978 article for the *New York Times*, "Essentially he [Hovhaness] is a consummate melodist who uses the modal scales and instrumental textures of Eastern music within a framework of Western counterpoint and structure."[6] While in terms of melody Kostelanetz could just as well have been describing El-Dabh's style, the statement does not accurately describe El-Dabh's harmonic conception. Whereas Hovhaness generally augments his melodies with fairly traditional chordal progressions, El-Dabh prefers to interweave melodic lines without regard to the vertical harmonic structure, often producing dissonant clashes, or "frictions" (which he terms heteroharmony"). Further, El-Dabh's music is also noted for its rhythmic complexity, use of unusual percussive techniques, and inclusion of instruments from other cultures. Kostelanetz continued, "Though tonal music as such is scarcely unfamiliar, he [Hovhaness] has nonetheless created a musical style that is instantly recognizable, largely because of its synthesis of Oriental and Occidental characteristics. Among American tonal composers, only Aaron Copland has created so much uniquely identifiable music."[7]

How interesting it is that Copland had such a major impact on El-Dabh's early musical expressions in the United States, and that Copland remained a loyal and staunch champion of El-Dabh's work throughout his career. What is equally interesting, however, is that El-Dabh, in my opinion, has not established a "uniquely identifiable music." This is the heart of what I believe lost him the fame that was once so very close at hand. In El-Dabh's music one may seem to hear references to Bartók, Stravinsky, and Hovhaness. However, one is stymied as to what is the quintessential El-Dabh style. The very chameleon-like qualities that one observes in El-Dabh the man, one may also discern in El-Dabh's music. The very qualities that were at first his great assets, the very essence of what opened the doors of opportunity that this young farmer had never dared to imagine in the late 1940s and early 1950s, proved to be his greatest liabilities in terms of recognition and longevity.

In explaining El-Dabh's life from both psychological and sociological perspectives, interesting correlations arise. Why is there no "instantly recognizable" style in El-Dabh's compositions? Why would one speak of "chameleon-like qualities" in both the man and his music? I believe the root of these questions lies within the fertile soil of his Egyptian homeland. El-Dabh, the youngest of nine children, was the only one of his family to be born in Cairo; growing up in the house on the Street of the Beautiful, in the heart of old Cairo, had a major influence on this man who first experienced the world through the eyes of the Orange Man, the puppeteers, his mother, and his older siblings.

This is the child who at the tender age of four attended a nearby school and began speaking Hebrew; this is the young boy who later studied at the Jesuit school Khouranfish and learned to speak French; and this is the young man who worshiped with all his friends, regardless of their religious beliefs. El-Dabh is a man who embraced all sides of his heritage, all sides of his personality; he soaked in his experiences like a sponge. When one contemplates El-Dabh's native Egypt, one immediately notes the myriad elements that make that wonderfully eclectic country as historically rich and colorful as it is. Be it the wonders of ancient Egypt—gods, goddesses, or pharaohs and their queens—or the political and economic events of the 1940s throughout the Arab world, it is evident that these forces had an impact on the composer. El-Dabh came of age during a time when "the potency of Turkey and things Turkish waned in Egypt—for instance, as the wealthy began to vacation in Europe rather than on the Bosphorus, and as economic and political power began to pass from the hands of the Turkish elite into those of native Egyptians."[8] El-Dabh's life changed when he won the opportunity to travel to the United States on his first Fulbright in 1950, just two years shy of the Egyptian revolution of 1952, which resulted in the Egyptian leader being addressed as "president" rather than "king."

I would argue that most Americans do not fully appreciate, if they are aware of it at all, Egypt's contribution to the modern world. In my undergraduate world music survey course I have asked students about their experiences outside the United States, and often in recent years an eager student has proudly reported traveling to the Middle East during the Desert Storm conflict. However, I am disheartened when the student invariably speaks of Cairo as being in the "heart of the Middle East." One certainly cannot deny the Arabic influences on the land, and one cannot quibble with the fact that Africa is most often discussed in terms of sub-Saharan countries. However, Cairo, this metropolitan delight, this mecca of diversity, this model for longevity and historical pride, creates a cultural paradox.

One is instantly aware of the conflict within which El-Dabh was reared, and I remember the cautionary words of Stephen Blum: "We have good reason to be suspicious of those who claim that a culture 'speaks' through a single voice."[9] How often we pigeonhole composers, cultures, and historical eras for pedagogical purposes. How much easier it is for educators to focus on the big picture and to dismiss the myriad individual small details that constitute a style. Certainly it is much easier for educators to argue that students need to understand the precise dates of stylistic periods or to equate Impressionism with France, then compare and contrast it with Germanic Expressionism. Of course, it is easier to define something by contrasting it with some other entity that we feel we know. In simplistic terms, American students often make ethnocentric value judgments based on their own experiences and then attempt to define other ways of making meaning by referring to the other as opposite, or empirically wrong.

Cairo cannot easily be stereotyped and neither can the musical style of Halim El-Dabh. His remarkable career began in 1942 when he walked away with the first prize in the composers' competition at the Egyptian Opera House, and he began devoting more of his time to music. Five years later he captured the attention of a young prince, who, in a flashy red sports car, sped El-Dabh to his palace in Abdeen to perform his music for the royal family. The critical juncture occurred in February 1949, at the Assembly Hall of All Saints' Cathedral in Cairo, when he premiered his piano work "It Is Dark and Damp on the Front." The excitement generated by the performance brought him to the attention of the American cultural attaché, a man so impressed with El-Dabh that he himself filled out the Fulbright application form for the young man whose English skills were then not good. Despite failing the written portion of the test, El-Dabh was selected to be one of the seven chosen from over five hundred applicants. This was very special treatment.

His six-week stay at the University of Denver afforded El-Dabh the opportunity to attend the Aspen Music Festival, where by happenstance he met Igor Stravinsky and served as his personal assistant for several days. The special treatment continued when one of the cultural attaché's assistants flew from Cairo to Denver to show El-Dabh how to operate his kitchen. During his course of study at the University of New Mexico, the American Cultural Center in Cairo was greatly interested in El-Dabh's progress, and a group was sent to observe how he was developing. When El-Dabh experienced friction with a faculty member, the International Institute contacted the University of New Mexico to insist that he receive better treatment. This was very special treatment.

On hearing El-Dabh's "It Is Dark and Damp on the Front," Irving Fine offered him a scholarship to study at the Berkshire Music Center at Tanglewood, which in turn led to an extension of his Fulbright support for another year. In the Berkshires he studied with Fine, Aaron Copland, and Luigi Dallapiccola. Because the Egyptian was viewed as a rarity, Voice of America broadcast many interviews with El-Dabh and aired some of his compositions. This again was very special treatment.

Irving Fine was instrumental in arranging for El-Dabh to pursue a master's degree in music at the New England Conservatory, studying theory and composition with Francis Judd Cooke. Recognizing El-Dabh's talent, Cooke made many allowances for his prized pupil that he never would have considered for the average composition student. As El-Dabh was finishing his graduate degree at the New England Conservatory, he received an invitation to study with Nadia Boulanger at Fontainebleau; although El-Dabh knew that an opportunity to study with this influential and respected conductor and teacher was a dream come true, he became sidetracked and never took advantage of it. Fine urged El-Dabh to pursue an advanced degree at the new School of Music at Brandeis University, and although El-Dabh was interested in the offer, he had promised to stay with his mother in Egypt until December. Fine assured El-Dabh that he would hold a place for him at Brandeis until his return. This was very special treatment.

In 1956 El-Dabh was invited for six months to the MacDowell Colony, where Otto Luening and Vladimir Ussachevsky encouraged him to experiment in the electronic music studio there. Shortly thereafter, El-Dabh made a conscious decision to go to New York. Upon his arrival, El-Dabh contacted the artist Leon Polk Smith, a fellow resident at MacDowell, who threw a huge party in his honor. During the party El-Dabh met Eugene Lester, Martha Graham's musical director, who promised to arrange a meeting between the composer and the choreographer. He also met the owners of the Edward B. Mark Music Publishing Company, who offered El-Dabh the keys to their penthouse on the corner of 12th Street at Fifth Avenue and asked him to stay there while they were in Los Angeles for the next three months. This was very special treatment.

His successful collaboration with Martha Graham in the creation of *Clytemnestra* led to his being invited to Oscar Williams's apartment in the Wall Street district for a party honoring Arthur Miller and his second wife, Marilyn Monroe. At this time the United Nations Orchestra was forming, and El-Dabh was commissioned by the Contemporary Music Society to compose a work for it to be conducted by Leopold Stokowski. Because many of the composers at Columbia University, including Otto Luening, attended the performance and were impressed, El-Dabh was invited to the Columbia-Princeton Electronic Music Center, receiving both a Guggenheim award and a small grant from the university. This was very special treatment.

Following a joint concert in 1950 with Alan Hovhaness at the Living Theatre, El-Dabh secured the services of the prestigious C. F. Peters music publishing company. Excited by El-Dabh's success in New York, the United

Arab Republic's minister of culture invited the El-Dabh family to travel to Egypt to stay indefinitely as his guests. El-Dabh was given an office in the former Abdeen Palace; when he became discontented, the minister of culture found him a beautiful office in the Institute of Filmwork, where he had access to a piano, his beloved pyramids, and no telephone—as he requested. It is no wonder that El-Dabh's special treatment created jealousy among and tension with his colleagues around the office. Eventually he was chosen to write the *Music of the Pyramids* (1960) for the Sound and Light Show at Giza, and this opportunity took him to Paris to work with the Radiodiffusion Française. This was very special treatment.

Returning from his success in Egypt, El-Dabh relocated his family in New Jersey to reestablish himself in New York. Shortly he was commissioned by choreographer Jerome Robbins to compose *Yulei, the Ghost* (1960), and he also reconnected personally with Martha Graham, who commissioned him to collaborate on two new works. During this phase of his career, a chance encounter with the chief program director of the Rockefeller Foundation led to sponsorship for research in Ethiopia. Again, this was very special treatment.

The research trip to Ethiopia brought El-Dabh a two-year relationship with Haile Selassie University in Addis Ababa, where he was offered a large salary as a professor, a furnished apartment, a cook, a private car, and a Land Rover. Again, his treatment was far and away above that afforded the average colleague—and by now he was quite used to it.

It seems clear that it was when he made the conscious decision to leave New York and shifted his focus into the academic world that he truly walked away from his opportunity for great fame. It is also apparent that it was uprooting his family so frequently in such a short period of time and never consulting with his wife, which resulted in the crumbling of his marriage, although the couple stayed together for several more years before they finally divorced.

The special treatment did not cease for him in the academic realm, however. While associated with Howard University from 1966 to 1969, El-Dabh was invited by many universities to lecture and to perform, invitations that gave him opportunities to engage in creative and intellectual debate. El-Dabh was sponsored by a second Fulbright Fellowship (1967) to conduct research in French-speaking Africa. At Howard he was essentially given free rein in teaching his classes—again, allowances that the average professor is not afforded. The chair of the School of Music at Kent State University persistently courted El-Dabh, finally traveling to meet El-Dabh when it appeared that El-Dabh would not respond. In his early days at Kent State University, El-Dabh again received star treatment, which was not appreciated by his colleagues.

The shooting deaths of the four students on May 4, 1970, had a tremendous impact on El-Dabh, and I believe this changed his behavior. Events in his personal life also resulted in lost opportunities. In 1975 his collaboration with Martha Graham in *Lucifer* was not especially well received although it was a major success in terms of the celebrity trappings that surrounded it. At the time El-Dabh and his first wife were in the throes of their divorce; he did not even attend the premiere of *Lucifer.* El-Dabh's remarkable experiences continued under the sponsorship of the Smithsonian Institution from 1974 to 1981. His work as a research consultant with the Smithsonian Institution and the preparations for the U.S. bicentennial celebration made this a very fulfilling time for him; however, his personal life had disintegrated. For the first time he had no one to look after him, to coddle or spoil him. His second marriage and the birth of his son were certainly happy events, but he was changed, and his decision to settle in Kent instead of continuing the peripatetic life he had known took him from the spotlight.

Halim El-Dabh has composed a vast amount of music, and although not all has been published, he is proud that nearly all of it has been performed. For him what is most meaningful is that his music has been heard. El-Dabh has asked, "If people do not have the opportunity to experience the music, what is the point? . . . There is a constant relationship, because if the composer does not get feedback from the audience, then what does he or she get?"[10] This constant feedback, this interaction, is an important part of El-Dabh's life as a contemporary composer. The artist gives to the community, and the public gives back to the artist. Whether teaching Egyptian songs to elementary schoolchildren, collaborating with professional dance ensembles, composing for professional musicians, recounting the chronology of his life for a university colleague, imbuing young African American college students with a sense of self and purpose, taking a trip to a car show with his son, or sharing a relaxed evening with friends, El-Dabh discovers vital sources of inspiration.

For El-Dabh's entry in the *International Dictionary of Black Composers* (Fitzroy Dearborn, 1999), I wrote that "for El-Dabh, the composer/ performer/teacher cannot be separated from El-Dabh the man. All is integral to the whole."[11] All of his life experiences have gone into the creation of his music. One cannot be divorced from the other. Earlier I argued that there is no single style characterizing his music; however, one finds common threads interwoven in the tapestry. Much has been written of his penchant for large, dramatic works, and his greatest fame was linked to these creations. However, I think the enduring pieces, those that warrant the greatest attention, are his piano works. I believe the essence of El-Dabh's music is found in his creative approach to piano composition.

Whether examining "It Is Dark and Damp on the Front" (1949), the piece that without question opened the first major door for him, or analyzing "Evolution and Decadence," a piece that examined the idea of the evolution of music, one sees a fresh approach to sound sources, combinations of tones with views that have been unshackled by conventional thinking or Western chordal progressions. In "Evolution and Decadence" (1949) El-Dabh played with the idea that sounds were developed in ancient Egypt and that when these sounds reached Europe they were further developed there. His philosophy suggests that the elements that cause a tone to evolve are also the elements that make it decay. El-Dabh focuses on surprising timbres and textures. He writes intriguing melodies, coupled with interesting rhythmic energy; in his pieces there is no focus on vertical harmonies. His utilization in his compositions of sound for sound's sake is fascinating and compelling. There is an originality in his music that cannot be denied. These ideas are heard throughout the piano work "Meditation on the Nile" (1951), which depicts the mystery of the Pyramids as well as the watery timbres of the great river. El-Dabh utilizes the sonorities of his Egyptian heritage throughout his piano works. The essence of mbiras, marimbas, xylophones, harps, lyres, dulcimers, psalteries, and lutes resonates in his piano pieces.

El-Dabh's three 1954 piano works, "Arabiyaat," "Ifriqiyaat," and "Misriyaat," capture the spirit of Arabic dance rhythms, African drumming ensembles, and the harplike effects of lyres, psalteries, and lutes that are heard throughout the Nile region. These works are unique for the manner in which El-Dabh treats the piano like a large, drumlike percussion instrument, employing a barrage of tone clusters, harmonies, and sonic textures, including plucking, strumming, and slapping the strings, as well as striking the body of the piano. Hearing these works in recital, one is amazed that only a single performer is playing; I believe this is the result of how El-Dabh combines his melodic lines and uses timbres with such sensitivity to how the sonorities vibrate one with the other. El-Dabh is very skillful in creating the exact tonal shades he seeks for his expression.

One is most aware of this in his pinnacle keyboard pieces collectively known as *Mekta' in the Art of Kitá'* (1955). I have emphasized that these works are the basis of El-Dabh's compositional style. These pieces truly convey El-Dabh's emphasis on melody and rhythm while allowing a new harmony to develop from the friction around the points of unison. For the Western-trained musician, the works are appealing because they convey an Eastern sound of one linear melody superimposed on another linear melody. The resulting harmony is not conventional, but it is not too harsh or too far out of the ordinary for the Western-trained ear. El-Dabh employs the piano in different ways—utilizing superimposed chords, playing inside the piano, modifying the sound of the piano by inserting various items between the strings, and by affixing various African percussion instruments to the body of the piano. Throughout his piano compositions, he effectively expands the sonic possibilities available to him.

As a contemporary composer and as a teacher Halim El-Dabh has spent countless hours enabling others to reach heightened senses of self-awareness, teaching that insight into a particular culture may be achieved through understanding that culture's music. Whether instructing in a formal classroom setting or marching with groups of students playing musical instruments through the streets of downtown Kent,[12] he has found, in interaction with his students, energy that has sustained his vigor, a vigor that today belies his advanced years. El-Dabh asserts that:

> a culture erodes, when positive, creative concepts are not nurtured due to neglect and lack of awareness. Many fantastic cultural events happen throughout society at the grassroots level, but because they do not receive monetary and public support they are not known to others outside a limited venue. . . . [T]his is stifling to our young people. Most high school students are exposed to the arts in the manner of fast food consumption. Most marching bands are provided with canned arrangements of popular movie soundtracks and Broadway show tunes. This is the music that is marketed and circulated for them to ingest. The problem is each school produces the same commodity as the next. Each band sounds exactly the same as the others. Creativity is stifled, not for lack of talent, but because the artistry is not generated from the school itself.[13]

In El-Dabh's ideal world, the arts would be part of an integrated curriculum rather than a curricular supplement that can be eliminated at any time. El-Dabh fears that corporate management controls all aspects of the humanities now; unfortunately, business-oriented administrators of universities and other artistic institutions do not always place a high enough emphasis on culture. It is not that the managers are uncultured themselves; on the contrary, most administrators possess a great deal of erudition. However, once they congregate, they tend to think corporately and to focus primarily on monetary factors. As soon as managers begin thinking in terms of box office returns, they lose themselves and their original goals.

A case in point is El-Dabh's relationship with C. F. Peters, a company that has changed considerably over the years and that El-Dabh regards as having shifted from an intimate, personal friendship with him to a more businesslike relationship. El-Dabh was saddened to receive in June 1996 a letter from the president of C. F. Peters requesting that he not send "more material to be engraved until further notice, because we are overwhelmed with a huge backlog of material and unable to meet the demands."[14] El-Dabh understands the situation and appreciates the company's dilemma, but it was never publication of his music that drove him as a composer. It has always been the relationships that he cultivates with individuals and within communities that have stimulated his creativity. El-Dabh asserts that publishers must be made aware that great creativity continues to thrive in these small pockets of communities; sitting behind their desks, publishers are separated from that creativity. The C. F. Peters Corporation first published El-Dabh not because he sought it out but because Walter Hinrichsen happened to hear his music at a concert in 1959. Today's publishers need to be reminded that there are many such aspiring composers throughout the world who could benefit from similar encouragement.

It is my hope that this biography and its companion CD will place the musical world of Halim El-Dabh in the proper context of twentieth-century music and allow him to be recognized for his many innovations and contributions to our collective creative world. I believe Halim El-Dabh to be a genius—and genius is difficult to define. How can we expect a genius to behave as the rest of us do? How can we have the temerity to ask a genius to conform to our methods of understanding, when the genius understands the world in ways unattainable to most?

Halim El-Dabh transcends the confines that ordinary people place upon themselves. He was born into a large family, where the responsibilities faced by the older siblings were not imposed on him. By the time the ninth child comes along (and a mother is giving birth to children born

Halim El-Dabh with a West African harp-lute (2001). (Photo by Gary Harwood.)

after her eldest daughter's children have been born) the sense of perspective changes within the family. El-Dabh enjoyed a freedom that his older siblings did not; he also was bossed around by the older children—all had a vested interest in the young boy's upbringing. He was coddled, he was doted on, and yes, he was spoiled. However, this spoiling was not necessarily a negative. He had the talent and the freedom to pursue his dreams, and his life has been full of remarkable opportunities of which he took full advantage. Chance, happenstance, and good fortune have all played roles in shaping the career of Halim El-Dabh. Clearly he received special treatment, and allowances were made for him. Clearly, star treatment has been bestowed upon Halim El-Dabh all his life. He has the personality of a star, he has the charm of a celebrity, and he has the charisma of an icon, but—and this is most important—he has talent that warrants it.

I believe it is fair to say that most people would be overwhelmed by such treatment. Surprisingly El-Dabh has remained a very simple, unassuming man. Yet he does live his life in a very nonconformist way. He is used to people responding favorably to him; he expects people to make allowances for his talent. He is always courteous and polite. He would never dream of being late for an appointment or of inconveniencing anyone. However, he never could have survived the tedious rise through the academic ranks, the usual process of tenure and promotion. He never could have lived a home life that most Americans would find appropriate. He twice married American women, and he acquired American citizenship, but I do not believe he thinks of himself as an American. He has no need for such labels, and he does not categorize his music in such a restrictive manner.

Perhaps Francis Judd Cooke's words of comfort to his discouraged student provide the best insight into Halim El-Dabh's music: "Don't worry. God is sitting at your elbow. Let the others worry. You know, there are thousands of theorists who will figure it out, but it's perfect."[15] Cooke's supportive comment had a tremendous effect on El-Dabh's compositional life. I believe that someday the musical world of Halim El-Dabh will be better understood, that it will take a deservedly distinguished place in the history of twentieth-century musical composition, and that we all will be the better for it.

Music List

The Music of Halim El-Dabh

CHAMBER—SOLO INSTRUMENT

FLUTE

"To the Letter of His Name: Raymond DeMattia." Score. 1995.

GUITAR

"A Triptych to Segovia." Score. 1953. Contains three separate works: "Rhythm in Space," "Parallelism," and "Toccata."

"My Foot Jarred the Stone." Score. 1973.

"Wedding Time." Score. 1984. To be played by Shadia at Amira and Tom's wedding.

ORGAN

"March." Score. 1947.

PERCUSSION

"Diversions." Score. 1965.

"Drum-Takseem." Score. 1951.

"Secrets of the Sky and Earth." Solo marimba. Score. 1996.

"Sonic No. 7." *Sonics.* Score. 1955. New York: C. F. Peters, 1965.

"Sonic No. 10." *Sonics.* Score. 1955. New York: C. F. Peters, 1965.

PIANO

"Arabiyaat." Score. 1954.

"Berceuse Amira." Score. 1959. Also in a version for voice and piano.

"Berceuse Shadia." Score. 1955. Also in a version for voice and piano.

"Coma Dance." Score. 1950.

"Egyptian Suite Ballet." Score. 1947.

"Eulogy to Cairo's Earthquake Victims and Their Families." Score. 1992.

"Evolution and Decadence." Score. 1949.

"Fantasia-Amira." Score. 1946.

"Felucca, the Celestial Journey." Score. 1953.

"Fikra." Score. 1950.

"Ifriqiyaat." Score. 1954.

"It Is Dark and Damp on the Front." Score. 1949.

"Meditation on the Nile." Score. 1951. New York: C. F. Peters, 1951.

Mekta' in the Art of Kita.' Score. 1955. New York: C. F. Peters, 1961. Recorded: NCG 2000. Book III only.

Mekta' in the Art of Kita': "Geometrical Circles with Feelings." Score. 1998. Book IV.

"Misriyaat." Score. 1954.

"Prelude Sheroude." Score. 1946.

"Soufiane." Score. 1961.

"Spectrum No. 1: Symphonies in Sonic Vibration." Strings of the piano and drums of wood and pottery. Score. 1955. Arranged for four harps and violins. Recorded: Folkways FX-6160, 1958.

"Walking in the Neighborhood." Score. 1997?

ZHENG (21-STRING CHINESE ZITHER)

"Dragons and Floating Lilies." Score. 1991.

"Kalabsha on River Nile." Score. 1991.

ELECTRONIC MUSIC

"Diffusion of Bells." Score. 1959? Cowritten with Otto Luening. Recorded in the *Electricity* compilation. Pointless Music, 1993 (as realized by Mike Hovancsek).

"Electronic Fanfare." Tape. Score. 1959. Cowritten with Otto Luening.

"Element, Being and Primeval." Tape. Score. 1959. Version for tape and ensemble flute, oboe, clarinet, horn, two trumpets, piano, percussion, and mezzo-soprano. Score. 2002.

"Leiyla and the Poet." Tape. Score. 1959. Recorded: Columbia ML-5966.

"Meditation on White Noise." Tape. Score. 1959. Recorded: Without Fear.

"Pirouette Continuum." Tape. Score. 1974. Cowritten with George Faddoul.

"Three Time Frames." Tape. Score. 1991. Cowritten with Mike Hovancsek. Recorded on *Postal Sound Surgery.* Cassette tape. No catalog number. Pointless Music, 1992. *Paradoxes of Enlargement* CD accompanies *Bananafish Magazine* 16 (2002). Tedium House Publications.

"The Word." Tape. Score. 1959.

PERCUSSION ENSEMBLE

"Hindi-Yaat No. 1." Cymbal-bells, medium-high drums, jingles, metallic discs, woodblocks/clappers. Score. 1965. New York: C. F. Peters, 1965.

"Juxtaposition No. 1." Two timpani, xylophone, marimba. Score. 1959. New York: C. F. Peters, 1965. Recorded: Indiana University School of Music Program, 1984–85. No. 832.

"Juxtaposition No. 2." Harp, timpani, tom-tom-xylophone, marimba. Score. 1959.

"Mosaic No. 1." Piano, double traps. Score. 1965. New York: C. F. Peters, 1965.

"Music for Oriental Percussion Instruments in the Traditional and Modern Manner." Piano, percussion ensemble. Score. 1960.

"Tabla-Dance." Piano, Indian drums, cymbals. Score. 1961. New York: C. F. Peters, 1965.

"Tabla-Tahmeel No. 1." Percussion ensemble. Score. 1965.

CHAMBER—TWO OR MORE INSTRUMENTS

"Big Tooth Aspen." Flute, *derabucca*. Score. 1995.

"Ceremonial Fattening for Death and Resurrection." Bassoon ensemble. Score. 1991.

"Dialogue for Double Bass and Ceramic Egyptian Drum." *Derabucca,* double bass. Score. 1991.

"Duo for African and Contemporary Marimbas." Score. 2000.

"Egueypto-Yaat." Two trumpets, crash cymbals. Score. 1963.

"Frieze in Body Movement." Violin, harp, piano, timpani. Score. 1954. Originally titled "Impressions from Gaugin, Léger and Dali."

"Global Order for Two Tubas and Egyptian Drum." Score. 1993. Commissioned by the Delta Omicron chapter at Kent State University.

"Habeeb's Lullaby and Rebuttal." Alto saxophone, bassoon ensemble. Score. 1991.

"Homage to Muhammad Ali al-kabir." Violin, cello, piano. Score. 1946.

"Journey through the Centers of Being." Violin, percussion. Score. 1988.

"Monotone, Bitone, and Polytone." Alt: "Thumaniya" Wind sextet flute, oboe, clarinet, horn, two trumpets, percussion. Score. 1952. Rev.1985.

"Multicolored Sonata." Two trumpets. Score. 1996.

"Osmo-Symbiotic" or "Duo-Tahmeel No. 1." Two pianos. Score. 1952.

"Rivers in Confluence." Violin, piano. Score. 2001.

"Shadows on Water." *Dàn bâu* (Vietnamese monochord), piano. Score. 2000.

"Spiral Spirit." *Dàn bâu* (Vietnamese monochord), piano. Score. 2001.

String Quartet No. 1: Metamorphosis and Fugue on Egyptian Folklore. Score. 1951.

"Sweet and Prickly Pear." Violin, *derabucca.* Score. 2002.

"Theme Song: The New Renaissance." Flute, cello, piano. Score. 1991.

"Three Pharaonic Themes." Two flutes. Score. 1972.

"Thulathiya." Violin, oboe, piano. 1954. New York: C. F. Peters, 1960.

"Thumaniya." Two trumpets, percussion. Score. 1984.

"Tonography." Clarinet, bassoon, marimba/percussion. Score. 1980. Rev. "Tonography III," 1984. Rev. for solo clarinet, 1991.

STRING ORCHESTRA

Aria for Strings. Score. 1949.

Atshan Ya Sabaye. Score. 1947.

The Reappearance of the Lotus Flower. Score. 2002. Commissioned by the Bibliotheca Alexandrina.

ORCHESTRA

Afra. Score. 1965. New York: C. F. Peters. n.d. Chamber orchestra.

Bacchanalia. Excerpt from *Clytemnestra.* Score. 1958. New York: C. F. Peters, 1961.

Ballet Suite No. 2. Score. 1958.

Cleopatra. Score. 1961. Rev. 1983.

Cleo's Suite. Score. 1999. To the discovery of Cleopatra's tomb in Alexandria, Egypt. Originally the incidental music to *Antony and Cleopatra,* 1996.

Gahmela. Score. 1960.

The Legend. Score. 1952.

National Anthem for Egypt for President Naguib. Score. 1952.

New Pharaohs Suite. In twelve movements. Score. 1996. Premiere: Cleveland Art Museum in conjunction with the Ethiopian exhibit from the Louvre, 1996.

Ramesses the Great: Symphony No. 9. Score. 1987. Commissioned by the Memphis Symphony Orchestra.

Rhapsodia Egyptia-Brasileira. Score. 1985 Unfinished.

Symphony No. 1. Score. 1950.

Symphony No. 2. Score. 1951.

Symphony No. 3 of Thirty-seven Years. Score. 1953. New York: C. F. Peters, n.d. Rental. Master's thesis, Brandeis University, 1954.

"Tahmeela." Flute, oboe, clarinet, bassoon, horn, violin, and strings. Score. 1958. New York: C. F. Peters, n.d.

"Tahmeela." *Derabucca* and strings. Score. 1958.

Unity at the Crossroad. Score. 1978.

Ya Gamul Ya Nasser. Score. 1947.

CONCERTO

Bahia: Father of the Orisha. Concerto for trombone and orchestra. Score. 1986.

Concerto. Derabucca, clarinet, string orchestra. Score. 1981.

Fantasia-Tahmeel: Concerto for Derabucca and Strings. Score. 1958. New York: C. F. Peters, n.d.

Surrr-Rah: Concerto for Piano and Orchestra. Score. 2000. Also in a version for piano, oboe, English horn, violin, and percussion.

Tahmeela, Concerto Grosso. Timpani and orchestra. Score. 1986.

WIND ENSEMBLE/BAND

Conversations with Shu. Score. 1990.

Five Etudes. Score. 1989.

Harmonies of the Spheres: Ten Nations Rejoice. Score. 1991. Commissioned for Middfest International Celebration, Middletown, Ohio.

Nomadic Waves. Score. 1962. Rev. 1981. New York: C. F. Peters. Rental. Also in a version for double-wind orchestra and percussion.

Voyages. Score. 1973 Used in the film *The Journey: The Geneva Semester on the United Nations System.* Dir. Cory Lash. 1974.

Voice with Instrument(s)

"Befen, Tefen and Five More Scorpions." Messo-soprano, flute. Score. 1990.

"Born from the World." Bass, sacred drums, cymbals, jingles. Score. 1967. Commissioned by Howard University.

"É Certo." Soprano, marimba. Score. 2000.

"Go Down Moses; the Planet Earth Is the Promised Land." Soprano, baritone, piano. Score. 1991.

"Hajer." Soprano, piano. Score. 1979.

"I Touched a Single Ray." Tenor, viola. Score. 2001.

"Isis and the Seven Scorpions." Soprano, flute, harpsichord, *derabucca*. Score. 1975.

"The Jade Flute." Soprano, trumpet, piano. Score. 1989.

"Juxtaposition No. 3." Mezzo-soprano, two harps, timpani, cymbals, bells, triangle, xylophone, marimba. Score. 1959.

"Ogún: Let Him, Let Her Have the Iron." Dramatic soprano, flute, clarinet, trumpet, violin, marimba, Nigerian percussion (batá, agogo), piano. Score. 2000.

"On This Planet We Call Home." Mezzo-soprano, flute, piano. Text provided by Dr. Giovanna Jackson to fit the founding of *Beta Zeta* chapter *Phi Beta Delta*.

Partita Poly-Obligati in Song Cycle. Soprano, violin, piano. Score. 1961.

"Shadia's Song." Voice, guitar. Score. 1980. Based on the tune "Berceuse Shadia."

Choral Music

"Abongila's Love." Three drums, shakers, and chorus of boys and men. Commissioned by Girard Bank. Score. 1974.

"Kyrie for the Bishop of Ghana." SATB, African percussion, African wind instruments. Score. 1968.

"Leiyla." Mezzo-soprano, men's chorus, piano, double bass, percussion. Score. 1965.

Mass. SATB, organ, African percussion. Score. 1974.

"Palm Sunday." SATB, keyboard. Score. 1969.

"Salma Ya Salama." Score. 1979.

"Shades and Shadow." TB, drums, jingles. Score. 1965.

"Shadows in Gallinia." Score. 1947.

Dramatic Music

Antony and Cleopatra. Incidental music. Score. 1996.

The Birds. Flute, piano, synthesizer, percussion, choruses, singers, actors, dancers. Score. 1988. Commissioned by Youngstown State University.

Black Epic. Chamber opera. Score. 1968. Commissioned by Howard University.

Black Genesis. Opera. Score. 1975.

Blue Sky Transmission: A Tibetan Book of the Dead. Score. 2002.

Clytemnestra. Ballet. Score. 1958. Rev. 1983. New York: C. F. Peters, n.d. Rental. Commissioned by Martha Graham. Broadcast on the Public Broadcasting System program *Dance in America.* New York: WNET, 1979 or 1980.

Drink of Eternity. Flutes, ceramic pots, shakers, bells, narrator, dancers. Score. 1981.

The Eye of Horus. Bass, percussion. Score. 1967.

Impromptu Africaine. Singers, dancers, multimedia. Score. 1972.

In the Valley of the Nile. Ballet. Score. 1999. Commissioned by Cleo Parker Robinson.

A Look at Lightning. Ballet. Score. 1961. Commissioned by Martha Graham. Premiere: 1962.

Lucifer. Ballet. Score. 1975. Commissioned by Martha Graham.

Lucy, Come Back. Singers, dancers, drummers, multimedia. Score. 1993.

Memphis Blues, Long Gone. Pageant. Score. 1976.

Music of the Pyramids. 1960. Rev. 1983. New York: C. F. Peters, n.d. Rental. Sound and Light Music of the Pyramids of Giza. Performed daily. Contains the following: *Prière au Sphynx, Pyramide Pierre Jusqu'au ciel, Trois themes pharaoniques, Gloria Aton,* and *Lamentation de Pharaon.*

Of Gods and Men. Concert play for singers, dancers, and chamber ensemble. Score. 1972.

One More Gaudy Night. Ballet. 1961. New York: C. F. Peters, n.d. Rental. Commissioned by Martha Graham.

Opera Flies. Score. 1971. Rev. 1995. Commissioned by the Hawthorne School.

Prometheus Bound. Score. 1969. Premiere, 1969.

Ptah-mose and the Magic Spell. Opera trilogy. Score. 1972. Contents: *The Osiris Ritual; Aton, the Ankh, and the World;* and *The Twelve Hours Trip.* Commissioned by the Hawthorne School.

Saladin and the Citadel. Ballet of lights. Score. 1960. To be performed at Sound and Light Music of Cairo's ancient Citadel.

Sobek the Crocodile. Children's opera. Score. 1992. Commissioned by the city of Cleveland for the museum's Egyptian exhibit.

Theodora in Byzantium (Doxastiko). TB, soprano, orchestra. Score. 1965. Commissioned by Rallou Manou.

Unnatural Acts. Flute, clarinet, cello, violin, marimba, electronic music. Score. 1986. Commissioned by director Lou Salerni for the Porthouse Theater production.

The Untold. Pageant for singers and dancers. Score. 1996.

Wa Ka Na. Dancers-singers, voice, drums, magnetic tape. Score. 1966.

Yulei, the Ghost. Soprano, oboe, clarinet, horn, trumpet, strings. 1960. Commissioned by Jerome Robbins.

FILM SCORES

Azhar wa Ashwaq. (Roses and Thorns). Dir. Husayn Helmy. Score (lost). 1946?

The Journey: The Geneva Semester on the United Nations System. Dir. Cory Lash. Score. 1974. Consists of the jazz band compositions *Voyages.* 1973.

Annotated Discography

Recordings of Halim El-Dabh, compiled by David Badagnani

Arabic and Druse Music: Recorded in Palestine by Sam Eskin. 1956. Ethnic Folkways Library. LP. New York: Folkways Records P 480 (reissued in 1961 as FE 4480). Program notes (4 pp.) by Halim El-Dabh including English translations of the song texts.

Sounds of New Music. 1957. LP. New York: Folkways Records FX 6160. Includes the piano piece *Symphonies in Sonic Vibration* from *Spectrum No. 1*, performed by the composer. The enclosed program notes state, mistakenly, that Halim El-Dabh was born in India.

Here History Began. 1961. Two 10-inch sound discs. S.l (Cairo?): Egyptian Ministry of Culture and National Guidance (no catalog number). A document of the music and narration created to accompany the Sound and Light Spectacular at the site of the Pyramid Complex at Giza, Egypt, officially inaugurated in April 1961. The music, although originally composed by Halim El-Dabh, was added to by French film composer Georges Delerue, and it is this version, containing elements of both composers' work, that is contained on this release. (The two segments by El-Dabh include *Lamentation de Pharaon* and *Pyramide pierre jusqu'au ciel*). The music was recorded in Paris by the orchestra and chorus of the O.R.T.F. (*l'Orchestre philharmonique de la radiodiffusion française*) and conducted by Delerue. The liner notes (in English) mistakenly spell El-Dabh's name "el Dabe" and Delerue's name as "Delraux."

Columbia-Princeton Electronic Music Center. 1964. LP. New York: Columbia Masterworks ML 6566 (also ML 5966 [mono] and MS 6566 [stereo]). Includes El-Dabh's electronic opera *Leiyla and the Poet* (1959) (5:20), as well as works by Bülent Arel, Vladimir Ussachevsky, Milton Babbitt, Mario Davidovsky, and Otto Luening. The record jacket states that *Leiyla and the Poet* is for "tape-transformed voice and instruments." The back of the jacket contains one paragraph of (uncredited) notes about *Leiyla and the Poet*.

Ptah mose and the Magic Spell (Part One: *The Osiris Ritual*). 1972. LP. n.p. [Washington, D.C.]: n.p. [The Hawthorne School] [no catalog number]. Performed by students of the Hawthorne School, a private high school in Washington, D.C., for whom the work was composed. There were probably less than 200 copies of this disc made, primarily for the students and their families, and no copies exist in libraries in North America. Engineered by Curt Wittig.

Auricular Monthly Audio Magazine no. 8 *(Auricular #8).* [1991?]. Cassette. San Francisco: Auricular Records. A cassette tape from a monthly series of experimental music releases, packaged in a burlap bag with the title stamped on the outside and a booklet with information on each artist. In addition to works by other composers, the cassette contains two pieces by Halim El-Dabh, as restored by Mike Hovancsek: *Pirouette and Meditation on White Sound. (Meditation on White Sound* is mislabeled as *Meditation on a White Sound.)* Although there is no release date listed, the cassette probably came out in 1991, the year Mike Hovancsek began restoring El-Dabh's electronic work. (Also, there is a note in the booklet that states that an upcoming CD release "should be available in February of 1991.")

El Dabh [*sic*], Halim. *Xango Ka O.* 1991. Cassette. Kent, Ohio: Pointless Music [no catalog number]. Produced and recorded by Mike Hovancsek, this cassette features Halim El-Dabh's storytelling and improvisations on piano and other instruments. El-Dabh's last name is spelled without a hyphen on this release.

Crossing into the Electric Magnetic. 1992. Cassette. Kent, Ohio: Pointless Music [no catalog number]. Represents the first release of nearly all of Halim El-Dabh's pioneering electronic and electroacoustic compositions, dating from the 1940s through the 1970s. The recordings were transferred from archival reel-to-reel tapes and remastered by Mike Hovancsek.

Postal Sound Surgery. 1992. Cassette. Kent, Ohio: Pointless Music [no catalog number]. A series of experimental collaborative pieces created with Mike Hovancsek and a wide assortment of musicians. The track with Halim El-Dabh is titled "Three Time Frames" (4:12). In it, El-Dabh and Hovancsek took elements from three different periods in time and combined them. The three time periods are represented this way: 1) electronic sounds that El-Dabh recorded at the Columbia-Princeton Electronic Music Center in 1959; 2) creaking and banging sounds from a sound sculpture recorded in a New York art gallery by El-Dabh in 1974; 3) live tape manipulation of the above two elements by El-Dabh and Hovancsek at the Kent State University department of audio visual services in 1992. El-Dabh's last name is spelled without a hyphen on this release.

Autophagia. 1993. Cassette. Kent, Ohio; Columbus, Ohio: Pointless Music/Luna Bisonte Prods [no catalog number]. A collaboration between poet John M. Bennett and multiinstrumentalist Mike Hovancsek, with several other musicians on other tracks. "Autophagia 7" (5:53) features Halim El-Dabh on prepared piano. El-Dabh's last name is spelled without a hyphen on this release.

The Avant World Jazz Noise Project: An Experimental Music Compilation. 1993.

Cassette. Kent, Ohio: Pointless Music [no catalog number]. Contains Halim El-Dabh's *Frolicsome Games No. 2,* as well as works by a number of other composers and musical groups.

Electricity (an electronic music compilation produced by Mike Hovancsek). 1993. Cassette. Kent, Ohio: Pointless Music [no catalog number]. Contains *Diffusion of Bells,* by Otto Luening and Halim El-Dabh (as realized by Mike Hovancsek) (3:12), as well as electronic works by a number of other artists and groups.

Toy Vox. 1995. Cassette. Kent, Ohio: Pointless Music [no catalog number]. A compilation of experimental vocal music by various composers, compiled by Mike Hovancsek. Contains two compositions by Halim El-Dabh: *Excerpt: Tower of Babel and Venice* (1960), a field recording made at the Basilica San Marco in Venice.

IDEAMA Target Collection: CD 066. 1996. Karlsruhe, Germany: Zentrum für Kunst und Medientechnologie Karlsruhe/ZKM/Mediathek-Audiothek CD 066. This compilation (released without liner notes) includes El-Dabh's electronic opera *Leiyla and the Poet* (1961) (5:20), as well as electronic works by Harvey Sollberger, William O. Smith, Milton Babbitt, and Edgard Varèse. All works created at the Columbia-Princeton Electronic Music Center with the exception of the Varèse work, created at the Philips' Gloeilampenfabrieken. Track 1 (*Leiyla and the Poet*) is reserved for the mixed mode CD format. The recording of *Leiyla and the Poet* is the same as that released on the 1964 Columbia Masterworks LP.

Gilbertson, Nancy. *Mediterranean Magic.* 2000. CD. Moravia, New York: Nancy Cody Gilbertson NCG 2000. This compilation of piano solos by Italian, Israeli, Spanish, Egyptian, and Greek composers includes the world premiere recording of Book III of the piano suite *Mekta' in the Art of Kita'.* The performer, Wells College piano professor and Kent State University graduate Nancy Gilbertson, worked closely with Halim El-Dabh during her studies at Kent State University. The CD was recorded in Alice Barler Hall, Wells College (Aurora, New York), October 1999.

Throwing Silverware Down Stairs. 2001. CD. Kent, Ohio: Pointless Orchestra [no catalog number]. This collection includes works by Kent, Ohio, ensemble Pointless Orchestra recorded from 1994 through 2001. The one track featuring Halim El-Dabh, an improvisation entitled "206 Bones," was recorded live at Kent State University's Carl F. W. Ludwig Recital Hall in 1994. The piece features Halim El-Dabh on piano with Mike Hovancsek on slide tambura, David Badagnani on zheng, psaltery, and saw u, and Mike Foster on sampler.

Crossing into the Electric Magnetic. 2001. CD. Cleveland, Ohio: Without Fear Recordings <http://purpleman.com/withoutfear> WFR003. This reissue of the 1992 Pointless Music release of the same title with new cover art and liner notes is the first full-length CD of El-Dabh's music ever released and contains nearly all of his pioneering electronic and electroacoustic compositions dating from the 1940s through the 1970s. The recordings were transferred from archival reel-to-reel tapes and remastered by Mike Hovancsek. The CD version (73 minutes and 35 seconds) is shorter than the original cassette version (90 minutes). Some of the repetitive or damaged segments are not included on the CD version.

Paradoxes of Enlargement. 2002. CD. San Francisco: Tedium House Publications, accompanies *Bananafish* magazine 16. Includes "Three Time Frames" (1991) by Halim El-Dabh and Mike Hovancsek (4:42). The liner notes state: "Halim El-Dabh, electronics, sound sculpture, tape manipulation; Mike Hovancsek, tape manipulation, live sound mix." In this piece, El-Dabh and Hovancsek took elements from three different periods in time and combined them. The three time periods are represented this way: 1) electronic sounds that El-Dabh recorded at Columbia-Princeton in 1959; 2) creaking and banging sounds from a sound sculpture recorded in New York by El-Dabh in 1974; 3) live tape manipulation of the above two elements by El-Dabh and Hovancsek at the Kent State University department of Audio Visual Services in 1992. Mike Hovancsek writes in *Bananafish* 16 (released April 2002): "In 1991 I spent several months restoring the master tapes from Halim El-Dabh's early electronic work. When the project was nearly finished, I found that I had a number of raw components on the tape that were pretty interesting. These 'components' were scraps of sound that Halim had recorded but that he never got around to using. The scraps were interesting enough that I hated to see them filed away and forgotten. I invited Halim into the Kent State Audio Visual Department so he and I could do a 'live' tape manipulation jam session with these components. 'Three Time Frames' is the result. The piece was originally released in a different version on my own 'Postal Sound Surgery' release. The version that appears on this *Bananafish* compilation has never appeared anywhere else" (page 24).

El-Dabh, Halim. *Live at Starwood.* CD. 2002. Cleveland Heights, Ohio: The Association for Consciousness Exploration (ACE) [no catalog number]. Document of a live performance by Halim El-Dabh with the drumming and performance group Seeds of Time, two guest drummers and singers, and dancers from the Middle Eastern–Central Asian ensemble Turku. Consists of extended performances of Yoruba, Nubian, and Ethiopian traditional pieces for voices, African and Middle Eastern percussion and flutes, and dancers, each preceded by a verbal introduction. Recorded July 27, 2002, at the Association for Consciousness Exploration's Starwood Festival, Bushwood Folklore Center Pavilion, Sherman, New York. [Date and location of recording not listed in liner notes.] Available directly from the Association for Consciousness Exploration at <www.rosencomet.com> or <ace@rosencomet.com>.

Violin Music by Kent State University Composers. 2003 [forthcoming]. CD. St. Paul, Minnesota: Innova Recordings <http://innova.mn/Innova 574>. Includes "Sweet and Prickly Pear" for violin and *derabucca.* Jameson Cooper, violin, and Halim El-Dabh, *derabucca.*

Notes

1. From Childhood to Young Manhood

1. The Egyptian *mizmar* is an ancient folk oboe with a stepped conical bore, a flattened reed, which is placed completely in the mouth, and seven finger holes plus one thumbhole.

2. *Naqqarah* is Arabic for "kettledrum." In the Islamic world, they are widely used in military as well as in religious and ceremonial music. They are often symbols of royalty and are sometimes accompanied with trumpets.

3. A citadel is a fortress that commands a city and is used to control the inhabitants and for defense during attack or siege.

4. A *swazzle* is a small device that when placed in the puppeteer's mouth and properly used generates the unique sound of the puppet's voice.

5. Egyptian women had succeeded in their suffragist movement in 1912, and they were not required to cover. During the years of King Fu'ad (1868–1936), who reigned from 1922 to 1936, and King Farouk (1920–65), who reigned from 1936 until his abdication in 1952, older women would cover part of their faces in public to show that they were worthy of respect. In the villages older women would place a small covering on their faces to signify their position in society—that they were married and had children. When Mohammed Naguib (1901–84) overthrew King Farouk in a bloodless revolution that changed the government from a monarchy to a republic, Halim El-Dabh composed a work entitled the *National Anthem for Egypt for President Naguib* (1952), for full orchestra. Naguib, who was premier of Egypt from 1952 to 1953 and president from 1953 to 1954, projected a very positive, fatherly figure and was well liked by the Egyptian people, and the *National Anthem for Egypt for President Naguib* reflects the optimistic sentiments of the time.

6. Interview with El-Dabh, September 13, 1996. All such interviews are between the author and El-Dabh unless otherwise noted.

7. Ismailia is named after Ismail Pasha (1830–95) who, as viceroy and khedive of Egypt from 1863 to 1879, built the Suez Canal.

8. An *ud*, or *oud*, is a musical instrument of the Middle East and North Africa belonging to the lute family.

9. Ludwig van Beethoven (1770–1827) was a German composer who is widely recognized as one of the greatest composers in the history of Western music. His bagatelle *Albumblatt,* or *Für Elise,* is one of the best-known works for piano.

10. Béla Bartók (1881–1945) was a Hungarian composer, pianist, ethnomusicologist, and teacher. He was noted for the Hungarian flavor of his major musical works.

11. Paul Hindemith (1895–1963) was one of the principal German composers of the first half of the twentieth century. He was a leading musical theorist who sought to revitalize tonality.

12. *Berseem,* a clover of Egypt and Syria, is similar to alfalfa.

13. A *arghul* is a double folk clarinet with a cylindrical bore, composed of melody pipe and drone pipe, each with single beating reeds.

14. Giuseppe Verdi (1813–1901) was a celebrated Italian opera composer. His *Aida* remains a staple of the opera repertoire.

15. A "tone cluster" is a dissonant group of tones lying close together and produced, usually on the piano, by depressing a segment of the keyboard with the fist, forearm, or a board of specified length. The term was invented by Henry Cowell (1897–1965), who along with Charles Ives (1874–1954) and Bartók used the device extensively.

16. Virginia Danielson, *The Voice of Egypt: Umm Kulthum, Arabic Song, and Egyptian Society in the Twentieth Century* (Chicago: University of Chicago Press, 1997), 87.

17. Ibid.

18. Ibid.

19. A *shisham* is a smoking apparatus, like a *hookah* or *narghile,* in which the smoke is drawn through a container of water and cooled before reaching the mouth.

20. Gamal Abdel Nasser (1918–70) was prime minister of Egypt (1954–56), president of Egypt (1956–58), and president of the United Arab Republic (1958–70).

21. Muhammad Ali al-kabir (1769–1849) was set up by the Ottoman Turks as the pasha of Egypt in 1805. He proved to be a very strong ruler and was the father of Ismail Pasha.

22. Danielson, *The Voice of Egypt,* 166.

23. Interview, October 4, 1996.

24. Telephone conversation, June 10, 1996.

25. A. J. Patry, *La Bourse Egyptienne,* February 15, 1949, 1.

26. Dietrich Buxtehude (1637–1707) was a Danish organist and composer of church music who lived in Germany after 1668. He was one of the most esteemed and influential composers of his time.

27. Johann Sebastian Bach (1685–1750) was a German organist and composer whose contrapuntal works typify the late-Baroque style.

2. Denver, New Mexico, and Boston

1. In addition to *Amreeka,* meaning America, the westernmost point of Africa is known as *Amreeka* or *Maghreeba.* A reference to Morocco, Maghreeba (or

Maghreb) means "where the sun sets." It is the contact with Europe, where Spain and North Africa touch.

2. There used to be an area on the George Washington Bridge where pedestrians were allowed to walk. There was a kiosk-like cover on the side, and this is where Halim El-Dabh would stand.

3. Arnold Schoenberg (1874–1951), an Austrian composer who lived in the United States, was one of the most influential teachers of the twentieth century. He created a new method of composition, serialism, based on a row, or series, of twelve tones. Among his most significant pupils were Alban Berg and Anton Webern. Schoenberg's *Pierrot Lunaire* (1912, op. 21) is a work consisting of twenty-one short pieces for a narrator employing *Sprechstimme,* a use of the voice midway between speech and song, and five instrumentalists (three of whom double: flute/piccolo, clarinet/bass clarinet, violin/viola, cello, piano), on poems by Albert Giraud in a German translation by Otto Erich Hartleben.

4. Igor Stravinsky (1882–1971) was a Russian composer, later of French (1934) and U.S. (1945) citizenship. His work had a revolutionary impact on music at the time of World War I.

5. Ernst Krenek (1900–91) was an Austrian composer who later became a U.S. citizen. He was one of the prominent exponents of the serial technique of Arnold Schoenberg.

6. Alban Berg (1885–1935) was an Austrian composer who wrote in the atonal style derived from that of Schoenberg.

7. Hugh Milton Miller (1908–86) was an American-born music history professor whose two works, *An Outline—History of Music* and *Introduction to Music: A Guide to Good Listening,* were published by Barnes and Noble in 1947 and 1958, respectively.

8. John Donald Robb (1892–1989) was an American composer who was educated at Yale and Harvard. He practiced law until 1941, when he moved to Albuquerque to serve as head of the music department at the University of New Mexico until his retirement in 1957.

9. Interview, October 4, 1996.

10. American composer, teacher, and conductor, Howard Hanson (1896–1981) so disliked El-Dabh's *Symphony No. 2* that he refused to perform it. This caused great consternation, because the committee at the New England Conservatory had chosen this work for representation at the festival in Rochester. However, Hanson was adamant; he did not like the work, and he did not like El-Dabh.

11. Cole Porter (1891–1964) was an American composer and lyricist who brought sophistication to the American musical theater.

12. Irving Fine (1914–62) was an American composer, teacher, and conductor who was influenced by Stravinsky and Paul Hindemith. He taught at Harvard from 1939 to 1950 and was chairman of the Brandeis School of Creative Arts at the time of his death.

13. Aaron Copland (1900–90) was an American composer who utilized American themes in a modern style.

14. Luigi Dallapiccola (1904–75) was an Italian composer and pedagogue.

15. The Voice of America (VOA) was the radio broadcasting network of the U.S. government. Its first broadcast, in German, took place on February 24, 1942; it was intended to counter Nazi propaganda among the German people.

16. *Handshakes across the Ocean* was one of the 3,200 programs in forty languages broadcast by the Voice of America every week to promote understanding of the United States and to spread American values.

17. Klaus George Roy, "New Music by Student Composers for Symposium," *Christian Science Monitor*, March 2, 1953, 4. Roy (b. 1924) is an Austrian-born American composer, writer, and program annotator. He was a music critic for the *Christian Science Monitor* from 1950 to 1957.

18. Francis Judd Cooke (1910–95) was an American composer and teacher.

19. Harold Rogers, "Young Composers Gain a Hearing: Seven New Works Performed at New England Conservatory," *Christian Science Monitor*, December 16, 1952, 7.

20. Giovanni Pierluigi da Palestrina (1525–94) was an Italian Renaissance composer of more than 105 masses and 250 motets. He was a master of contrapuntal composition.

21. Interview, May 30, 1996.

22. A *Meistersinger* (master singer) was a member of one of the guilds, chiefly of working men, established during the fourteenth, fifteenth, and sixteenth centuries in the principal cities of Germany for the cultivation of poetry and music.

23. A troubadour was a member of a class of medieval lyric poets who flourished principally in southern France from the eleventh to thirteenth centuries, writing songs and poems of a complex metrical form in *langue d'oc*, chiefly on themes of courtly love.

24. The concerto grosso is a musical form, common in the Baroque period, in which contrasting sections are played by full orchestra and by a small group of soloists.

25. Darius Milhaud (1892–1974) was a French composer who lived in the United States beginning in 1940.

26. The first violinist was Ma Si-Hon, who later was on the music faculty at Kent State University with El-Dabh.

27. John Cage (1912–92) was an American avant-garde composer whose compositions and unorthodox ideas profoundly influenced twentieth-century music.

28. Gian Carlo Menotti (b. 1911) is an American opera composer born in Italy. His realistic operas represent a successful combination of twentieth-century dramatic situations with the traditional form of Italian opera.

29. Vincent Persichetti (1915–87) was an American composer noted for his succinct polyphonic style, forceful rhythms, and generally diatonic melodies.

30. The fermata is a musical symbol indicating that a tone or rest is to be held beyond its written value, at the discretion of the performer.

31. From the title page of *The Legend* (1952) by El-Dabh.

32. Nadia Boulanger (1887–1979) was a French conductor and one of the most influential teachers of musical composition of the twentieth century.

33. Arthur Berger (b. 1912) is an American composer, teacher, critic, and author.

He was also cofounder of *Perspectives of New Music* and edited the journal from 1962 to 1963.

34. Harold Shapero (b. 1920) is an American composer, pianist, and teacher. By 1949, Aaron Copland was including him in what he called the American Stravinsky School, along with Irving Fine.

35. Milton Babbitt (b. 1916) is an American composer who has taught at both Princeton University and at Juilliard as professor of composition. In 1959 he became one of the founders of the Columbia-Princeton Electronic Music Center.

36. Leonard Bernstein (1918–90) was an American conductor, composer, and pianist noted for his accomplishments in both classical and popular music, for his flamboyant conducting style, and for his concerts for young people.

37. Ra, also known as Re, was the sun god of Heliopolis, a universal creator once worshiped throughout Egypt. He is typically represented as a hawk-headed man bearing on his head the solar disk and the uraeus (the symbol of the sacred asp or cobra on the headdress of ancient Egyptian rulers).

38. Nut, Egyptian goddess of the sky, is sometimes shown as a cow bearing Ra on her back and the stars on her underside.

39. The article continued, "20,000 jam Public Gardens Art Festival were not satisfied in looking only at the 338 works by local Artists, for they stayed late into the night to listen to Halim El-Dabh, Egyptian composer, play a four part piano solo."

40. Martha Graham (1894–1991) was an influential American dancer, teacher, and pioneering choreographer of modern dance.

41. (Eugène Henri) Paul Gauguin (1848–1903) was one of the leading French painters of the post-Impressionist period.

42. Fernand Léger (1881–1955) was a French artist who, deeply influenced by modern industrial technology, developed "machine art."

43. Salvador Dali (1904–89) was a Spanish Surrealist painter and illustrator. He was influential for his explorations of subconscious imagery.

44. *Symphony No. 3* (1953), for full orchestra, was part of El-Dabh's master's thesis at Brandeis University. El-Dabh reworked the piece many times over the years. It was finally premiered in 1990 in Springfield, Ohio, under the title *Symphony No. 3 of Thirty-seven Years*, a reference to the time that had lapsed from its creation until its premiere. (Track No. 8 on companion CD.)

3. MASSACHUSETTS AND NEW YORK

1. Shadia El-Dabh Kirk is a banker in Chicago. Romanticizing about his beautiful, brown-eyed baby daughter, Halim El-Dabh composed "Berceuse Shadia" (1955), for solo piano. He later wrote a version of this piece for voice and piano.

2. "Thulathiya" was originally listed incorrectly in the C. F. Peters catalogue as a trio for viola, oboe, and piano.

3. Harold Rogers, *Christian Science Monitor*, November 18, 1955.

4. *Derabucca* is the Arabic name of a single-headed Egyptian drum with a ceramic body in the shape of a vase. El-Dabh had studied and performed on this instrument from an early age.

5. Harold Rogers, "New Music in Brookline," *Christian Science Monitor*, February 14, 1957, 7.

6. Eric Salzman, "Music of El-Dabh in Concert: Egyptian's Works, Others by Hovhaness Offered by Living Theatre," *New York Times*, February 17, 1959, 28.

7. Moses Asch (1905–86) founded Folkways Records in 1948. The 2,168 titles Asch released on Folkways include traditional and contemporary music from around the world. In 1987, the Smithsonian Institution acquired Folkways Records and the label's business papers and files.

8. *Sounds of New Music*, Folkways Records FX 6160, 1958 (sound recording).

9. Interview, May 30, 1996.

10. Tempered tuning is the tuning of a keyboard instrument in accordance with something other than "just," or "pure," intervals. It is especially used in equal temperament. Temperament is the modification of tuning in order to lessen dissonance, which results from the acoustical phenomenon of beats, the interference between sound waves of close frequencies. Consonance, therefore, is the absence of beats.

11. Interview, May 30, 1996.

12. Ibid.

13. Ibid.

14. Edward MacDowell (1860–1908) was an American composer and pianist.

15. Otto Luening (1900–96) was an American composer, conductor, and flutist noted for his innovative experiments in composition employing the tape recorder.

16. Vladimir Ussachevsky (1911–90) was a Russian-born American composer known for his experiments with music for the tape recorder, often combined with live sound.

17. The Columbia-Princeton Electronic Music Center was founded in 1959 by Luening, Ussachevsky, and Milton Babbitt.

18. Interview, September 27, 1996.

19. Robert A. Wilkin, "'Artists' Colony: MacDowell Idyll Revisited," *Christian Science Monitor*, September 2, 1958, 2.

20. Ibid.

21. Leon Polk Smith (b. 1906) is an American painter in the abstract style.

22. Interview, October 11, 1996.

23. Dada was a nihilistic movement of a group of artists, writers, etc., of the early twentieth century who exploited accidental and incongruous effects in their work and who programmatically challenged established canons of art, thought, morality, etc.

24. Piet Mondrian (1872–1944) was a Dutch painter who was the leading exponent of the Dutch abstract art movement known as *de Stijl*. His work exerted a profound influence on twentieth-century art, architecture, and graphic design.

25. Eugene Lester (1921–97) was an American composer and pianist who specialized in writing for and working with ballet companies, most notably Martha Graham's company and the Ballet Hispanico.

26. Wole Soyinka (b. 1934) is a Nigerian playwright, poet, novelist, and critic who received the Nobel Prize in literature in 1986.

27. Interview, October 11, 1996.

28. Ibid.

29. Mysia was an ancient country in northwest Asia Minor. A geographic rather than a political territory, it encompassed Aeolis, Troas, and the region surrounding Pergamum.

30. Howard Taubman, "Young Composers in America between 20–35: Roll-Call of Young Composers in U.S. Makes an Impressively Long List," *New York Times*, August 4, 1957, sec. 2, p. 7.

31. Marcelle Hitschmann, *Foreign Press News* 77 (April 1958).

32. Kabuki is a popular drama of Japan, developed chiefly in the seventeenth century, characterized by elaborate costuming, rhythmic dialogue, stylized acting, music, and dancing and by the performance of both male and female roles by male actors.

33. John Martin, "Dance: Miss Graham's 'Clytemnestra,'" *New York Times*, April 2, 1958, 37.

34. Martin, "Dance: Graham—'Clytemnestra': An Epic Full-Evening Work by a Modern Master," *New York Times*, April 6, 1958, sec. 2, p. 12.

35. Walter Terry, "Graham: Monumental Dance," *New York Herald Tribune*, April 6, 1958, sec. 4, p. 6.

36. Miles Kastendieck, "Martha Graham's 'Clytemnestra': Fortnight of Repertory Begins in New York," *Christian Science Monitor*, April 5, 1958, 10.

37. Geor, "Dance Review: Martha Graham Co.," *Variety*, April 9, 1958, 114.

38. "'Clytemnestra': Martha Graham's Art Effective," *New York Journal-American*, April 2, 1958, 20.

39. Y. Boehm, "'Clytemnestra' Is More Myth Than Dance," *Jerusalem Post*, September 26, 1958, 11.

40. In her autobiography, *Choros: ou ton radion—ousan ten technen (Dance Is Not Better Than Art)*, Rallou Manou (1915–87) wrote of El-Dabh and *Theodora in Byzantium*. El-Dabh's photo appears on page 126. Unfortunately, because of its complexity, *Theodora in Byzantium* has been seldom performed since its premiere.

41. Carlos Salzedo (1885–1961) was born and educated in France but emigrated to the United States as a young man. An internationally renowned performer, teacher, composer, arranger and innovator for the harp, Salzedo founded the harp department at the Curtis Institute of Music in Philadelphia.

42. A *sistrum* was called *shesheset* by the ancient Egyptians. In its basic shape it resembled the *ankh*, the symbol of life. The *sistrum* was a musical instrument, a sticklike wooden or metal object with a frame and small metal disks that rattled when the instrument was shaken by hand. It produced a soft jingling sound resembling that of a breeze blowing through papyrus reeds.

43. Isamu Noguchi (1904–88) was an American sculptor and designer. He was one of the strongest advocates of the expressive power of organic abstract shapes in twentieth-century American sculpture.

44. Oscar Williams (1900–64) was an American anthologist.

45. Arthur Miller (b. 1915) is a Pulitzer Prize–winning American playwright.

46. Marilyn Monroe (1926–62) was an American movie actress.

47. Leopold Stokowski (1882–1977) was an American orchestra conductor born in England. He was known for his flamboyant showmanship and the rich sonorities of his orchestras.

48. Henry Cowell (1887–1965) was among the most innovative American composers of the twentieth century.

49. Francis D. Perkins, "Near and Far East Music at Metropolitan Museum," *New York Herald Tribune,* December 4, 1958, 24.

50. The origin of the Japanese bamboo flute known as the *shakuhachi,* according to one theory, has been traced back as far as ancient Egypt. The instrument is presumed to have migrated through India and China before entering Japan in the sixth century.

51. An echo chamber is a room or studio with resonant walls for broadcasting or recording echoes or hollow sound effects.

52. Tape looping is a technique in which a segment of tape is played over and over in a continuous, circular manner, which produces a repetitive pattern, or ostinato.

53. Interview, January 27, 2000.

54. Interview, September 20, 1996.

55. Yuriko Kikuchi (b. 1920), known to audiences worldwide by her stage name, Yurika, has been a star dancer and award-winning choreographer. A native of San Jose, California, she spent her childhood in Japan.

56. Interview, September 20, 1996.

57. White noise is random noise with a uniform frequency spectrum over a wide range of frequencies.

58. Edgard Varèse (1883–1965) was an American composer born in France. He was an innovator in twentieth-century techniques of sound production.

59. Interview, September 20, 1996.

60. Interview, September 27, 1996.

61. Amira El-Dabh Ranney, a physical therapist with her own business in Asheville, North Carolina, has two children.

62. There is another version of this work for voice and piano.

63. Alan Hovhaness (1911–2000) was an American composer of Armenian and Scottish descent. He was notable for his eclectic choice of material from non-European traditions.

64. On Monday evenings the theater was transformed into a concert hall; the rest of the week it served as a theater.

65. Eric Salzman (b. 1933) is an American composer and critic. He studied under Luening and Ussachevsky at Columbia University and under Babbitt at Princeton. He wrote music criticism for the *New York Times* (1958–62) and the *New York Herald Tribune* (1963–64, 1965–66) and wrote several reviews of El-Dabh's compositions.

66. Salzman, "Music of El Dabh Heard in Concert: Egyptian's Works, Others by Hovhaness Offered by Living Theatre," *New York Times,* February 17, 1959, 28.

67. Walter Hinrichsen (1907–69) founded the C. F. Peters Corporation in New York in 1949. Today Peters ranks among the most prominent houses dedicated to publishing the works of contemporary American composers.

68. Salzman, "Forum Is Shared by Two Composers: Egyptian, American Offer Works at Program Given in McMillin Theatre Here," *New York Times*, January 19, 1959, 23.

4. Egypt, New York, and Ethiopia

1. Abdeen Palace, located in a district of Cairo known as El Rodah, was built by Khedive Ismail to replace the Citadel as the official government headquarters. Noted for its adornments, paintings, and large number of clocks scattered throughout its parlors and wings, most of them decorated with pure gold, Abdeen palace is considered one of the most elegant in the world.

2. From 1938 until it was disbanded in 1974, the Office de Radiodiffusion Télévision Française, under the direction of the minister of information, oversaw all aspects of French broadcasting.

3. Because he left most of his scores with his family during this stay, many of Halim El-Dabh's scores have been lost in Egypt.

4. When El-Dabh returned to the United States near the end of 1960, he composed some pieces for the New York Percussion Trio, consisting of pianist David Shapiro and percussionists Ronald Gould and Arnold Goldberg. Although these works have been lost, an extant program sponsored by the South Mountain Association of Pittsfield, Massachusetts, reveals that the group performed El-Dabh's "Music for Oriental Percussion Instruments in the Traditional and Modern Manner" (1960) on a Family Music Day concert.

5. Jerome Robbins (1918–98) was one of the most popular and imaginative American dancers and choreographers of the twentieth century.

6. Noh is a classical drama of Japan, developed chiefly in the fourteenth century, employing verse, prose, choral song, and dance in highly conventionalized formal and thematic patterns derived from religious sources and folk myths.

7. Bertram Ross, Ethel Winter, and Anita Ellis performed in the premiere of *Yulei, the Ghost* with Yuriko.

8. Walter Terry, "Dance: Martha Graham," *New York Herald Tribune*, April 26, 1960, 15.

9. John Martin, "Dance: A Greek Drama Is Retold: Graham Troupe Seen in 'Clytemnestra,'" *New York Times*, April 26, 1960, 41.

10. Terry, "Dance: Martha Graham," 15.

11. Martin, "Graham Dancers in 'Clytemnestra,'" *New York Times*, April 20, 1961, 28.

12. The title *One More Gaudy Night* was suggested by Shakespeare's lines in *Antony and Cleopatra*:

Antony: Let's have one other gaudy night.—Call to me
All my sad captains; fill our bowls; once more

Let's mock the midnight bell.
Cleopatra: It is my birthday:
I had thought to have held it poor; but, since my lord
Is Antony again, I will be Cleopatra.

13. Interview, September 27, 1996.

14. Martin, "Dance: Graham Novelties," *New York Times,* March 11, 1962. 12X.

15. Joseph Kaye, "Egyptian Writes Dance Music for Martha Graham," *Kansas City Star,* March 11, 1962. 5E.

16. Martha Graham's *Blood Memory* was published by Doubleday in 1991.

17. The term "partita" has been used at different times throughout history to refer to either a variation, piece, set of variations, suite, or other multimovement genre. The term "obbligato" refers to an independent part in concert music, ranking in importance just below the principal melody and not to be omitted.

18. Kevin Kelly, "Brink-Barker-Burton Concert at Jordan Hall," *Boston Globe,* January 20, 1962, 12.

19. "Music: 2 Premieres Feature Jordan Hall Concert," *Boston Herald,* January 20, 1962, 18B.

20. Louis Chapin, "El-Dabh Song Cycle Featured in Première," *Christian Science Monitor,* January 20, 1962.

21. Ibid.

22. Eric Salzman, "Program Is Sung by Miriam Burton: Soprano Offers Ravel, Gluck, and Spanish Folk Songs," *New York Times,* February 3, 1962, 12.

23. A copy of the note from Eleanor Roosevelt is in the possession of the author. The original note was discovered in El-Dabh's office by David Badagnani on June 12, 2002.

24. When El-Dabh left Ethiopia in July 1964, he sold the Nagra, purchased for six hundred dollars, to the Ethiopian telephone company for twelve hundred dollars. The company offered to pay more for it, because it would have taken several years to acquire such a high-caliber piece of equipment from Switzerland. This profit enabled El-Dabh to ship some of his belongings back to the United States.

25. Some of the relics of Saint Mark were finally returned to Egypt by Pope Paul VI in 1968 from the Basilica San Marco at the request of Pope Kyrillos VI.

26. The *Bambuti,* or *Mbuti,* are a group of pygmies of the Ituri Forest of the Democratic Republic of the Congo. In stature, they are the shortest pygmies in Africa. Their music is complex in rhythm and harmony, but visual art is virtually nonexistent among them. Music, dance, and mime provide means of reinforcing accepted values and form the basis of religious expression.

27. Interview, October 18, 1996.

28. Ibid.

29. A *bouzouki* is a long-necked, fretted lute of modern Greece, of Turkish origin.

30. Today Haile Selassie University is known as Addis Ababa University.

31. The *azmari* are wandering Ethiopian folk musicians who sing lengthy historical epics and strophic love songs while accompanying themselves with

mazenko (one-string fiddle) or *krar* (lyre). A historian of the people, the *azmari* fiddle player possessed a very powerful capability to praise or to condemn, much like the *jali* (griot) of West Africa.

32. The only truly Ethiopian organization El-Dabh worked with was the Institute of Ethiopian Studies, which became the recipient of some of the many field recordings he made while in Ethiopia.

33. Kassa Wolde-Mariam became Haile Selassie's son-in-law when he married Princess Seble Desta.

34. Haile Selassie I (1892–1975), emperor of Ethiopia from 1930 to 1974, sought to modernize his country. Born Tafari Mekonnen, he took the name Haile Selassie, "Might of the Trinity," when he was crowned emperor.

35. Some of the musicians later formed a group that toured all over Canada and the United States. Four years after El-Dabh left Ethiopia, while teaching at Howard University in Washington, D.C., he learned that an Ethiopian troupe would be performing in the auditorium. El-Dabh was amazed when he attended the performance and recognized his musicians. When they in turn noticed El-Dabh in the audience, they jumped from the stage and carried him throughout the auditorium as if he were a chief they wanted to repatriate to Ethiopia.

36. It took El-Dabh thirteen hours traveling in the papyrus boat to make a return trip that had taken him two hours in his fiberglass boat.

37. Lalibela is a religious and pilgrimage center in north-central Ethiopia. It was named for its most distinguished monarch, who according to tradition built the eleven monolithic churches for which the place is famous. The churches, which attract thousands of pilgrims during the major holy day celebrations, are tended by more than a thousand Coptic priests.

38. Abu Simbel is famous for a set of two temples hewn from rock near the border of Egypt and Sudan. It was constructed for the pharaoh Ramesses II, who reigned for sixty-six years during the sixteenth century BCE (Nineteenth Dynasty).

39. Interview, October 25, 1996.

5. Greece, Germany, and Washington, D.C.

1. At another of the monasteries, Halim El-Dabh was unnerved when a monk approached him and announced that El-Dabh was indeed a Monophysite. El-Dabh asked his meaning and learned that Egyptian Coptics are Monophysites, whereas Greek Orthodox monks were Diophysites. El-Dabh, who did not understand the point the monk was attempting to make, thought that perhaps the monk was insulting him. Undaunted, El-Dabh stated that he was enjoying himself eating good food and drinking good wine; therefore, the monk could say anything he wanted as far as he was concerned. Eventually El-Dabh determined that a Monophysite believes that the two natures of Jesus, the divine and the worldly, are one. In contrast, a Diophysite believes that the two natures of Jesus are separate and that one is either divine or worldly; one cannot combine the worldly with the divine.

2. Alain Daniélou (1907–94) was a French musicologist who specialized in Asian music. He published on various aspects of Indian civilization and edited

collections of discs of Asian and African music for the series *UNESCO Anthology of the Orient.*

3. El-Dabh later learned that as soon as he drove the Mercedes out of Berlin, it became worth six thousand dollars. He fleetingly toyed with the idea of entering the automobile export business.

4. Built by a wealthy Roman as a memorial to his wife in 161 C.E., Herodes Atticus was a five-thousand-seat conventional Roman theater, except that the semicircular auditorium had been hollowed out of the rock, was roofed in cedar, and had a three-story facade of arches. It is now used for the Athens Summer Festival of Music and Drama.

5. Greek composer [Michael George] Mikis Theodorakis (b. 1925), a political activist, was imprisoned and his music banned when Greece fell under right-wing rule in 1967. He was released in 1970 following worldwide appeals. During his time in Greece, El-Dabh was invited by Theodorakis to many performances at Greek amphitheaters.

6. Manos Hadjidakis (1925–94) was a Greek composer and administrator known for his film scores for many Greek and international films.

7. Henry David Thoreau (1817–1862) was an American naturalist, philosopher, and writer.

8. As in his piano pieces composed in 1954 ("Arabiyaat," "Ifrikiyaat," and "Misriyaat"), El-Dabh added *yaat*, the Arabic way of identifying something's source, to the titles of some of these percussion pieces. This suffix is also used in the title of the *Rubaiyat*, the famous epic by Persian poet and mathematician Omar Khayyám (d. 1123?), from which El-Dabh would often read before performing with his *derabucca* at both musical and literary gatherings in museum halls throughout Boston and New York. Following one such performance, a record company approached El-Dabh to read and perform the *Rubaiyat*, but as the fee El-Dabh requested was exorbitant, the project never materialized.

9. This "Leiyla" is a completely different work from the composer's similarly titled "Leiyla and the Poet."

10. In late 1959 El-Dabh became interested in writing for percussion ensembles. He composed several pieces that he called Juxtapositions, explaining that the word "juxtaposition" reflected the interchange of ideas among different instruments. "Juxtaposition No. 1" (1959), for two timpani, xylophone, and marimba, was recorded by the Indiana University School of Music Program 1984–85, no. 832. "Juxtaposition No. 2" (1959) is scored for harp, timpani, tom-tom, xylophone, and marimba. "Juxtaposition No. 3" (1959) includes voice and is written for mezzo-soprano, two harps, timpani, cymbals, bells, triangle, xylophone, and marimba.

11. Bruno Nettl (b. 1930) is an American ethnomusicologist of Czech birth. Several of his works have become basic to the study of ethnomusicology.

12. Sviatoslav Soulima Stravinsky (b. 1910) is a Russian pianist who appeared frequently with his famous father performing works for two pianos.

13. Carl P. Snyder, "New Concept in Theatre Getting Showing Here," *Gloucester Daily Times*, May 25, 1966, 1.

14. Ibid.

15. Margo Miller, "From Work in Africa Egyptian Composer Comes to Rockport," *Boston Globe*, April 16, 1966. 10.

16. Snyder, "New Concept in Theatre Getting Showing Here," 2.

17. Joan B. Cass, "Dance: New Art Form Fuses Music and Movement," *Boston Herald*, September 2, 1966, 14C.

18. Ibid.

19. Ibid.

20. The Tuareg are a nomadic, Muslim, Berber-speaking people of the western and central Sahara and Sahel.

21. The Hawthorne School was located in the Old Summer School Building, 17th and M Streets, N.W., Washington, D.C.

22. Jean Battey, "Ballet, Music Blend in Graham's 'Clytemnestra,'" *Washington Post*, February 26, 1967, G-5.

23. Ibid.

24. Henrietta Buckmaster, "Martha Graham," *Christian Science Monitor*, December 27, 1973, B7.

25. A basso profundo is a singer with a bass voice of the lowest range.

26. Guus Hoekman (1913–96) was a Dutch bass who sang most of the great bass roles, both comic and serious. He also had an extensive concert and oratorio repertory.

27. Rena Fruchter, "Glee Club of Wheelock Presents Chamber Opera," *Boston Herald Traveler*, November 9, 1967, C27.

28. Ibid.

29. Theodore Price, "'Eye of Horus' Has Wide-Open Quality," *Akron Beacon Journal*, February 27, 1971, B14.

30. Ibid.

31. Warner Lawson (1903–71), affiliated with Howard University for over thirty years, was head of Howard's choral activities and dean of the School of Music.

32. [Olu] Fela Sowande (1905–87) was a Nigerian composer who studied in Lagos and in London at Trinity College of Music and London University.

33. Amos Tutuola (1920–97) was a Nigerian writer who gained fame for his works based on Yoruba folktales.

34. Wole Soyinka, born Oluwa Akinwande Soyinka in 1934, received a Nobel Prize for literature in 1986. His *The Lion and the Jewel* was first performed in Ibadan in 1959.

35. Stokely Carmichael (1941–98), born in Trinidad and later known as Kwame Ture, was an American civil-rights leader. He was chairman of the Student Nonviolent Coordinating Committee from 1966 to 1967 and originator of the slogan "black power."

36. Negritude was a literary movement among black francophones that addressed the historical, cultural, and social heritage considered common to all blacks.

37. Leopold Sédar Senghor (1906–2001) was Senegal's president from 1960 to 1981 and one of Africa's most skilled and brilliant poets. He became the first African member of the Académie Française.

38. The Yoruba are one of the two largest ethnic groups of Nigeria. They speak

a language of the Kwa branch of the Niger-Congo family, which has an extensive literature of poetry, short stories, myths, and proverbs. Although some Yoruba are now Christians or Muslims, belief in their traditional religion continues. The traditional religion has an elaborate hierarchy of deities, which includes a supreme creator and some four hundred lesser gods and spirits, most of whom are associated with their own cults and priests.

39. Kiswahili, a Bantu language that originated as a trading language on the East African coast, is used also as a lingua franca in Tanzania, Kenya, and parts of the Democratic Republic of Congo.

40. E. Lindsey Merrill (b. 1925) was director of the School of Music at Kent State University from fall 1967 to spring 1970.

41. John Flower (b. 1921) served as dean of the College of Fine and Professional Arts at Kent State University from fall 1966 to spring 1971.

6. The Hawthorne School and Kent State University

1. This was not Halim El-Dabh's first trip to the Cleveland area, however. While a student at the University of New Mexico, he had received a cable to attend the hundredth anniversary ceremony of the YMCA, which was held in Cleveland. Because he had participated in many activities and performances at the YMCA as a young boy, and because he was already in the United States, he was selected to serve as a representative from Cairo.

2. Robert Finn, "B-W Group Is Told Music of Africa Challenges Theory," *Cleveland Plain Dealer*, February 14, 1969, 14.

3. From a publicity poster advertising the Hawthorne School's twentieth-year celebration with benefit performances of El-Dabh's *Opera Flies* on June 5 and 6, 1976, at the Baird Auditorium of the Smithsonian Institution's Natural History Building.

4. The thirteen seconds of firing by the Ohio National Guard into the crowd of Kent State University students on May 4, 1970, left four dead (Allison Krause, Jeffrey Miller, Sandra Scheuer, and William Schroeder) and nine wounded (Alan Canfora, John Cleary, Thomas Mark Grace, Dean Kahler, Joseph Lewis, Donald MacKenzie, James Dennis Russell, Robert Stamps, and Douglas Wrentmore). Kahler was left paralyzed.

5. El-Dabh always appreciated the talent and diversity of the Kent culture. He especially enjoyed the variety afforded by working with his colleagues William M. Anderson, Terry E. Miller, and Kazadi wa Mukuna, co-directors of Kent State University's Center for the Study of World Musics. Anderson is currently associate dean for research and graduate studies. He is an adjunct professor in curriculum and instruction and is professor of music with an interest in the music of India. Miller, professor of ethnomusicology, is a Southeast Asia specialist. Kazadi wa Mukuna, with doctorates in both ethnomusicology and sociology, is a specialist in African urban music and Brazilian music.

6. Donald Henahan, "Kent State Composer Threads Tragedy into Opera," *New York Times*, May 31, 1971, 10.

7. Interview, November 12, 1996.

8. See author, "Halim El-Dabh," *The International Dictionary of Black Composers*, ed. Samuel A. Floyd Jr. (Chicago: Fitzroy Dearborn, 1999).

9. Lyrics to "I Strolled in Jello" from *Opera Flies* by El-Dabh, 1970.

10. Henahan, "Kent State Composer Threads Tragedy into Opera," 10.

11. K. T. Maclay, "Bringing It All Back Home: The Diary of an Experience," *New York Herald,* May 16, 1971, sec. 2, 11.

12. Henahan, "Kent State Composer Threads Tragedy into Opera," 10.

13. Ibid.

14. Joy Billington, "Opera Tells Story of Kent State," *Washington Evening Star,* May 3, 1971, B-10.

15. Henahan, "Kent State Composer Threads Tragedy into Opera," 10.

16. Joel Taylor, "Opera by KSU Prof: 'Flies' Premieres in U. Aud.," *Daily Kent Stater,* May 7, 1971, 8.

17. Ibid.

18. Matthew B. Brady (1823?–96) was an American photographer, especially known for his photographs of President Abraham Lincoln and the Civil War.

19. Billington, "Opera Tells Story of Kent State," B-10.

20. Henahan, "Kent State Composer Threads Tragedy into Opera," 10. After the publication of Filo's photograph, Mary Ann Vecchio returned to her parents' home in Opa-Locka, Florida. She was confined to a youth institution following a barrage of abusive letters.

21. Billington, "Opera Tells Story of Kent State," B-10.

22. Wilma Salisbury, "KSU Guest Opera Woefully Unmusical," *Cleveland Plain Dealer,* May 10, 1971, 10B.

23. Ibid.

24. Ibid.

25. Ibid.

26. "Aleatoric" refers to the element of chance in the choice of indeterminate elements in a musical composition. Tones, rests, durations, rhythms, dynamics, etc., are left for the performer to realize.

27. Daniel Webster, "Two Student Pianists Make Debut," *Philadelphia Inquirer,* March 14, 1974, 5-C.

28. James Felton, "New Music Applauded by Youngster," *Philadelphia Evening Bulletin,* March 14, 1974, 40A.

29. Ibid.

30. Marsha Liston Wright, "'Abongila's Love': Brotherhood," *Philadelphia Tribune,* March 23, 1974, 8.

31. Edward Kennedy "Duke" Ellington (1899–1974) was an American jazz pianist, composer, arranger, and conductor. He was one of the founders of big-band jazz, which typified the Swing Era, and is generally considered the most important composer in the history of jazz.

32. Marian McPartland (b. 1918) is an English-born jazz pianist and composer; her birth name was Margaret Turner. Living in the United States since 1946, she has performed at many important jazz venues and has established her own record

company, Halcyon. Since 1979 she has been the host of the popular National Public Radio program, *Piano Jazz*.

33. Billy Taylor (b. 1921) is an American pianist and educator. He was house pianist at the Birdland jazz club in 1951. At the University of Massachusetts he earned a doctorate in music education (DME) in 1975; his dissertation was entitled "The History and Development of Jazz Piano: A New Perspective for Educators."

34. Rudolf Nureyev (1938–93), a Russian ballet dancer and choreographer known for his suspended leaps and fast turns, became an Austrian citizen in 1982.

35. British ballerina Margot Fonteyn (1919–91) was recognized as the outstanding ballerina of the British stage.

36. Anna Kisselgoff, "Nureyev and Fonteyn Go Modern for Graham," *New York Times*, June 15, 1975, 8D.

37. Ibid., 1D.

38. Leandro V. Locsin (1928–94) saw his work as a link between the past and the future of Filipino architecture. He built five churches, over thirty office buildings, over seventy residences, and the Cultural Center of the Philippines (a major national landmark). In his early career, he worked for the largest firm in the Philippines, Ayala and Company. In 1959, Locsin came to the United States to tour architectural sites. By the time he returned, Locsin had found the inspiration for Filipino architecture in the modern age through the combination of modern techniques and indigenous elements.

39. Fashion designer Halston (1932–90) was born Roy Halston Frowick in Des Moines, Iowa. He was chief custom milliner for Bergdorf Goodman (1959–68) before heading his own fashion house (1968–84). He dressed many socialites and entertainers in the trademark understated designs that earned him four Coty Awards.

40. Murray Schumach, "Gala and Glamour Leap for Miss Graham," *New York Times*, June 20, 1975, 22L.

41. Ibid.

42. Frances Herridge, "The Dance: Golden Tribute," *New York Post*, June 20, 1975, 19.

43. Ibid.

44. Alan M. Kriegsman, "'Lucifer': Startling Détente of Dance," *Washington Post*, June 21, 1975, C3.

45. Clive Barnes, "The Dance: Graham Gala—Fonteyn and Nureyev in 'Lucifer' Premiere," *New York Times*, June 21, 1975, 21.

46. Barnes, "Galas Are Good but Seasons Are Better," *New York Times*, June 29, 1975, 8D.

7. KENT, OHIO

1. Glenn A. Olds served as president of Kent State University from 1971 to 1977.

2. "Far-out Music: Halim Searches for Cultural Links," *Record-Courier*, November 20, 1975, 30.

3. Ibid.

4. Ibid.

5. Interview, March 6, 2000.

6. The *atumpan* talking drums of the Ashanti of Ghana are barrel-shaped, with a narrow, cylindrical, open foot at the base and are played in pairs.

7. From a Hawthorne School publicity flyer announcing the twentieth-anniversary celebration of the school in 1976.

8. Sterling Brown (1901–89) was an influential African American author, teacher, and literary critic whose poetry was rooted in black folklore and dialect.

9. Mobutu Sese Seko (1930–97) became president of Zaire when he seized power in a 1965 coup and ruled dictatorially for some thirty-two years (until 1991) before being ousted by a rebellion in 1997.

10. Henry A. Kissinger (b. 1923) became President Richard Nixon's secretary of state in 1973. He was awarded the Nobel Peace Prize in that same year for his Vietnam War negotiations.

11. Interview, November 22, 1996.

12. Ibid.

13. Ibid.

14. Following a traditional Egyptian wedding ceremony, the two families would "fight" over who was more important, the bride or the groom. While praising their respective attributes, the two groups danced with large canes and attempted to strike each other in the manner of a martial art. The only ceremony having greater importance than the marriage ceremony was the circumcision ceremony, in which the entire village was involved.

15. Letter dated February 28, 1977, to Halim El-Dabh from Fr. Mikhail E. Mikhail.

16. *Unity at the Crossroad* was later performed at Kent State University in 1986 under the direction of John Ferritto.

17. Interview, November 12, 1996.

18. Habeeb, who studied automotive technology in college, now lives in Guadalupe, Arizona, a suburb of Phoenix.

19. Interview, November 22, 1996.

20. Title page from "Tonography."

21. A *jallabiyah* is a long, loose cotton gown reaching to the ankles, worn in Arabic countries.

22. Hamza El-Din is a Sudanese composer, singer, and master of the *ud*. Originally trained as an engineer, he enrolled in the Middle Eastern School of Music and later won a fellowship to study Western classical music in Italy. He gained fame in the United States in the mid-1960s, when his music was introduced to American folk musicians Joan Baez and Bob Dylan.

23. Civil-rights activist Bernice Johnson Reagon (b. 1942) is a leading member of the African American women's vocal group Sweet Honey in the Rock, which was formed in 1973 at the Black Repertory Theater Company in Washington, D.C.

24. Interview, December 20, 1996.

25. Ravi Shankar (b. 1920) is an Indian sitarist, composer, and founder of the National Orchestra of India. He was influential in stimulating Western appreciation for Indian music.

26. Anna Kisselgoff, "The Dance: 'Clytemnestra' Revived," *New York Times*, March 9, 1984, C19.

27. Heitor Villa-Lobos (1887?–1959) was a Brazilian composer of great renown.

28. *Cachaça* is a Brazilian liquor made from sugar cane.

29. Interview, December 20, 1996.

30. Itaparica Island is one of the larger islands off the coast of Bahia, Brazil. The colonial town of Itaparica is known for its mineral water springs, with legendary rejuvenating properties.

31. The *Egungun* ancestral masqueraders are a feature of many West African religious societies. Four main types of masqueraders are identified by the roles they play: those who make sacrifice to deities, those who embody the ancestral spirits, those who placate the spirits, and those who perform principally as entertainers.

32. Interview, December 20, 1996.

33. Syncretism is the reconciliation or union of different or opposing belief systems, principles, practices, and parties.

34. Program notes for the premiere of *Bahia: Father of the Orisha* by El-Dabh, December 7, 1986, Carl F. W. Ludwig Recital Hall, Kent State University; John Ferritto, conductor.

35. *Umbanda,* practiced in urban areas such as Rio de Janeiro and São Paulo, is considered to be more sophisticated than *candomblé* and reflects Hindu and Buddhist influence. Its appeal has spread to the white middle class.

36. David Henry Hwang (b. 1957) is an American playwright of Chinese immigrant parents. In 1978 he had already written his first play, *FOB (Fresh Off the Boat)*, which won the 1981 Obie Award as the best new play of the season when Joseph Papp brought it to off-Broadway in New York.

37. Leonard Burkat, program notes for the May 1, 1987, premiere of *Ramesses the Great: Symphony No. 9* (1987) by El-Dabh, commissioned by the Memphis Symphony Orchestra, Alan Balter, conductor.

38. Ibid.

39. The *maqam*, a system of tonal and compositional structure dating back to seventh-century Islamic musical practice, is similar in some ways to scale or modal systems in Western music or to the ragas of India. The *maqam* system influenced a broad range of art music in North Africa, the Middle East, Asia Minor, Central Asia, and Eastern Europe.

40. Interview, December 20, 1996.

41. Kisselgoff, "Dance: A Classic by Graham," *New York Times*, October, 17, 1987, 12.

42. Ibid.

43. Ibid.

44. Musical Instrument Digital Interface (MIDI) is a standard protocol of communication between electronic musical instruments and computers.

45. T'ai Chi Ch'uan is a Chinese system of physical exercises designed for self-defense and meditation.

46. Robert Finn, "A Seldom-Heard but Pleasing Mix," *Cleveland Plain Dealer*, March 6, 1990, 7D.

47. Ibid.

48. Ibid.

49. Klaus George Roy (b. 1924) in 1953 wrote about El-Dabh and his music for the *Christian Science Monitor*. From 1958 to 1988 he served as program annotator for the Cleveland Orchestra, during which time he continued to follow El-Dabh's career.

8. Retirement

1. Manuel Noriega (b. 1939) was a Panamanian soldier and politician, born in Panama City. He was recruited by the Central Intelligence Agency in the late 1960s and supported by the U.S. government until 1987. Alleging involvement in drug trafficking, U.S. authorities ordered his arrest in 1989. American troops invaded Panama, and Noriega, after taking refuge for ten days in the Vatican nunciature, surrendered in January 1990. He was taken to the United States for trial, found guilty in 1992, and sentenced to forty years' imprisonment.

2. Saddam Hussein (b. 1937) has been president of Iraq since 1979. His attack on Iran in 1980, supported by the U.S. government, led to a war of attrition that ended in 1988. He invaded Kuwait in 1990 but was forced to withdraw when he was defeated by a coalition of Arab and Western forces in Operation Desert Storm (1991). For continued breaching of the peace terms he brought further military strikes against his country in 1993, and his failure to comply with United Nations weapons inspectors led to further strikes led by the United States in 1998.

3. Latvian-born ballet dancer Mikhail Baryshnikov (b. 1948) defected to the United States via Canada in 1974 and joined the American Ballet Theater, where his dazzling style catapulted him to international stardom.

4. Halim El-Dabh had not been involved actively with Middletown from 1992 to 2001. In 2002 he returned to Middletown where, together with local public-school students, he created an original "Map Rap" as a method of teaching the children about geography. For Middfest International's Twenty-Year, Twenty-Nations celebration in October 2002, El-Dabh presented several workshops and participated in the festival's final percussion extravaganza, performing together with drummers from Japan, Korea, India, and several other nations.

5. Madonna Louise Veronica Ciccone (b. 1958) is a successful and popular singer-actress. She is known professionally by her first name only.

6. Interview, November 12, 1996.

7. Donald Johanson (b. 1943) is an American anthropologist who has conducted fieldwork in the Afar Triangle region of Ethiopia. In 1981 he, along with M. A. Edey, published *Lucy: The Beginnings of Humankind*, a book documenting his famous research discovery.

8. El-Dabh enjoyed Foster's company and permitted him to share his office in the School of Music at Kent State University.

9. In his book *Schumann: The Inner Voices of a Musical Genius*, Peter Ostwald recounts a letter Robert Schumann (1810–56) wrote to Henriette Voigt in September 1834, in which he explained the origins of his piano suite, *Carnaval*: "'I have

just discovered that the name [of Ernestine von Fricken's hometown] ASCH is very musical and contains letters that also occur in my name. They were musical symbols.' [In German, "As" stands for A-flat, "Es" (pronounced S) for E-flat, and "H" is B; "C" is, of course, C.] By playing with these ciphers he found he could generate numerous tone sequences, and he used them in melodies and chords throughout the twenty "little scenes" *(scènes mignonnes)* of *Carnaval*."

10. Neale Donald Walsch (b. 1943) is best known for his three books in the series entitled *Conversations with God: An Uncommon Dialogue.* James Redfield's (b. 1950) works include: *The Secret of Shambhala: In Search of the Eleventh Insight; The Celestine Prophecy: An Adventure;* and *The Tenth Insight: Holding the Vision.*

11. Timothy Leary (1920–96) was an American psychologist and author who was a leading advocate for the use of LSD and other psychedelic drugs. His phrase "turn on, tune in, drop out" became a popular counterculture slogan in the 1960s.

12. Interview, November 12, 1996.

13. E-mail correspondence with Mike Hovancsek, February 14, 2000.

14. Born Richard Starkey on July 7, 1940, Ringo Starr became the drummer of the famed rock band The Beatles on August 18, 1962.

15. E-mail correspondence with Hovancsek, February 14, 2000.

16. In the 1990s El-Dabh granted permission for Kent State University student Hovancsek to release his early electronic compositions and other works on Hovancsek's record label, Pointless Music, which was later co-opted by Without Fear Recordings. Hovancsek released two full-length sound recordings of El-Dabh's music. The first, *Xango Ka O,* contains improvisations for piano and African traditional instruments. The second, *Crossing into the Electric Magnetic,* comprises most of El-Dabh's pioneering electronic works. In preparation for their second release, Hovancsek spent months attempting to organize and restore El-Dabh's source material, and the two became very close. Hovancsek, in an e-mail correspondence on February 14, 2000, compared the experience to an "archaeological dig with sound."

17. E-mail correspondence with Hovancsek, February 14, 2000.

18. Interview, May 2, 2000.

19. Program notes for *Opera Flies,* Carl F. W. Ludwig Recital Hall, Kent State University, March 22, 1995.

20. Ibid.

21. Marc Vincent, "May 4 Opera Returns to Kent State," *Daily Kent Stater,* January 27, 1995, 5.

22. Ibid.

23. Hovancsek, "Ordeals in New Music: Bringing Halim El-Dabh's Opera Back to Life," unpublished account.

24. Ibid.

25. Ibid.

26. Ibid.

27. Interview, May 5, 2000.

28. Daniel Ryan, telephone conversation, February 7, 2000.

29. Program notes for *Opera Flies.*

30. Hovancsek, "Ordeals in New Music."

31. Prominent in the physiological practices of certain forms of Hinduism and Buddhism, the seven *chakra*s are focal points in the human body where psychic forces and bodily functions merge with and interact with one another. Each of the major *chakras* is associated with a specific color, shape, organ, natural element, and deity.

32. The party occurred February 9, 1996, and was sponsored by Key Bank.

33. The premiere did not utilize the tomb of Akhenaton, which was created only for the first gala party.

34. David Birney is an award-winning actor and director whose extensive stage credits include starring roles on Broadway, the American Shakespeare Festival, the New York Shakespeare Festival, and Lincoln Center. He has starred in many television movies and series.

35. Interview, February 7, 1997.

36. Actress Annalee Jefferies was educated at the Royal Academy of Dramatic Art in London. Now in her twelfth season at Houston's Alley Theatre, she has done off-Broadway, television, and film work.

37. Interview, February 7, 1997.

38. Born Maria Muchin in Kiev, Ukraine, Masha Archer emigrated to the United States in 1949. She studied at the Pratt Institute in New York City. She later worked as a restorer and exhibitor at the Museo Nacional de Mexico, Mexico City, and designed jewelry and clothing in Tucson and San Francisco. Archer created fifty original necklaces for the Great Lakes Theater Festival's production of Shakespeare's *Antony and Cleopatra.*

39. Interview, February 7, 1997.

40. Chris Maderasz, "'Untold' Shows Africa's Spirit," *Daily Kent Stater,* November 21, 1996, 1.

41. Ibid.

42. Marc Shulgold, "A Dance Tribute to Egypt," *Denver Rocky Mountain News,* September 17, 1999, 18D.

43. Glenn Giffin, "Valley Girl: Troupe to End Millennium with a Vision of Egypt's Isis," *Denver Post,* September 17, 1999, E1.

44. Giffin, "Rhythms of Egypt: Composer Teaches Young Dancers the Intricacies of Music," *Denver Post,* July 23, 1999, 20F.

45. Ibid.

46. Program notes for *Meet the Composer: Halim El-Dabh,* Carl F. W. Ludwig Recital Hall, Kent State University, February 5, 2000.

47. Ibid.

48. Ibid.

49. Interview, March 6, 2000. The name of French film composer Georges Delerue (1925–92) was mistakenly spelled as "Delraux" in the record's liner notes.

50. From the opening pages of the score to "Ogún: Let Him, Let Her Have the Iron." Unpublished manuscript.

51. Program notes for *An Afternoon of Piano and Chamber Music of Halim El-Dabh,* Hiram College, April 1, 2001.

52. The accepted international spelling for this instrument should be *riq*, with a "q" representing the Arabic letter *qoph*. El-Dabh spells it *rik* in his compositions.

53. Program notes for *Halim El-Dabh 80th Birthday Gala Concert*, Kent State University, April 17, 2001.

54. In the program notes for *Halim El-Dabh 80th Birthday Gala Concert*, "Sonic No. 7" is attributed with the composition date of 1961; however, the *Sonics* were composed in 1955, and El-Dabh premiered them in 1959. "Sonic No. 7" and "Sonic No. 10" were published by C. F. Peters in 1965.

55. In the program notes for *Halim El-Dabh 80th Birthday Gala Concert*, "Dialogue for Double Bass and Ceramic Egyptian Drum" is identified only as "Dialogue."

56. In the program notes for *Halim El-Dabh 80th Birthday Gala Concert*, "Tonography" is given a composition date of 1979, revised in 1991. In fact, however, the work was originally composed for clarinet, bassoon, marimba, and percussion in 1980; revised as "Tonography III" in 1984; and revised for solo clarinet in 1991.

57. In the program notes for *Halim El-Dabh 80th Birthday Gala Concert*, "Ifriqiyaat" is assigned a composition date of 1940, revised 2001, and "Misriyaat" is given a composition date of 1936. However, both works, along with the piano piece "Arabiyaat," were actually composed and premiered in 1954. The earlier dates are references to incipient works of the same names that the composer was experimenting with in the beginning stage of his compositional life in Egypt.

58. For the gala performance celebrating El-Dabh's eightieth birthday, "Electronic Fanfare" (1959), originally composed with Otto Luening for electronic tape, was performed live with El-Dabh performing on theremin, Hovancsek playing *zheng* and waterphone, and Blake Tyson on *derabucca*.

59. Program for *Kent State University's Two Hundred Eighth Commencement*, May 12 and 13, 2001.

60. Program for *Composition in Africa and the Diaspora*, Churchill College, University of Cambridge, August 2–4, 2001.

61. Ibid.

62. David Badagnani specializes in new and improvised music for oboe and English horn and a variety of wind and string instruments from China and Thailand. Badagnani holds degrees from Florida State University and Kent State University, where he is currently an instructor and doctoral candidate and where his research focuses on global rap music and intercultural musical collaboration. He has recorded for the Without Fear, Manifold, Pointless Music, Yucca Tree, and Uphrania labels.

Hardin Butcher holds a bachelor's degree in trumpet performance from Youngstown State University and is currently a graduate assistant in trumpet and orchestral conducting at Kent State University. Butcher's most recent orchestral performances have included the Kent Blossom Festival Orchestra, the Youngstown Symphony Orchestra, and the Warren Philharmonic Orchestra. His commercial musical credits include the Glenn Miller Orchestra, Carnival Cruise Lines, and the recently released *Strings Attached* CD, featuring the legendary Cleveland rock band Glass Harp and the Youngstown Symphony Orchestra.

Charles (Al) Couch joined the trumpet section of the Cleveland Orchestra in 1972. The following year he became assistant principal, the position he currently holds. In addition to his duties with the orchestra, he serves on the faculty of Cleveland State University as trumpet instructor. Couch and his wife, Joanne, a soprano, perform works for trumpet and soprano as the duo The Bright Seraphim. Couch also appears as a soloist and chamber music player as his schedule permits.

Kent Larmee is associate professor of horn at Kent State University. He holds degrees in music education and horn performance and pedagogy from the Ohio State University and has attended the Aspen Music Festival and Blossom Festival School. His professional performing experience includes playing principal horn with the Ohio Chamber Orchestra, Cleveland Opera and Ballet, Sinfonia da Camera (of Illinois), and the Champaign-Urbana Symphony. He was also a charter member of the Pro Musica Chamber Orchestra (of Columbus, Ohio).

Dennis Nygren has been professor of clarinet at Kent State University since 1983. Prior to this he was a faculty member at Northern Michigan University and served as solo clarinet and soloist with the North American Air Defense (NORAD) Band. He was the first clarinetist to earn a doctor of music degree in performance from Northwestern University, where he also attained a bachelor of music degree; his master's degree is from Michigan State University.

Tuyen Tonnu, a native of Vietnam, moved to the United States in 1982, where she received her B.M. degree from Pacific Lutheran University, M.M. degree from the Eastman School of Music, and artist diploma from the Cleveland Institute of Music. She gives regular recitals on both the west and east coasts of North America and in Asia. A recipient of numerous awards and fellowships, including a full scholarship to study at the Hochschule für Musik in Freiburg, Germany, in 1989, Tonnu was named "Vietnamese Woman of the Year" in 1993 by *Women's Magazine* in Hanoi, Vietnam.

Blake Tyson is currently assistant professor of percussion at the University of Central Arkansas. He received a D.M.A. from the Eastman School of Music, an M.M. from Kent State University, and a B.M. from the University of Alabama. While at Eastman, he also received the prestigious Performer's Certificate. He has served on the faculties of New Mexico State University and the University of Alabama. Also a composer, Tyson's most recent works include *Anubis*, for solo marimba, and *Fabric of Time*, for solo oboe, viola, and percussion. Tyson is an active concert artist and clinician for the Malletech and Zildjian companies.

Liana Tyson is currently assistant professor of flute and music theory at Boise State University. She received a D.M.A. from the Eastman School of Music, an M.M. from the University of Michigan, and a B.M. from the University of Alabama. While in Alabama, she was a member of the Tuscaloosa Symphony Orchestra under the direction of Ransom Wilson. Tyson performs as a solo artist throughout the United States and also with the flute and percussion duo Imbate with her husband, Blake Tyson.

Joel Jacobson is an instructor in the Department of Pan-African Studies and works with the Family Tree Program. In this class, he works with students to produce a television program that is broadcast on the university's student-operated station. Jacobson is currently working on a DVD documentary about El-Dabh. He graduated from Kent State University in 1998, where he is completing a master's degree in education.

Julie Grant has been a news reporter and producer at WKSU-FM, an affiliate of National Public Radio, based in Kent, Ohio, since 2000. She worked for six years at WCBE-FM, an NPR station in Columbus, Ohio, four years of that as news director. She has won numerous awards for her work, most recently a Regional Murrow award, a Press Club of Cleveland award, and an Ohio Professional Writers award. She is currently working on a graduate degree in philosophy and environmental science at Kent State University.

The author (Denise Seachrist) is associate professor of music at the Kent State University Trumbull Campus. She holds degrees in vocal performance from Heidelberg College and the Dana School of Music at Youngstown State University and a Ph.D. in musicology-ethnomusicology from Kent State University. The author is considered a specialist in the music of both historical and living German religious communities in Pennsylvania.

63. Copy of an e-mail correspondence from the Misr Company for Sound and Light to Badagnani, dated March 21, 2002. In the possession of the author.

64. Copy of an e-mail correspondence from Badagnani to the Misr Company for Sound and Light, dated March 21, 2002. In the possession of the author.

65. Samha El-Kholy is the former director of the Cairo Conservatory and former president of the Egyptian Academy of Arts at the Ministry of Culture. She is the widow of acclaimed Egyptian composer Gamal Abdel-Rahim (1924–1988).

66. Rageh Daoud (b. 1954) belongs to the third generation of modern Egyptian composers, which consists of those born between 1950–1970.

67. (Daniel) Louis Armstrong (1900-1971) was a United States jazz trumpeter and bandleader, considered a formative figure in the history of jazz.

68. Qtd. in Isabella Brega, *Egypt Past and Present* (Vercelli, Italy: White Star S.r.l., 1998), 73. Dominique Vivant Denon was one of the scholars who took part in the ill-fated expedition of the French military leader Napoleon Bonaparte (1769–1821) in 1798. Bonaparte later crowned himself emperor in 1804.

69. Khafre (Chephren) was the Egyptian king of the fourth dynasty (late twenty-sixth century B.C.E.) and the son of Khufu (Cheops). Khafre was the builder of the second pyramid at Giza.

70. The fact that the reconstructed Bibliotheca Alexandrina is very close to the location of the Old Library in the Ancient Royal Quarter was verified by a 1993 archeological survey.

71. "Bibliotheca Alexandrina: A Return to the Golden Past," *Horus* 20, no. 2 (April/June 2002): 22.

72. A few days after El-Dabh and his party returned to the United States (April 2, 2002), it was reported that a student had been shot and killed by police officers during a protest near Alexandria University.

73. "Mary El-Dabh, 79: Former Kentite Dies in N.C.," *Record-Courier*, April 5, 2002, A5.

Postscript

1. Martha Graham, *Blood Memory* (New York: Doubleday, 1991).

2. Otto Luening, *The Odyssey of an American Composer: The Autobiography of Otto Luening* (New York: Scribner, 1980).

3. George Crumb (b. 1929) is a U.S. composer who represents the American postwar avant-garde. He makes powerful use of amplification effects.

4. Charles Ives (1874–1954) was a U.S. composer who frequently employed or quoted American folksongs, popular songs, and hymns in his highly dissonant and often electric music.

5. Denise A. Seachrist, "Halim El-Dabh," *The International Dictionary of Black Composers*, ed. Samuel A. Floyd Jr. (Chicago: Fitzroy Dearborn, 1999).

6. Qtd. in "Alan Hovhaness, Prodigious Composer Who Drew on Eastern Music, Dies at 89," obituary, *New York Times*, June 22, 2000. Unsigned article form an on-line edition only.

7. Ibid.

8. Virginia Danielson, *The Voice of Egypt: Umm Kulthum, Arabic Song, and Egyptian Society in the Twentieth Century* (Chicago: University of Chicago Press, 1997), 99.

9. Stephen Blum, "Conclusion: Music in an Age of Cultural Confrontation," *Musical Cultures in Contact: Collisions and Convergences*, ed. Margaret Khartoum and Stephen Blum (Sydney: Currency Press and Gordon & Breach, 1993), 252.

10. Interview, November 12, 1996.

11. Seachrist, "Halim El-Dabh."

12. In the 1970s, inspired by his experiences of public music making in Africa and Europe, El-Dabh created and taught a popular course, Street Music, in which he led students throughout the campus and city streets while playing a variety of conventional and unconventional musical instruments.

13. Interview, November 12, 1996.

14. Letter to El-Dabh from Stephen Fisher, June 1996.

15. Interview, May 30, 1996.

Selected Bibliography

Abazah, al-Amir Sulayman Muhammad. *Amir 67.* al-Qahirah: Dar al-Taawun, 1997.

'Abd al-Wahhāb, Muhammad. *Mudhakkirāt Muhammad 'Abd al-Wahhāb* (The memoirs of Muhammad 'Abd al-Wahh̄ab). Ed. Muhammad Rif'at al-Muhāmī. Beirut: Dār al-Thaqāfa, n.d.

Abu-Lughod, Ibrahim. "The Mass Media and Egyptian Village Life." *Social Forces* 42 (1963): 97–104.

Abu-Lughod, Janet. "Migrant Adjustment to City Life: The Egyptian Case." *American Journal of Sociology* 47 (1961): 22–32.

Abu-Lughod, Lila. "Bedouins, Cassettes and Technologies of Public Culture." *Middle East Report* 159 (1989): 7–11, 47.

——. *Veiled Sentiments: Honor and Poetry in a Bedouin Society.* Berkeley: Univ. of California Press, 1986.

Abū 'l-Majd, Sabrī. *Zakariyyā Ahmad.* Cairo: al-Mu'asassa al-Misriyya at-'Āmma lil-Ta'līf wa-'l-Tarjama wa-'l-Tibā'a wa-'I-Nashr, 1963.

Āl Ahmad, Jalāl. *Gharbzadagi: Weststruckness.* Trans. John Green and Ahmad Alizadeh. Lexington, Ky.: Mazda, 1982.

Ako, Edward Oben. "The Harlem Renaissance and the Negritude Movement: Literary Relations and Influences." Ph.D. diss., Univ. of Illinois at Urbana-Champaign, 1982.

Altorki, Soraya. *Women in Saudi Arabia: Ideology and Behavior among the Elite.* New York: Columbia Univ. Press, 1986.

American Society of Civil Engineers. *George Washington Bridge across the Hudson River at New York, N.Y.* Published by American Society of Civil Engineers in Collaboration with the Port of New York Authority. New York: Port of New York Authority, 1933.

Ansari, Hamied. *Egypt: The Stalled Society.* Albany: State Univ. of New York Press, 1986.

Antelme, Ruth Schumann. *Becoming Osiris: The Ancient Egyptian Death Experience.* Trans. from the French by Jon Graham. Rochester, Vt.: Inner Traditions, 1998.

'Arafa, 'Abd al-Mun'im. *Tārīkh A'lām al-Mūsīqa 'l-Sharqiyya* (The history of the stars of oriental music). Cairo: Matba'at 'Anānī, 1947.

Aria, Barbara. *Misha: The Mikhail Baryshnikov Story.* New York: St. Martin's Press, 1989.

Auboux, François, and Nicolas Klotz. *Pandit Ravi Shankar* [videorecording]: *The Man and His Music.* Princeton, N.J.: Films for the Humanities and Sciences, 1994.

'Awad, Mahmūd. *Umm Kulthūm allātī lā Ya'rifuhā Ahad* (The Umm Kulthūm nobody knows). Cairo: Mu'assasat Akhbār al-Yawm, 1971.

Azzam, Nabil. "Muhammad 'Abd al-Wahhāb in Modern Egyptian Music." Ph.D. diss., University of California, Los Angeles, 1990.

Babbitt, Milton. *A Life of Learning.* [New York]: American Council of Learned Societies, 1991.

Badawi, M. M. *A Critical Introduction to Modern Arabic Poetry.* Cambridge: Cambridge Univ. Press, 1975.

Badran, Margot, and Miriam Cooke, eds. *Opening the Gates: A Century of Arab Feminist Writing.* Bloomington: Indiana Univ. Press, 1990.

Baines, Anthony, ed. *The Oxford Companion to Musical Instruments.* Oxford: Oxford Univ. Press, 1992.

Barbour, Neville. "The Arabic Theatre in Egypt." *Bulletin of the School of Oriental Studies* 8 (1935–37): 173–87, 991–1012.

Bascom, William Russell. *Shango in the New World.* Austin: African and Afro-American Research Institute, Univ. of Texas at Austin, 1972.

Beck, Lois, and Nikki R. Keddie, eds. *Women in the Muslim World.* Cambridge, Mass.: Harvard Univ. Press, 1978.

Bedier, Shafia. *Die Rolle des Gottes Geb in den ägyptischen Tempelinschriften der griechisch-römischen Zeit.* Hildesheim: Gerstenberg Verlag, 1995.

Behrens-Abouseif, Doris. *Azbakiyya and Its Environs from Azbak to Ismā'īl, 1476–1879.* Cairo: Institut Français d'Archéologie Orientale, 1985.

Beinhorn, Gabriele. *Das Groteske in der Musik: Arnold Schönbergs "Pierrot Lunaire."* Pfaffenweiler: Centaurus-Verlagsgesellschaft, 1989.

Bengio, Ofra. *Saddam's Word: Political Discourse in Iraq.* New York: Oxford Univ. Press, 1998.

Berggruen and Cie. *Fernand Léger: Gouaches, Aquarelles & Dessins.* Paris: Berggruen, 1996.

Berlan, Édouard. *Addis-Abeba, la Plus Haute Ville d'Afrique: étude géographique.* Grenoble: n.p., 1963.

Bernstein, Leonard. *Findings.* New York: Anchor Books, 1993.

Berque, Jacques. *Egypt: Imperialism and Revolution.* Trans. Jean Stewart. London: Faber and Faber, 1972.

Bidder, Irmgard. *Lalibela: The Monolithic Churches of Ethiopia.* Trans. from the German by Rita Grabham-Hortmann. Cologne: M. D. Schauberg, 1958.

Bietak, Manfred. *Theben-West (Luqsor). Vorbericht über die ersten vier Grabungskampagnen (1969–1971).* Wien: Böhlau in Komm, 1972.

Billington, Joy. "Opera Tells Story of Kent State." *Washington (D.C.) Evening Star,* May 3, 1971.

Bird, Dorothy, and Joyce Greenberg. *Bird's Eye View: Dancing with Martha Graham and on Broadway.* Pittsburgh: Univ. of Pittsburgh Press, 1997.

Blum, Stephen. "Conclusion: Music in an Age of Cultural Confrontation." In *Musical Cultures in Contact: Collisions and Convergences,* edited by Margaret Kartomi and Stephen Blum. Sydney: Currency Press and Gordon and Breach, 1993.

———. "In Defense of Close Reading and Close Listening." *Current Musicology* 53 (1993): 41–54.

———. "Musics in Contact: The Cultivation of Oral Repertories in Meshed, Iran." Ph.D. diss., Univ. of Illinois, 1972.

———. "Prologue: Ethnomusicologists and Modern Music History." In *Ethnomusicology and Modern Music History,* edited by Stephen Blum, Philip V. Bohlman, and Daniel M. Neuman. Urbana: Univ. of Illinois Press, 1991.

———. "Towards a Social History of Musicological Technique." *Ethnomusicology* 19 (1975): 207–31.

Blum, Stephen, Philip V. Bohlman, and Daniel M. Neuman, eds. *Ethnomusicology and Modern Music History.* Urbana: Univ. of Illinois Press, 1991.

Boolaky, Ibrahim. "Traditional Muslim Vocal Art." *Arts and the Islamic World* 1 (Winter 1983–84): 52–55.

Booth, Marilyn. *Bayram al-Tunisi's Egypt: Social Criticism and Narrative Strategies.* Exeter: Published for the Middle East Centre, St. Anthony's College, Oxford by Ithaca Press, 1990.

———. "Colloquial Arabic Poetry, Politics, and the Press in Modern Egypt." *International Journal of Middle East Studies* 24 (1992): 419–40.

Boretz, Benjamin, ed. *Sounds and Words: A Critical Celebration of Milton Babbitt at 60.* Annandale-on-Hudson, N.Y.: Perspectives of New Music, 1977.

Bourdieu, Pierre. "Outline of a Sociological Theory of Art Perception." *International Social Science Journal* 20/4 (1968): 589–612.

Boyd, Douglas A. *Broadcasting in the Arab World: A Survey of Radio and Television the Middle East.* Philadelphia: Temple Univ. Press, 1982.

———. *Egyptian Radio: Tool of Political and National Development.* Journalism Monographs no. 48. Lexington, Ky.: Association for Education in Journalism, 1977.

Braitsch, Hans, and Kale Kypros. *Mikis Theodorakis: Leben für Musik und Freiheit.* Hamburg: vpm, 1995.

Braune, Gabriele. *Die Qasida im Gesang von Umm Kultūm: Die arabische Poesie im Repertoire der grossten ägyptschen Sängerin unserer Zeit. Beiträge zur Eth-16.* 2 vols. Hamburg: Karl Dieter Wagner, 1987.

Breaux, Charles. *Journey into Consciousness: The Chakras, Tantra, and Jungian Psychology.* York Beach, Me.: Nicolas-Hays, 1989.

Bredel, Marc. *Edgar Varèse.* Paris: Mazarine, 1984.

Briner, Andres. *Paul Hindemith.* [Zürich] Atlantis [-Verlag] Mainz: Schott, 1971.

Brown, Diana DeGroat. *Umbanda: Religion and Politics in Urban Brazil.* Ann Arbor, Mich.: UMI Research Press, 1986.

Brown, Nathan J. *Peasant Politics in Modern Egypt: The Struggle against the State.* New Haven, Conn.: Yale Univ. Press, 1990.

Browning, Robert. *Justinian and Theodora.* New York: Thames and Hudson, 1987.

Burstein, Stanley, ed. *Ancient African Civilizations: Kush and Axum.* Princeton, N.J.: Markus Wiener, 1998.

Butcher, E. L. *The Story of the Church of Egypt.* New York: AMS Press, 1975.

Butrus, Fikrī *A'lām al-Mūsīqa wa-'l Ghinā' '/-'Ababī, 1867–1967* (Stars of Arabic music and song, 1867–1967). Cairo: al-Hay'a al-Misriyya al-'Āmma lil-Kitāb, 1976.

Cachia, Pierre. "The Egyptian Mawwal: Its Ancestry, Its Development, and Its Present Forms." *Journal of Arabic Literature* 8 (1977): 77–103.

———. *Taha Husayn: His Place in the Egyptian Literary Renaissance.* London: Luzac, 1956.

Cachin, Françoise. *Gauguin.* Paris: Flammarion, 1988.

Capoeira, Nestor. *Pequeno Manual do Jogador de Capoeira.* Trans. Alex Ladd. Berkeley, Calif.: North Atlantic Books, 1995.

Carson, Neil. *Arthur Miller.* New York: St. Martin's Press, 1982.

Chabrier, Jean-Claude. "Music in the Fertile Crescent." *Cultures* 1 (1974): 35–58.

Chelbi, Moustapha. "Um Kalthoum, la Voix d'Or de la Conscience Arabe." In *Les Africans,* edited by Charles-André Julien et al. Vol. 3. [Paris]: Éditions J.A., 1977.

Clifford, James. "Introduction: Partial Truths." In *Writing Culture: The Poetics and Politics of Ethnography,* edited by James Clifford and George E. Marcus. Berkeley: Univ. of California Press, 1986.

———. *The Predicament of Culture: Twentieth-Century Ethnography, Literature, and Art.* Cambridge, Mass.: Harvard Univ. Press, 1988.

Connelly, Bridget. *Arab Folk Epic and Identity.* Berkeley: Univ. of California Press, 1986.

Cooke, Harold P. *Osiris: A Study in Myths, Mysteries and Religion.* Chicago: Ares, 1979.

Copland, Aaron, and Vivian Perlis. *Copland.* New York: St. Martin's Press, 1984.

———. *Copland: Since 1943.* New York: St. Martin's Press, 1989.

Corzo, Miguel Angel, and Mahasti Afshar, eds. *Art and Eternity: The Nefertari Wall Paintings Conservation Project, 1986–1992.* [Santa Monica, Calif.]: J. Paul Getty Trust, 1993.

Cox, Dennis K. "Aspects of the Compositional Styles of Three Selected Twentieth-Century American Composers of Choral Music: Alan Hovhaness, Ron Nelson, and Daniel Pinkham." D.M.A. thesis, Univ. of Missouri, Kansas City, 1978.

Crabbs, Jack. "Politics, History, and Culture in Nasser's Egypt." *International Journal of Middle East Studies* 6 (1975): 386–420.

Crapanzano, Vincent. *Tuhami: Portrait of a Moroccan.* Chicago: Univ. of Chicago Press, 1980.

El-Dabh, Halim. Interviews with Denise A. Seachrist, May 30, 1996; September 13, 20, 27, 1996; October 4, 11, 18, 25, 1996; November 12, 22, 1996; December 20, 1996; January 24, 1997; February 7, 1997; January 27, 2000; March 6, 2000; May 2, 5 2000.

————. *The Derabucca: Hand Techniques in the Art of Drumming.* New York: C. F. Peters, 1965.

Dagan, Esther A. *Emotions in Motion: Theatrical Puppets and Masks from Black Africa: La magie de l'imaginaire: marionnettes et masques théâtraux d'Afrique noir.* Montréal: Galerie Amrad African Arts, 1990.

Danielson, Virginia. "Artists and Entrepreneurs: Female Singers in Cairo during the 1920s." In *Women in Middle Eastern History: Shifting Boundaries in Sex and Gender,* edited by Nikki R. Keddie and Beth Baron. New Haven, Conn.: Yale Univ. Press, 1991.

————. "The Qur'ān and the Qasīdah: Aspects of the Popularity of the Repertory Sung by Umm Kulthūm *Asian Music* 19/1 (1987): 26–45.

————. "Shaping Tradition in Arabic Song: The Career and Repertory of Umm Kulthūm." Ph.D. diss., Univ. of Illinois, 1991.

————. *The Voice of Egypt: Umm Kulthūm, Arabic Song, and Egyptian Society in the Twentieth Century.* Chicago: Univ. of Chicago Press, 1997.

Daniélou, Alain. *The Way to the Labyrinth: Memories of East and West.* Translated by Marie-Claire Cournand. New York: New Directions, 1987.

Davis, Eric. *Challenging Colonialism. Bank Misr and Egyptian Industrialization, 1920–1941.* Princeton, N.J.: Princeton Univ. Press, 1983.

————. "Religion against the State." In *Religious Resurgence: Contemporary Cases in Islam, Christianity, and Judaism,* edited by Richard T. Antoun and Mary Elaine Hegland. Syracuse, N.Y.: Syracuse Univ. Press, 1987.

De la Motte-Haber, Helga, and Klaus Angermann. *Edgard Varèse, 1883–1965: Dokument zu Leben und Werk.* Frankfurt: P. Lang, 1990.

Delphin, G., and L. Guin. *Notes sur la Poésie et la Musique Arabes dans le Maghreb Algérien.* Paris: Leroux, 1886.

The Diagram Group. *Musical Instruments of the World: An Illustrated Encyclopedia.* New York: Sterling, 1997.

Diehl, Gaston. *F. Léger.* New York: Crown, 1985.

Dombrowski, Joanne Carol. "Excavations in Ethiopia: Lalibela and Natchabiet Caves, Begemeder Province." Master's thesis, Boston University, Boston, 1971.

Dreyfus, Hubert L., and Paul Rabinow. *Michel Foucault: Beyond Structuralism and Hermeneutics.* Chicago: Univ. of Chicago Press, 1982.

Duff, Gordon, and Lady Lucie. *Letters from Egypt.* London: Virago Press, 1983.

Duffy, Kevin. *Children of the Forest.* New York: Dodd, Mead, 1984.

Dunsby, Jonathan. *Schoenberg: Pierrot Lunaire.* Cambridge: Cambridge Univ. Press, 1992.

During, Jean. *Introduction au Muqam Ouïgour.* Bloomington: Indiana University, Research Institute for Inner Asian Studies, 1991.

Dwyer, Kevin. *Moroccan Dialogues.* Baltimore: Johns Hopkins Univ. Press, 1982.

Edgerton, William Franklin. *Historical Records of Ramses III.* Chicago: Univ. of Chicago Press, 1936.

Edward MacDowell Association. *The Edward MacDowell Association . . . 1907–1932.* Peterborough, N.H.: The Association, 1932.

Egypt. Ministry of Finance. *The Census of Egypt Taken in 1907.* Cairo: National Printing Department, 1909.

———. *The Census of Egypt Taken in 1917.* Cairo: Government Press, 1920.

Eichelmann, Toni. *Berchtesgadner Sagen.* Berchtesgaden: L. Vonderthann und Sohn, 1932.

Eisner, Jürgen. "Ferment nationalen Bewüsstseins: die Musikkultur Algeriens." *Musik und Gesellschaft* 33/8 (1983): 456–63.

Erlmann, Viet. *African Stars: Studies in Black South African Performance.* Chicago: Univ. of Chicago Press, 1991.

———. "Conversation with Joseph Shabalala of Ladysmith Black Mambazo: Aspects of African Performers' Lifestories." *World of Music* 31/1 (1989): 31–58.

Etherington-Smith, Meredith. *Dali: A Biography.* London: Sinclair-Stevenson, 1992.

Fakhouri, Ham. *Kafr el-Elow: An Egyptian Village in Transition.* New York: Holt, Rinehart and Winston, 1972.

Al Faruqi, Lois Ibsen. *An Annotated Glossary of Arabic Musical Terms.* Westport, Conn.: Greenwood Press, 1981.

———. "Music, Musicians and Muslim Law." *Asian Music* 17 (1985): 3–36.

———. "The Nature of the Musical Art of Islamic Culture: A Theoretical and Empirical Study of Arabian Music." Ph.D. diss., Syracuse Univ., Syracuse, N.Y., 1974.

———. "Ornamentation in Arabian Improvisational Music: A Study in Interrelatedness in the Arts." *World of Music* 20 (1978): 17–32.

———. "The Status of Music in Muslim Nations: Evidence from the Arab World." *Asian Music* 12 (1979): 56–84.

Feld, Steven. "Communication, Music, and Speech about Music." *Yearbook for Traditional Music* 16 (1984): 1–18.

———. *Sound and Sentiment.* 2nd ed. Philadelphia: Univ. of Pennsylvania Press, 1990.

Fernea, Elizabeth Warnock, and Basima Qattan Bezirgan, eds. *Middle Eastern Muslim Women Speak.* Austin: Univ. of Texas Press, 1977.

Fleming, Richard, and William Duckworth. *John Cage at Seventy-Five.* Lewisburg, Penn.: Bucknell Univ. Press, 1989.

Floyd, Samuel A., Jr., ed. *The International Dictionary of Black Composers.* Chicago: Fitzroy Dearborn, 1999.

Fonteyn, Margot. *Margot Fonteyn: Autobiography.* New York: Alfred A. Knopf, 1976.

Foucault, Michel. *The History of Sexuality.* Vol. 1: *An Introduction.* Trans. Robert Hurley. New York: Vintage Books, 1978.

Fraser, John. *Private View: Inside Baryshnikov's American Ballet Theatre.* New York: Bantam Books, 1988.

Frith, Simon. "Essay Review: Rock Biography." *Popular Music* 3 (1983): 276–77.

———. "Why Do Songs Have Words?" In *Lost in Music: Culture, Style, and the Musical Event,* edited by A. L. White. London: Routledge and Kegan Paul, 1987.

Fu'cd, Ni'māt Ahmad. *Umm Kulthūm wa-'Asr min al-Fann* (Umm Kulthūm and an era of art). Cairo: al-Hay'a al-Misriyya'l-'Āmma lil-Kitāb, 1976.

Gabbin, Joanne V. *Sterling A. Brown: Building the Black Aesthetic Tradition.* Charlottesville: Univ. Press of Virginia, 1994.

Gaines, Steven S. *Simply Halston.* New York: Jove Books, 1993.

Gaitachew, Bekele. *The Emperor's Clothes: A Personal Viewpoint on Politics and Administration in the Imperial Ethiopian Government, 1941–1972.* East Lansing: Michigan State Univ. Press, 1993.

Gauthier, Guy. *Justinien: le Rêve Impérial.* Paris: Editions France-Empire, 1998.

Geertz, Clifford. *The Interpretation of Cultures: Selected Essays.* New York: Basic Books, 1973.

Geiss, Josef. *Obersalzberg: The History of a Mountain.* Berchtesgaden: J. Geiss, 1964.

Ghiryani, Yusuf. *Abd al-Nasir fi al-mizan: Hasanatuhu wa-akhtauhu wa-ayyuhuma arjah.* Iskandariyah: Wakalat Misr lil-Sihafah wa-al-Ilan, 1990.

Gibbons, Dana Lyn. "Shango Altar Ensembles as Embodiments of Yoruba Duality and Balance." Master's thesis, Ohio Univ., Athens, 1996.

Gibbs, James. *Wole Soyinka.* New York: Grove Press, 1986.

Giddens, Anthony. *The Constitution of Society: Outline of the Theory of Structuration.* Berkeley: Univ. of California Press, 1984.

―――. *Profiles and Critiques in Social Theory.* Berkeley: Univ. of California Press, 1982.

Giles, Frederick John. *The Amarna Age: Eastern Asia.* Warminster: Aris and Phillips, 1997.

Gilman, Lawrence. *Edward MacDowell: A Study.* New York: Da Capo Press, 1969.

Goffmann, Erving. *Frame Analysis: An Essay on the Organization of Experience.* Boston: Northeastern Univ. Press, 1986.

Goldberg, Ellis. "Leadership and Ideology in the 1919 Revolution." Paper presented at the Twenty-first annual meeting of the Middle East Studies Association of North America, Baltimore, 1987.

Goldschmidt, Arthur. *A Concise History of the Middle East.* 2nd ed. Cairo: American Univ. in Cairo Press, 1983.

Goldsmith, Peter David. *Making People's Music: Moe Asch and Folkways Records.* Washington, D.C.: Smithsonian Institution Press, 1998.

Gordon, Lewis R. *Bad Faith and Antiblack Racism.* Atlantic Highlands, N.J.: Humanities Press, 1995.

Graham, Martha. *Blood Memory.* New York: Doubleday, 1991.

Gronow, Pekka. "The Record Industry Comes to the Orient." *Ethnomusicology* 25 (1981): 251–82.

Gruen, John. *Menotti: A Biography.* New York: Macmillan, 1978.

Guiles, Fred Lawrence. *Legend: The Life and Death of Marilyn Monroe.* Chelsea, Mich.: Scarborough House, 1991.

Gutman, Bill. *Duke: The Musical Life of Duke Ellington.* New York: Random House, 1977.

Hāfiz Muhammad Mahmūd Sāmī. *Tārīkh al-Mūsīqá wa-'l-Gbinā'al-'Arabī* (History of Arabic music and song). Cairo: Maktabat al-Anjlū 'I-Misriyya, 1971.

Hāfiz N āhid Ahmad. "Al-Ughniyya al-Misriyya wa-Tatawwuruhā khilāl al-Qarnayn al-Tāsi' 'Ashar wa-'l-Ishrīn" (Egyptian song and its development through the nineteenth and twentieth centuries). Ph.D. diss., Hilwān Univ., Hilwān, Egypt, 1977.

Halbach, Helan. *Romance of the Rubaiyat: A Comprehensive Directory to the Myriad Editions of the Rubaiyat, the Ephemeron, Edward Fitzgerald, Omar Khayyam, and the Lesser Persian Poets.* Santa Barbara, Calif.: Halbach, 1975.

El-Hamamsy, Laila Shukrv. "The Assertion of Egyptian Identity." In *Ethnic Identity Cultural Continuities and Change,* edited by George De Vos and Lola Ranucci. Palo Alto, Calif.: Mayfield, 1975.

Hassan, Scheherazade Qassim. "Survey of Written Sources on the Irāqī Maqām." In *Regionale Maqām-Traditionen in Geschichte und Gegenwart,* edited by Jürgen Elsner and Gisa Jähnichen. Berlin, 1992.

Hasse, John Edward. *Beyond Category: The Life and Genius of Duke Ellington.* New York: Da Capo Press, 1995.

Hébert, Matthew Donald. "Henry Cowell's New Musical Resources and Rhythm: Theory and Practice." Master's thesis, Univ. of Cincinnati, 1996.

Hees, Julia van. *Luigi Dallapiccolas Bühnenwerk Ulisse: Untersuchungen zu Werk und Werkgenese.* Kassel: G. Bosse, 1994.

Hegland, Mary. "Introduction." In *Religious Resurgence: Contemporary Cases in Islam, Christianity, and Judaism,* edited by Richard T. Antoun and Mary Elaine Hegland. Syracuse, N.Y.: Syracuse Univ. Press, 1987.

———. "Conclusion." In *Religious Resurgence: Contemporary Cases in Islam, Christianity, and Judaism,* edited by Richard T. Antoun and Mary Elaine Hegland. Syracuse, N.Y.: Syracuse Univ. Press, 1987.

Henne, Rachel L. "Chinese American Literature: Constructing Identity and Breaking Silence." Master's thesis, Bowling Green State Univ., Bowling Green, Ohio, 1994.

Herride, Frances. *New York Post,* June 20, 1975.

Heyworth-Dunne, J. *An Introduction to the History of Education in Modern Egypt.* 1939. Reprint. London: Frank Cass, 1968.

Al-Hifnī, Mahmūd Ahmad, et al., eds. *Turāthunā 'l Mūsīqīmin al-Adwār wa-'l Muwashshahāt* (Our musical heritage of Adwār and Muwashshahāt). 4 vols. Cairo: al-Lajna al-Mūsīqiyya al-'Ulyá, 1969.

Hildebrand, William, H., Dean H. Keller, and Anita D. Herington, eds. *A Book of Memories: Kent State University, 1910–1992.* Kent, Ohio: Kent State Univ. Press, 1993.

Hitchcock, H. Wiley, and Stanley Sadie, eds. *The New Grove Dictionary of American Music.* London: Macmillan, 1986.

Hitschmann, Marcelle. *The Foreign Press News* 77 (April 1958).

Hock, Fritz. *Die Lyrik Otto Erich Hartlebens.* Nendeln, Liechtenstein: Kraus Reprint, 1967.

Hooke, S. H. *Middle Eastern Mythology.* Baltimore: Penguin, 1963.

Hopwood, Derek. *Egypt: Politics and Society, 1945–1981.* London: Allen and Unwin, 1982.

Hornbostel, Erich M. von. "Zum Kongress für arabische Musik-Kairo 1932." *Zeitschrift für Vergleichende Musikwissenschaft* 1 (1933): 16–17.

Houston, Jean. *The Passion of Isis and Osiris: A Union of Two Souls.* New York: Ballantine Books, 1995.

Hovancsek, Mike. E-mail correspondence to Denise A. Seachrist, February 14, 2000.

Hunter, Sam. *Isamu Noguchi.* New York: Abbeville Press, 1978.

Husayn, Tāhā. *An Egyptian Childhood.* Trans. E. H. Paxton. London: Heinemann, 1981.

———. *A Passage to France.* Trans. Kenneth Cragg. Arabic Translation Series of the *Journal of Arabic Literature* 4. Leiden: Brill, 1976.

———. *The Stream of Days: A Student at the Azhar.* Trans. Hilary Wayment. Cairo: al-Maaref, n.d.

Huwayri, Mahmud Muhammad. *Aswan fi al-Usur al-Wustá.* al-Haram: Ayn lil-Dirasat wa-al-Buhuth al-Insaniyah wa-al-Ijtimaiyah, 1996.

Ibn Abd al-Jalil, Abd al-Aziz. *Mujam Mustalahat al-musiqá al-Andalusiay al-Maghribiyah.* al-Rabat: Manshurat Mahd al-Dirasat wa-al-Abhath lil-Tarib, 1992.

Ibrahim, Muhammad Fuad. *Jamiat Sanjur bi-al-Iskandariyah: Amal Kabir . . . Wa-waqi Hazil.* al-Qahirah: al-Maktabah al-Akadimiyah, 1995.

Issawi, Charles. *Egypt at Mid-Century.* London: Oxford Univ. Press, 1954.

Jaffé, Hans Ludwig C. *Piet Mondrian.* New York: Harry N. Abrams, 1970.

Jayyusi, Salma Khadra. *Modern Arabic Poetry: An Anthology.* New York: Columbia Univ. Press, 1987.

———. *Trends and Movements in Modern Arabic Poetry.* 2 vols. Leiden: E. J. Brill, 1977.

Johnson, Jacqueline. *Stokely Carmichael: The Story of Black Power.* Englewood Cliffs, N.J.: Silver Burdett Press, 1990.

Jones, Eldred D. *The Writing of Wole Soyinka.* London: Heinemann, 1973.

Junker, Hermann. *Die Onurislegende.* Wien: In Kommission bei A. Hölder, 1917.

Kamil, Jill. *Aswan and Abu Simbel: History and Guide.* Cairo: American University in Cairo Press, 1993.

Kāmil, Mahmūd. *Al-Masrah al-Ghinā'ī 'l-'Arabī* (Arabic musical theater). Cairo: Dār al-Ma'ārif, 1977.

———. *Muhammad al-Qasabj ī.* Cairo: al-Hay'a al-Misriyya al-'Āmma lil-Kit b,1971.

———. *Tadbawwuq al-Musiqa 'I-'Arabiyya* (Savoring Arabic music). Cairo: Muhammad al-Amīn, n.d.

Kämper, Dietrich. *Gefangenschaft und Freiheit: Leben und Werk des Komponisten Luigi Dallapiccola.* Köln: Gitarre and Laute, 1984.

Kassel, Richard, ed. *Baker's Dictionary of Music.* New York: Schirmer Books, 1997.

———. *Webster's New World Dictionary of Music.* New York: Macmillan, 1998.

Keddie, Nikki R. "Introduction: Deciphering Middle Eastern Women's History." In *Women in Middle Eastern History: Shifting Boundaries in Sex and Gender*, edited by Nikki R. Keddie and Beth Baron. New Haven, Conn.: Yale Univ. Press, 1991.

Keddie, Nikki R., and Beth Baron, eds. *Women in Middle Eastern History: Shifting Boundaries in Sex and Gender.* New Haven, Conn.: Yale Univ. Press, 1991.

Kelly, Sean. *America's Tyrant: The CIA and Mobutu of Zaire: How the United States Put Mobutu in Power, Protected Him from His Enemies, Helped Him Become One of the Richest Men in the World, and Lived to Regret It.* Washington, D.C.: American Univ. Press, 1993.

Kennedy, Michael, ed. *The Oxford Dictionary of Music.* Oxford: Oxford Univ. Press, 1994.

Al-Khaṭīb, 'Adnān, ed. *Umm Kuthlūm: Mu'jizat al-Ghinā'al-'Arabī.* Damascus: Matba'at al-Ilm, 1975.

Khayrī, Badī'. *Mudhakkirat Badī'Khayrī. 45 Sana taht adwā'al-Masrah* (The memoirs of Badī Khayrī: Forty-five years under the lights of the theater). Ed. Mahmūd Rif'at al-Muhāmī. Beirut: Dār al-Thaqāfa, n.d.

El-Kholy, Samha Anun. "The Function of Music in Islamic Culture (Up to 1100 A.D.)." Ph.D. diss., Univ. of Edinburgh, 1953–54.

Khouri, Mounah. *Poetry and the Making of Modern Egypt* (1882–1922). Leiden: E. J. Brill, 1971.

Al-Khula'ī, Kamāl. *Al-Aghānī 'l-'Asriyya* (Contemporary songs). Cairo: Tab'at al-Sighāda, 1921; 2nd ed. Cairo: at-Maktaba al-Misriyya, 1923.

———. *Kitāb al-Mūsīqa 'l-Sharqī* (Book of oriental music). Cairo: Matba'at al-Taqaddum, ca. 1904–5.

Kinne, Aaron. *Sarah and Hagar, or, An Explanation of the Scripture Allegory, with Particular Reference to Infant Baptism.* New London, Conn.: Samuel Green, 1801.

Kirkpatrick, John, et al. *The New Grove Twentieth-Century American Masters: Ives, Thomson, Sessions, Cowell, Gershwin, Copland, Carter, Barber, Cage, Bernstein.* London: Macmillan, 1988.

Kitāb Mu'tamar al-Mūsīqá 'l-'Arabiyya (Book of the conference of Arab music). Cairo: al-Matba'a al-Amīryya, 1933.

Lacouture, Jean, and Simonne Lacouture. *Egypt in Transition.* Trans. Francis Scarfe, London: Methuen, 1958.

Laing, Dave. *The Sound of Our Time.* Chicago: Quadrangle Books, 1970.

Landau, Jacob M. *Studies in the Arab Theater and Cinema.* Philadelphia: Univ. of Pennsylvania Press, 1958.

Landes, David S. *Bankers and Pashas: International Finance and Economic Imperialism in Egypt.* Cambridge, Mass.: Harvard Univ. Press, 1958.

Lane, Edward William. *An Account of the Manners and Customs of the Modern Egyptians, Written in Egypt during the Years 1833–1835.* 1836. Reprint. The Hague and London: East-West, 1978.

Leakey, Richard E. *One Life: An Autobiography.* Salem, N.H.: Salem House, 1984.

Lewis, John Lowell. *Ring of Liberation: Deceptive Discourse in Brazilian Capoeira.* Chicago: Univ. of Chicago Press, 1992.

Libman, Lillian. *And Music at the Close: Stravinsky's Last Years, a Personal Memoir.* New York: W. W. Norton, 1972.

Lockot, Hans Wilhelm. *The Mission: The Life, Reign and Character of Haile Sellassie I.* London: Hurst, 1989.

Locsin, Leandro. *The Architecture of Leandro V. Locsin.* New York: Weatherhill, 1977.

Logan, Rayford Whittingham. *Howard University: The First Hundred Years, 1867–1967.* New York: New York Univ. Press, 1969.

Luening, Otto. *The Odyssey of an American Composer: The Autobiography of Otto Luening.* New York: Scribner, 1980.

MacDonald, Duncan B. *Aspects of Islam.* 1911. Reprint. New York: Books for Libraries Press, 1971.

MacEwen Sally, ed. *Views of Clytemnestra, Ancient and Modern.* Lewiston, N.Y.: Edwin Mellen Press, 1990.

McBrien, William. *Cole Porter: A Biography.* New York: Alfred A. Knopf, 1998.

McDonald, John K. *House of Eternity: The Tomb of Nefertari.* Los Angeles: Getty Conservation Institute and J. Paul Getty Museum, 1996.

McKee, Nancy. *Valiant Woman.* San Antonio: Naylor, 1962.

Macaulay, Alastair. *Margot Fonteyn.* Stroud, U.K.: Sutton, 1998.

Madden, Dorothy Gifford. *You Call Me Louis, Not Mr. Horst.* Australia: Harwood Academic, 1996.

Mahdi, Salih. *al-Musiqá al-Arabiyah: Maqamat wa-dirasat.* Bayrut, Lubnan: Dār al-Gharb al-Islami, 1993.

Mahfūz, Najīb. *Bidāya wa-Nihāya.* Cairo: Dār Misr lil-Tibā'a, 1949.

———. Cairo Trilogy. New York: Doubleday, 1991–93.

Mandelbaum, David. "The Study of Life History: Gandhi." *Current Anthropology* 14/3 (1973): 177–206.

Mansī, Ahmad Abū 'l-Khidr. *Al-Aghānī wa-'l-Mūsīqá 'l-Sharqiyya, bayn al-Qadīm wa-'l-Jadīd* (Oriental songs and music between the old and the new). Cairo: Dār al-'Arab li-l-Bustānī, 1966.

Manou, Rallou. *Choros: ou ton radion—ousan ten technen.* Athena: Ekdoseis "Gnose." 1987.

Manuel, Peter. "Popular Music and Media Culture in South Asia: Prefatory Considerations." *Asian Music* 24/1 (1992–93): 91–99.

Marcus, Scott. "Arab Music Theory in the Modern Period." Ph.D. diss., Univ. of California, Los Angeles, 1989.

Marsot, Afaf Lutfi al-Sayyid. *Egypt in the Reign of Muhammad Ali.* Cambridge: Cambridge Univ. Press, 1984.

———. *Egypt's Liberal Experiment, 1922–1936.* Berkeley: Univ. of California Press, 1977.

———. "Religion or Opposition? Urban Protest Movements in Egypt." *International Journal of Middle East Studies* 16 (1984): 522–41.

———. *A Short History of Modern Egypt.* Cambridge: Cambridge Univ. Press, 1985.

———. "The Ulama of Cairo in the Eighteenth and Nineteenth Centuries." In *Scholars, Saints and Sufis: Muslim Religious Institutions in the Middle East since 1500,* edited by Nikki Keddie. Berkeley: Univ. of California Press, 1972.

Martin, John. "'Clytemnestra' An Epic Full-Evening Work by a Modern Master." *New York Times,* April 6, 1958.

Masabnī, Badī'a. *Mudhakkirāt Badī'a Masabnī* (The memoirs of Badī'a Masabnī).
    Ed. Nāzik Bāsīla. Beirut: Dār Maktabat al-Hayāh, n.d.

Al-Masrī, Khalīl and Mahmūd Kāmil. *Al-Nusūs al-Kāmila li-Jamī'Aghānī Kawakab
    al- Sharq Umm Kulthūm* (The complete texts for all of the songs of the star of
    the east, Umm Kulthūm). Cairo: Dār al-Tibā'a al-Hadītha, 1979.

Mernissi, Fatima. *Beyond the Veil: Male-Female Dynamics in Modern Muslim
    Society*. Bloomington: Indiana Univ. Press, 1987.

Middleton, Richard. "Articulating Musical Meaning/Reconstructing Musical His-
    tory/Locating the 'Popular,'" *Popular Music* 5 (1986): 5–43.

———. *Studying Popular Music*. Milton Keynes: Open Univ. Press, 1990.

Miller, Hugh Milton. *Introduction to Music: A Guide to Good Listening*. New
    York: Barnes and Noble, 1958.

———. *An Outline-History of Music*. New York: Barnes and Noble, 1947.

Miquel, André. *Deux Histoire d'amour: de Majnûn à Tristan*. Paris: Editions O.
    Jacob, 1996.

Mitchell, Timothy. *Colonising Egypt*. Cambridge: Cambridge Univ. Press, 1988.

Money, Keith. *Fonteyn & Nureyev: The Great Years*. London: Harvill, 1994.

Monroe, Robert C. "Howard Hanson: American Music Educator." Ph.D. diss.,
    Florida State Univ., Tallahassee, 1970.

Monsaingeon, Bruno. *Mademoiselle: Conversations with Nadia Boulanger*. Trans-
    lated by Robyn Marsack. Manchester: Carcanet, 1985.

Morehead, Philip D., with Anne MacNeil, eds. *The New International Dictio-
    nary of Music*. New York: Meridian, 1992.

Morell, Virginia. *Ancestral Passions: The Leakey Family and the Quest for Human-
    kind's Beginnings*. New York: Simon and Schuster, 1995.

Morella, Joe. *Genius and Lust: The Creativity and Sexuality of Cole Porter and
    Noel Coward*. New York: Carroll and Graf, 1995.

Mustafá, Zākī. *Umm Kulthūm: Ma'bad al-Hubb* (Umm Kulthūm: temple of love).
    Cairo: Dār al-Tibā'a al-Hadītha, [1975].

Naguib, Mohammed. *Egypt's Destiny: A Personal Statement*. Westport, Conn.:
    Greenwood Press, 1984.

Al-Najī , Kamāl. *Al-Ghinā' al-Misrī* (Egyptian song). Cairo: Dār al-Hilāl, 1966.

Al-Naqqāsh, Rajā'. "Aswāt atrabat Ajdādanā" (Voices that charmed our grandpar-
    ents). *Al-Kawākib* (1965). Reprinted in *Lughz Umm Kulthūm*. Cairo: Dār al-
    Hilāl, 1978.

———. "Liqā' ma'a Umm Kulthūm" (A meeting with Umm Kulthūm). *Al-Kawākib*
    (1965). In *Lughz Umm Kulthūm*. Cairo: Dār al-Hilāl, 1978.

———. "Lughz Umm Kulthūm" (The secret of Umm Kulthūm). In *Lughz Umm
    Kulthūm*. Cairo: Dār al-Hilāl, 1978.

———. "Al-Mashāyikh wa-'l-Fann" (The *mashāyikh* and art). *Al-Kawākib* (1965).
    Reprinted in *Lughz Umm Kulthūm*. Cairo: Dār al-Hilāl, 1978.

———. "Shawqī wa-Hayāt 'Abd al-Wahhāb" (Shawqī and the life of 'Abd al-Wahhāb).
    Al-Kawākib (1969). In *Lughz Umm Kulthūm*. Cairo: Dār al-Hilāl, 1978.

———. "Umm Kulthūm wa-'l-Muthaqqafūn" (Umm Kulthūm and the intellec-
    tuals), *al-Musawwar* (1968). In *Lughz Umm Kulthūm*. Cairo: Dār al-Hilāl, 1978.

Nelson, Cynthia. "Biography and Women's History: On Interpreting Doria Shafik." In *Women in Middle Eastern History: Shifting Boundaries in Sex and Gender*, edited by Nikkie R. Keddie and Beth Baron. New Haven, Conn.: Yale Univ. Press, 1991.

Nelson, Kristina. *The Art of Reciting the Qur'an*. Austin: Univ. of Texas Press, 1985.

Nettl, Bruno. *The Study of Ethnomusicology: Twenty-nine Issues and Concepts*. Urbana: Univ. of Illinois Press, 1983.

Nettl, Bruno, and Ruth M. Stone, advisory eds. *The Garland Encyclopedia of World Music*. New York: Garland, 1998-.

Nimri, Keram. "A Study of the Selective Theatrical Environment Exploring the Internal Symbols between Graham's Choreography and Noguchi's Set-Sculptures." Master's thesis, Ohio Univ., Athens, 1995.

Noriega, Manuel, and Peter Eisner. *America's Prisoner: The Memoirs of Manuel Noriega*. New York: Random House, 1997.

Ortner, Sherry B. "Theory in Anthropology since the Sixties." *Comparative Studies in Society and History* 26/1 (1984): 126–66.

Ostwald, Peter. *Schumann: The Inner Voices of a Musical Genius*. Boston: Northeastern Univ. Press, 1985.

Owens, Dewey. *Carlos Salzedo: From Aeolian to Thunder: A Biography*. Chicago: Lyon and Healy Harps, 1993.

Page, Malcolm. *Wole Soyinka: Bibliography, Biography, Playography*. London: TQ, 1979.

Patry, A. J. "Au Music and the Arts—un jeune compositeur égyptien: M. Halim El-Dabh et Mlle Linette Tamin." *La Bourse Egyptienne*, February 15, 1949.

Persichetti, Vincent. *The Music of Vincent Persichetti: Biographical Material, Complete Works, Records, Articles, and Books*. Philadelphia: Elkan-Vogel, n.d.

Peyser, Joan. *Bernstein: A Biography*. New York: Billboard Books, 1998.

———. *Twentieth-Century Music: The Sense behind the Sound*. New York: Schirmer Books, 1980.

Pincus, Andrew L. *Tanglewood: The Clash between Tradition and Change*. Boston: Northeastern Univ. Press, 1998.

Porzecanski, Teresa. *Rituales: Ensayos Antropológicos Sobre Umbanda, Ciencias Sociales y Mitologías*. Montevideo, Uruguay: L. A. Retta Libros, Editor, 1991.

Prasse, Karl. *The Tuaregs: The Blue People*. Copenhagen: Museum Tusculanum Press, Univ. of Copenhagen, 1995.

Qureshi, Regula. *Sufi Music of India and Pakistan: Sound, Context and Meaning in Qawwali*. Cambridge: Cambridge Univ. Press, 1986.

Racy, Ali Jihad. "Arabian Music and the Effects of Commercial Recording." *World of Music* 20 (1975): 47–58.

———. "Creativity and Ambience: An Ecstatic Feedback Model from Arab Music." *World of Music* 33/3 (1991): 7–28.

———. "Music." In *The Genius of Arab Civilization: Source of Renaissance*, edited by John R. Hayes. 2nd ed. Cambridge, Mass.: MIT Press, 1983.

———. "Music in Contemporary Cairo." *Asian Music* 12/1 (1981): 4–26.

———. "Musical Change and Commercial Recording in Egypt, 1904–1932." Ph.D. diss., Univ. of Illinois, 1977.

———. Review of "Waslah Ghinā'iyyah (Nefertiti), Līh Yā Banafsaj (Sono Cairo), Cinera-phone Presents Mary Gibran (Cineraphone), Cheikh Sayed Darwiche (Baidaphon)." *Ethnomusicology* 24 (1980): 603–7.

———. "Sound and Society: The *Takht* Music of Early Twentieth Century Cairo." *Selected Reports in Ethnomusicology* 7 (1988): 139–70.

———. "The Waslah: A Compound-Form Principle in Egyptian Music." *Arab Studies Quarterly* 5 (1983): 396–403.

———. "Words and Music in Beirut: A Study of Attitudes" *Ethnomusicology* 30 (1986): 413–27.

Rahman, Fazlur. *Islam*. 2nd ed. Chicago: Univ. of Chicago Press, 1979.

Randel, Don Michael, ed. *Harvard Concise Dictionary of Music*. Cambridge, Mass.: Belknap Press, 1978.

Raslan, Muhammad Said. *Majnun Laylá, Haqiqah am Khayal?* [Cairo]: Matbatt Isá al-Babi al-Halabi, 1982.

Ratib, Najla Abd Al-Hamid. *Azmat al-talim fi Misr: Dirasah Susyulujiyah fi Idarat al-azamat al-ijtimaiyah*. Al-Qahirah: Markaz al-Mahrusah lil-Buhuth wa-al-Tadrib wa-al-Nashr, 1998.

Rawnsley, Gary D. *Radio Diplomacy and Propaganda: The BBC and VOA in International Politics, 1956–65*. New York: St. Martin's Press, 1996.

Reagon, Bernice Johnson. *We Who Believe in Freedom: Sweet Honey in the Rock— Still on the Journey*. New York: Anchor Books, 1993.

Rego, Waldeloir. *Capoeira Angola: Ensaio Sócio-etnográfico*. Rio de Janeiro: Gráf. Lux, 1968.

Reich, Willi. *The Life and Work of Alban Berg*. Trans. Cornelius Cardew. New York: Da Capo Press, 1981.

Reyes Schramm, Adelaida. "Music and the Refugee Experience." *The World of Music* 32/3 (1990): 3–21.

Reynolds, Dwight. "Heroic Poets, Poet Heroes." Ph.D. diss., Univ. of California, Los Angeles, 1991.

Rice, Timothy. *May It Fill Your Soul: Experiencing Bulgarian Music*. Chicago: Univ. of Chicago Press, 1994.

Ricoeur, Paul. "The Model of the Text: Meaningful Action Considered as a Text." In *Interpretive Social Science: A Reader*, edited by Paul Rabinow and William M. Sullivan. Berkeley: Univ. of California Press, 1979.

Rizq, Qistandī. *Al-Mūsīqa 'l-Sharqiyya wa-'l-Ghinā' al-'Arabī* (Oriental music and Arabic song). 4 vols. Cairo: al-Matba'a al-'Asriyya, ca. 1936.

Robinson, Edwin Arlington. *The Peterborough Idea*. New York: North American Review, 1916.

Robinson, Simon, with Derek Robinson. *A Year with Rudolf Nureyev*. London: Robert Hale, 1997.

Roseman, Marina. "The New Rican Village: Artists in Control of the Image-Making Machinery." *Latin American Music Review* 4 (1983): 132–67.

Rosenstiel, Léonie. *Nadia Boulanger: A Life in Music*. New York: W. W. Norton, 1982.

Rouanet, Jules. "La musique arabe." *Encyclopédie de la Musique et Dictionnaire du Conservatoire.* Ed. A. Lavignac. Paris: Librairie Delagrave, 1922.

Ryan, Daniel. Telephone conversation with Denise A. Seachrist, February 7, 2000.

Sabrī, Muhammad, ed. *Al-Shawqiyyāt al-Majhūla.* 2 vols. Cairo: Matba'at Dār al-Kutub, 1961–62.

Sadie, Stanley, ed. *The New Grove Dictionary of Music and Musicians.* London: Macmillan, 1980.

———. *The New Grove Dictionary of Musical Instruments.* London: Macmillan, 1985.

El-Saghir, Mohammed. *Le camp romain de Louqsor: (Avec une étude des graffites gréco-romains du temple d'Amon).* [Cairo]: Institut français d'archéologie orientale, 1986.

Sahhāb, Ilyās. *Difā'an 'an al-Ughniyya al-'Arabiyya* (A defense of Arabic song). Beirut: al-Mu'assasa al-'Arabiyya lil-Dirāsāt wa-'l-Nashr, 1980.

Sahhāb, Victor. *Al-Sab'a al-Kibār fī'l-Mūsīqa 'l-'Arabiyya al-Mu'āsira* (The seven great ones in contemporary Arab music). Beirut: Dār al-Ilm lil-Malāyīn, 1987.

Saiah, Ysabel. *Oum Kalsoum: l'Étoile de l'Orient.* Paris: Denoël, 1985.

Samson, Julia. *Nefertiti and Cleopatra: Queen-Monarchs of Ancient Egypt.* London: Rubicon, 1990.

San Francisco Museum of Art. *Leon Polk Smith: An Exhibition.* [San Francisco: Museum of Art, 1968].

Santoni, Ronald. *Bad Faith, Good Faith, and Authenticity in Sartre's Early Philosophy.* Philadelphia: Temple Univ. Press, 1995.

Sawa, George Dimitri. *Music Performance Practice in the Early 'Abbasid Era 132–320 AH/750–932 ad.* Studies and Texts 92. Toronto: Pontifical Institute of Mediaeval Studies, 1989.

———. "Oral Transmission in Arabic Music, Past and Present." *Oral Tradition* 4/1–2 (1989): 254–65.

Saylor, Bruce. *The Writings of Henry Cowell: A Descriptive Bibliography.* Brooklyn: Institute for Studies in American Music, Dept. of Music, School of Performing Arts, Brooklyn College of the City Univ. of New York, 1977.

Schlundt, Christena L. *Dance in the Musical Theatre: Jerome Robbins and His Peers, 1934–1965, a Guide.* New York: Garland, 1989.

Schneegass, Christian. *Ugge Bärtle: das Zeichnerische Spätwerk des Bildhauers (1965–1984).* Tübingen: E. Wasmuth, 1985.

Schwab, Peter. *Ethiopia & Haile Selassie.* New York: Facts on File 1972.

Schwartz, Charles. *Cole Porter: A Biography.* New York: Dial Press, 1977.

Seeger, Anthony. *Why Suyá Sing: A Musical Anthropology of an Amazonian People.* Cambridge: Cambridge Univ. Press, 1987.

Seeger, Charles. *Studies in Musicology, 1935–1975.* Berkeley: Univ. of California Press, 1977.

Shakespeare, William. *Antony and Cleopatra.* Ed. Richard Madelaine. Cambridge: Cambridge Univ. Press, 1998.

Sharamon, Shalila, and Bodo J. Baginski. *The Chakra Handbook: From a Basic Understanding to Practical Application.* Wilmot, Wisc.: Lotus Light Publications, 1991.

El-Shawan, Salwa. "Al-Mūsīka al-ʿArabiyyah: A Category of Urban Music in Cairo, Egypt, 1927–77." Ph.D. diss., Columbia Univ., 1980.

El-Shawan Castelo Branco, Salwa. "Some Aspects of the Cassette Industry in Egypt." *World of Music* 29 (1987): 3–45.

Shawqi, Ahmad. *Al-Shawqiyyāt* (The works of Shawqī). 4 vols. Cairo: Matbaʿat al-Istiqāma, 1950.

Al-Shawwā, Sāmī. *Mudhakkirāt Sāmī al-Shawwī* (The memoirs of Sāmī al-Shawwā). Ed. Fuʾād Qassās. Cairo: Matābiʿ al-Sharq al-Awsat, 1966.

———. *Al-Qawāʾid al-Fanniyya fī ʾl-Mūsīqá ʾl-Sharqiyya wa-ʾl-Gharbiyya* (The artistic foundations of oriental and western music). Cairo: Jibrāʾil Fath Allāh Jabri wa-Walādihi, 1946.

Shelah, Aviva. *Musikah: Ieksikon Devir.* Tel-Aviv: Devir, 1990.

Shelemay, Kay Kaufman. "Response to Rice." *Ethnomusicology* 31 (1987): 489–90.

Sherwood, Keith. *Chakra Therapy: For Personal Growth & Healing.* St. Paul, Minn.: Llewellyn, 1988.

Shiloah, Amnon. "The Status of Art Music in Muslim Nations." *Asian Music* 12 (1979): 40–55.

Shūsha, Muhammad al-Sayyid. *Umm Kulthūm: Hayāt Nagham* (Umm Kulthūm: The life of a melody). Cairo: Maktabat Rūz al-Yūsuf, 1976.

Siliotti, Alberto. *Nefertari e la Valle delle Regine.* Firenze, Italy: Giunti, 1993.

Slawek, Stephen. "Ravi Shankar as Mediator between a Traditional Music and Modernity." In *Ethnomusicology and Modern Music History,* edited by Stephen Blum, Philip V. Bohlman, and Daniel M. Neuman. Urbana: Univ. of Illinois Press, 1991.

Slonimsky, Nicolas, ed. *Lectionary of Music.* New York: McGraw-Hill, 1989.

Slyomovics, Susan. *The Merchant of Art: An Egyptian Hilali Oral Epic Poet in Performance.* Berkeley: Univ. of California Press, 1987.

Smith, Charles D. "The 'Crisis of Orientation': The Shift of Egyptian Intellectuals to Islamic Subjects in the 1930s." *International Journal of Middle East Studies* 4 (1973): 382–410.

Smith, Leon Polk. *Leon Polk Smith.* New York: Galerie Denise René, 1973.

Smith, William Ander. *The Mystery of Leopold Stokowski.* Rutherford, N.J.: Fairleigh Dickinson Univ. Press, 1990.

Snyder, Carl P. "New Concept in Theatre Getting Showing Here." *Gloucester* [Mass.] *Daily Times,* May 25, 1966.

Soares, Janet Mansfield. *Louis Horst: Musician in a Dancer's World.* Durham, N.C.: Duke Univ. Press, 1992.

Solihin, Sohirin Mohammad. *Copts and Muslims in Egypt: A Study on Harmony and Hostility.* Markfield: Islamic Foundation, 1991.

Solla Olivera, Horacio. *Umbanda.* Montevideo: EPPAL, 1992.

Stewart, John L. *Ernst Krenek: The Man and His Music.* Berkeley: Univ. of California Press, 1991.

Stewart, Kathleen. "Backtalking the Wilderness: 'Appalachian' En-genderings." In *Uncertain Terms: Negotiating Gender in American Culture,* edited by Faye Ginsburg and Anna Lowenhaupt Tsing. Boston: Beacon Press, 1990.

Stodelle, Ernestine. *The First Frontier: The Story of Louis Horst and the American Dance.* [Cheshire, Conn.: n.p., 1964].

Strahle, Graham, ed. *An Early Music Dictionary: Musical Terms from British Sources, 1500–1740.* Cambridge: Cambridge Univ. Press, 1995.

Street, Douglas. *David Henry Hwang.* Boise, Idaho: Boise State Univ., 1989.

Sugarman, Jane. "The Nightingale and the Partridge: Singing and Gender among Prespa Albanians." *Ethnomusicology* 33 (1989): 191–215.

Sykora. D. *Reconnaissance Report of Damage to Historic Monuments in Cairo, Egypt following the October 12, 1992 Dahshur Earthquake.* Buffalo, N.Y.: National Center for Earthquake Engineering Research, 1993.

Al-Tābi'ī Muhammad. *Asmahān tarwi Qissatahā* (Asmahān tells her story). Cairo: Mu'assasat Rūz al-Yūsuf, 1965.

Tapper, Nancy, and Richard Tapper. "The Birth of the Prophet: Ritual and Gender in Turkish Islam." *Man*, n.s. 22 (1987): 69–92.

Taskin, Sefa. *Mysia ve Isik Insanlari.* Cagaloglu, Istanbul: Sel Yayincilik, 1997.

Terry, Walter. "Graham: Monumental Dance." *New York Herald Tribune*, April 6, 1958.

Teubal, Savina J. *Ancient Sisterhood: The Lost Traditions of Hagar and Sarah.* Athens: Swallow Press/Ohio Univ. Press, 1997.

———. *Hagar the Egyptian: The Lost Tradition of the Matriarchs.* San Francisco: Harper and Row, 1990.

Theodorakis, Mikis. *Hoi Dromoi tou Archangelou: Autoviographia.* Athena, Gr.: Kedros, 1987.

Thompson, Oscar, ed. *The International Cyclopedia of Music and Musicians.* New York: Dodd, Mead, 1985.

Threlfall, Tim. *Isamu Noguchi: Aspects of a Schulptor's Practice; a Continuity with Life.* Lewes, Sussex: Seagull, 1992.

Tobin, Jennifer. *Herodes Attikos and the City of Athens: Patronage and Conflict under the Antonines.* Amsterdam: Gieben, 1997.

Tomassoni, Italo. *Mondrian.* London: Hamlyn, 1970.

Toobin, Jerome. *Agitato: A Trek through the Musical Jungle.* New York: Viking Press, 1975.

Torpey, Glennis A. "A Comparative Study of the Physical Conventions of No and Kabuki." Master's thesis, Bowling Green State Univ., Bowling Green, Ohio, 1973.

Touma, Habib Hassan. "Die Musik der Araber im 19. Jahrhundert." In *Musikkulturen Asiens, Afrikas und Ozeaniens im 19. Jahrhundert*, edited by Robert Günther. Studien zur Musikgeschichte des 19. Jahrhunderts, Band 31. Regensburg: Gustav Bosse, 1973.

Turino, Thomas. "The Coherence of Social Style and Musical Creation among the Aymara in Southern Peru." *Ethnomusicology* 33/1 (1989): 1–30.

———. "The History of a Peruvian Panpipe Style and the Politics of Interpretation." In *Ethnomusicology and Modern Music History.* Ed. Stephen Blum, Philip V. Bohlman, and Daniel M. Neuman. Urbana: Univ. of Illinois Press, 1991.

———. "Structure, Context, and Strategy in Musical Ethnography." *Ethnomusicology* 34 (1990): 399–412.

Turnbull, Colin M. *The Mbuti Pygmies: Change and Adaptation.* Fort Worth, Tex.: Harcourt Brace Jovanovich, 1983.

———. *The Mbuti Pygmies: An Ethnographic Survey.* New York: American Museum of Natural History, 1965.

Tyldesley, Joyce A. *Nefertiti: Egypt's Sun Queen.* New York: Viking Press, 1999.

Umm Kulthūm: al-Nagham al-Khālid (Umm Kulthūm: the eternal melody). Alexandria: Hay'at al-Funūn wa-'l-Adab wa-'l-'Ulūm al-Ijtimā'iyya bil-Iskandriyya, 1976.

Umm Kulthūm: Qissat Hayātihā, Majmū'at Aghānīhā wa-ba'd Nukātihā wa-Wafātuhā (Umm Kulthūm: the story of her life, collection of her songs and some of her jokes, and her death). Beirut: Maktabat al-Hadīth, ca. 1975.

Umm Kulthūm: Qithārat al-Arab (Umm Kulthūm: lyre of the Arabs). Beirut: Maktabat al-Jamāhīr, 1975.

Univ. of New Mexico Fine Arts Library. *Puppetry Library: An Annotated Bibliography Based on the Batchelder-McParlin Collection at the University of New Mexico.* Comp. and ed. George B. Miller Jr., Janet Harris, and William E. Hannaford Jr. Westport, Conn.: Greenwood Press, 1981.

U.S. National Archives and Records Service. *Inspection Reports on Foreign Service Posts, 1906–1939.* Comp. George Brent and Kent Carter. Washington, D.C.: n.p., 1974.

Van Nieuwkerk, Karin. "Female Entertainment in Nineteenth and Twentieth-Century Egypt." *MERA Occasional Paper* 6, June 1990.

Vigreux, Philippe, ed. *Musique Arabe: Le Congrès du Caire de 1932.* Le Caire: CEDEJ, 1992.

Vinton, John, ed. *Dictionary of Contemporary Music.* New York: E. P. Dutton, 1974.

Voeks, Robert A. *Sacred Leaves of Candomblé: African Magic, Medicine, and Religion in Brazil.* Austin: Univ. of Texas Press, 1997.

Voll, John, "Islamic Renewal and the 'Failure of the West.'" In *Religious Resurgence: Contemporary Cases in Islam, Christianity, and Judaism,* edited by Richard T. Antoun and Mary Elaine Hegland. Syracuse, N.Y.: Syracuse Univ. Press, 1987.

Wachsmann, Klaus. "The Changeability of Musical Experience." *Ethnomusicology* 26 (1982): 197–216.

Wafer, James William. *The Taste of Blood: Spirit Possession in Brazilian Candomblé.* Philadelphia: Univ. of Pennsylvania Press, 1991.

Wahba, Magdi. "Cultural Planning in the Arab World." *Journal of World History* 14 (1972): 800– 813.

Waterman, Christopher Alan. *Jùjú: A Social History and Ethnography of an African Popular Music.* Chicago: Univ. of Chicago Press, 1990.

———. "Jùjú History: Toward a Theory of Sociomusical Practice." In *Ethnomusicology and Modern Music History,* edited by Stephen Blum, Philip V. Bohlman, and Daniel M. Neuman. Urbana: Univ. of Illinois Press, 1991.

Watson, Peter. *Nureyev: A Biography.* London: Hodder and Stoughton, 1994.

Widā'an 'an Umm Kulthūm (Farewell to Umm Kulthūm). Ed. Muhammad 'Umar Shatabū. Cairo: al-Markaz al-Misrī lil-Thaqāfa wa-l-I'lām, 1975.

Wilcox, Lee Owen. *Arab Republic of Egypt: A Study of the Educational System of the Arab Republic of Egypt and a Guide to the Academic Placement of Students in Educational Institutions of the United States.* Washington, D.C.: American Association of Collegiate Registrars and Admissions Officers, 1988.

Williams, David Russell. *Conversations with Howard Hanson.* Arkadelphia, Ark.: Delta, 1988.

Williams, Raymond. *Culture and Society, 1780–1950.* Garden City, N.Y.: Anchor Books, 1960.

———. *Marxism and Literature.* Oxford: Univ. Press, 1977.

Wissa, Hanna F. *Assiout: The Saga of an Egyptian Family.* Lewes, Sussex: Book Guild, 1994.

Witmer, Robert. "Stability in Blackfoot Songs, 1909–1968." In *Ethnomusicology and Modern Music History*, edited by Stephen Blum, Philip V. Bohlman, and Daniel M. Neuman. Urbana: Univ. of Illinois Press, 1991.

Witt, R. E. *Isis in the Ancient World.* Baltimore: Johns Hopkins Univ. Press, 1997.

Yeager, Cynthia H. "The Musical Ideas of the Futurists and Similar Expressions by American Composers in the First Half of the Twentieth Century." Master's thesis, Univ. of Cincinnati, 1979.

Yogananda, Paramahansa. *Wine of the Mystic: The Rubaiyat of Omar Khayyam, a Spiritual Interpretation.* Los Angeles: Self-Realization Fellowship, 1994

You Can Count on VOA: Voice of America. n.p. [Washington, D.C.?]: U.S. Information Agency, n.d.[1984?].

Al-Yūsuf, Fatma. *Dhikrayatī* (My memories). Cairo: Rūz al-Yūsuf, 1953.

Zakī,'Abd al-Hamīd Tawfīq. *A'lām al-Mūsīqa 'l-Misriyya 'abra 150 Sana.* Cairo: al-Hay'a al-Misriyya al-'Āmma lil-Kitāb, 1990.

Zayid, Mahmud. "The Origins of the Liberal Constitutionalist Party in Egypt." In *Political and Social Change in Modern Egypt: Historical Studies from the Ottoman Conquest to the United Arab Republic*, edited by P. M. Holt. London: Oxford Univ. Press, 1968.

Zemp, Hugo. "'Are'are Classification of Musical Types and Instruments." *Ethnomusicology* 22 (1978): 37–67.

———. "Aspects of 'Are'are Musical Theory." *Ethnomusicology* 23 (1979): 5–39.

Index

Contents of the Compact Disc

Produced, edited, and mastered by George Faddoul
in Kent, Ohio, November 2002

1. *Misriyaat* (1954) [excerpt]: 3:19
   Halim El-Dabh, piano
   recorded January 19, 1954, in the home of the composer's brother, Bushra El-Dabh, in Cairo, Egypt
2. Halim El-Dabh practicing and composing at the piano (1948): 3:10
   recorded in the home of the composer's brother, Bushra El-Dabh, in Cairo, Egypt
3. *Sonic No. 7* (1955): 2:59
   Halim El-Dabh, *derabucca*
   recorded live February 13, 1969, in Gamble Auditorium of Baldwin-Wallace College in Berea, Ohio
4. *Sweet and Prickly Pear* (2002) [excerpt]: 3:03
   Jameson Cooper, violin
   Halim El-Dabh, *derabucca*
   recorded in the Carl F. W. Ludwig Recital Hall of Kent State University in Kent, Ohio, by George Faddoul. Reproduced with kind permission from Frank Wiley and Innova Recordings <http://innova.mu/>
5. *It Is Dark and Damp on the Front* (1949) [excerpt]: 5:33
   Tuyen Tonnu, piano
   recorded live March 29, 2002, in the entrance hall of the Bibliotheca Alexandrina in Alexandria, Egypt, by Julie Grant for WKSU (89.7 FM, Kent, Ohio)
6. *Monotone, Bitone, and Polytone* (1952) [first movement: "Monotone"]: 6:12
   Liana Tyson, flute
   David Badagnani, oboe
   Dennis Nygren, clarinet
   Kent Larmee, horn
   Charles Couch, trumpet
   Hardin Butcher, trumpet

Blake Tyson, percussion

Denise Seachrist, conductor

recorded live March 31, 2002, in the entrance hall of the Bibliotheca Alexandrina in Alexandria, Egypt, by Joel Jacobson for the Department of Pan-African Studies, Dr. Diedre Badejo, chair, Kent State University

7. *Thulathiya* (1955) [third movement: "Allegro," excerpt]: 1:46

David Badagnani, oboe

Ahmed Fahmi, violin

Tuyen Tonnu, piano

recorded live March 31, 2002, in the entrance hall of the Bibliotheca Alexandrina in Alexandria, Egypt, by Julie Grant for WKSU (89.7 FM, Kent, Ohio)

8. Symphony No. 3 (*Symphony of 37 Years*) (1953, rev. 1992) [second movement: "Adagio sostenuto," excerpt]: 4:37

Springfield Symphony Orchestra

John E. Ferritto, music director and conductor

recorded live March 7, 1992, in the North High School Auditorium in Springfield, Ohio

9. *Clytemnestra*; music for the ballet by Martha Graham (1958) [excerpt]: 8:46 [Act II, "Curtain Prelude"; "Dance of Terror: The Ghost of Agamemnon"; "Electra and the Paid Mourners"; "Orestes"; "Recognition Scene"]

Bethany Beardslee, soprano

Halim El-Dabh, baritone

Orchestra comprised primarily of musicians from Arturo Toscanini's Symphony of the Air

Eugene Lester, conductor

studio recording made late March 1958 in New York City, (prior to the April 1, 1958, premiere)

10. *Meditation on White Noise* (1959) [excerpt]: 3:39

electronic tape

recorded at the Columbia-Princeton Electronic Music Center in New York City

11. *Leiyla and the Poet* (1959): 7:11

electronic tape (Halim El-Dabh, voice)

recorded at the Columbia-Princeton Electronic Music Center in New York City

12. *Pirouette Continuum* (1969; rev. 1974) [excerpt]: 3:04

musique concrète composition

created for the "Sound" Exhibition at the Museum of Contemporary Crafts of the American Crafts Council in New York City (October 25, 1969–January 4, 1970)

based on sounds from the construction of the stainless steel mobile sculpture, *Pirouette*, by Nicholas D. Ohly

recorded by Halim El-Dabh in the artist's studio in Sherburne (now Killington), Vermont

reworked with George Faddoul at the Kent State University Electronic Music Studio in Kent, Ohio

13. *Mekta' in the Art of Kita'* (1955): 7:56

Book III ["Basseet"; "Samaï"; "Nawakht"; "Sayera"; "Soufiane"]

Nancy Voigt, piano
recorded June 6, 1971, in the Metropolitan Auditorium of Cuyahoga Community College in Cleveland, Ohio, by George Faddoul

14. Ethiopian Field Recordings and Orchestra Ethiopia (1964) [excerpts]: 3:57
    1. Three malakat (royal trumpets)
       names of musicians unknown
       recorded outside the Cathedral of St. Mary of Zion, Axum, Tigray province, Ethiopia, by Halim El-Dabh
    2. thirty-three-year-old Dorze woman singing
       name of singer unknown
       recorded in Wollamo Sodo, Sidamo province, Ethiopia, by Halim El-Dabh
    3. Ethiopian Coptic chant, sung in Ge'ez
       names of male singers unknown, with kabaro (large barrel drums struck with the hands) and sanasel (sistrum)
       recorded inside the Cathedral of St. Mary of Zion, Axum, Tigray province, Ethiopia by Halim El-Dabh
    4. Untitled composition by Halim El-Dabh
       Orchestra Ethiopia
       Halim El-Dabh, conductor
       demonstrating El-Dabh's experiments in symphonic treatment of indigenous Ethiopian musical instruments: kabaro, washint (four-hole end-blown bamboo flute), masenqo (one-string spike fiddles), krar (lyres), and voices
       recorded outside El-Dabh's residence in the Janmeda District, Addis Ababa, Shewa province
    5. Untitled composition by Halim El-Dabh
       Orchestra Ethiopia
       Halim El-Dabh, conductor
       demonstrating El-Dabh's experiments in symphonic treatment of indigenous Ethiopian musical instruments: masenqo, washint, embilta (set of three side-blown bamboo flutes without fingerholes), clappers, and kabaro
       recorded outside El-Dabh's residence in the Janmeda District, Addis Ababa, Shewa province

15. *Opera Flies* (1970–71) [Act III, scene 2: "Rituals and Burials," excerpt]: 3:41
    soloists, chorus, and orchestra comprised of students, faculty, and staff of the Hawthorne School, Washington, D.C.
    recorded live May 9, 1971, in the University Auditorium of Kent State University in Kent, Ohio, by George Faddoul

16. *The Eye of Horus* (1967) [excerpt]: 2:17
    Guus Hoekman, bass
    The New Boston Percussion Ensemble:
    Allen Barker, piano and voice
    James Latimer, percussion and voice
    Everett Beale, percussion and voice
    recorded November 1967 at Wheelock College in Boston, Massachusetts

17. "Processional Invocation to Ptah," from *In the Valley of the Nile;* music for the ballet by Cleo Parker Robinson (1999) [excerpt]: 2:26
   Denise Seachrist, mezzo-soprano
   Emad Guergiss, baritone
   Liana Tyson, flute
   Dennis Nygren, clarinet
   Kent Larmee, horn
   Charles Couch, trumpet
   Hardin Butcher, trumpet
   Tuyen Tonnu, piano
   Blake Tyson, percussion
   Mohammed Seif El Yazal, double bass
   David Badagnani, conductor
   recorded live March 30, 2002, in the entrance hall of the Bibliotheca Alexandrina in Alexandria, Egypt, by Joel Jacobson for the Department of Pan-African Studies, Dr. Diedre Badejo, chair, Kent State University

18. *Ogún: Let Him, Let Her Have the Iron* (2000) [excerpt]: 2:23
   Denise Seachrist, mezzo-soprano
   Liana Tyson, flute
   Dennis Nygren, clarinet
   Charles Couch, trumpet
   Ahmed Fahmi, violin
   Tuyen Tonnu, piano
   Blake Tyson, percussion
   Kent Larmee, conductor
   recorded live March 29, 2002, in the entrance hall of the Bibliotheca Alexandrina in Alexandria, Egypt, by Julie Grant for WKSU (89.7 FM, Kent, Ohio)

19. "Baladi" (Egypt) from *Harmonies of the Spheres: Ten Nations Rejoice* (1991) [arrangement for orchestra]: 1:08
   Bibliotheca Alexandrina String Orchestra with
   Liana Tyson, flute
   Dennis Nygren, clarinet
   Kent Larmee, horn
   Charles Couch, trumpet
   Hardin Butcher, trumpet
   Tuyen Tonnu, piano
   Blake Tyson, percussion
   David Badagnani, percussion
   Denise Seachrist, percussion
   Sherif Mohie El Din, conductor
   recorded live March 29, 2002, in the entrance hall of the Bibliotheca Alexandrina in Alexandria, Egypt, by Julie Grant for WKSU (89.7 FM, Kent, Ohio)

20. *The Reappearance of the Lotus Flower* (2002) [first movement: "Facing the Ocean Waves," excerpt]: 2:33

Bibliotheca Alexandrina String Orchestra
Sherif Mohie El Din, conductor
recorded live March 29, 2002, in the entrance hall of the Bibliotheca Alexandrina
in Alexandria, Egypt, by Julie Grant for WKSU (89.7 FM, Kent, Ohio)

The original source recordings range from 1948–2002, and some of the older tapes
have been processed to a certain degree to improve the overall sound quality of
these historically important tapes.

Running Time: 79:49